Fluid Boundaries

Fluid Boundaries

Forming and Transforming Identity in Nepal

William F. Fisher

COLUMBIA UNIVERSITY PRESS   NEW YORK

COLUMBIA UNIVERSITY PRESS
Publishers Since 1893
New York, Chichester, West Sussex
Copyright © 2001 Columbia University Press

Library of Congress Cataloging-in-Publication Data

Fisher, William F., 1951–
  Fluid boundaries : forming and transforming
identity in Nepal / William F. Fisher
      p. cm.
  Includes bibliographic references and index.
  ISBN 0–231–11086–3 (cloth)
  ISBN 0–231–11087–1 (paper)
    Thakali (Nepalese people)—Ethnic identity.
2. Thakali (Nepalese people)—Social life and customs.
1. Title.

  DS493.9.T45 F57 2001
  305.891′495—dc21
                                    2001032461

∞

Columbia University Press books are printed on
permanent and durable acid-free paper.
Printed in the United States of America

c 10 9 8 7 6 5 4 3 2 1
p 10 9 8 7 6 5 4 3 2 1

You can't step into the same river twice.   —Heraclitus, "*Cratylus*"

Each time I remember Fragment 91 of Heraclitus: 'You will not go down twice to the same river,' I admire his dialectic still, because the facility with which we accept the first meaning ('The river is different') clandestinely imposes the second one ('I am different') and gives us the illusion of having invented it.
      —Jorge Luis Borges, "New Refutation of Time," Other Inquisitions

Contents

Maps and Tables

Maps

Tables

Preface

This book is based on almost twenty years of contact with the Thakali. It is rooted in intensely personal experiences and builds on my research among Thakali communities not only in Thaksatsae but also in Khani Khuwa, Kathmandu, Butwal, Bhairawa, Pokhara, and elsewhere. During the past seven years, overseas communities in Tokyo and Cambridge, Massachusetts, have also been included within the research scope. Throughout, the communities among which I have worked have been characterized by their openness to outsiders in general and to me specifically. My original research began among migrant Thakali communities in Khani Khuwa, and I have continued to maintain particularly close contacts with members of these communities.

The language of research was generally Nepali. Most Thakali living outside of Thaksatsae do not speak Thakali as their first language. In fact, many do not speak Thakali at all. I learned Thakali early on in my initial research period and have used it frequently for discussions of rituals and kinship, but it always remained the second language of my research. Some informants regularly and deliberately speak to me in Thakali, especially when they want to distinguish themselves from non-Thakali-speaking Thakali who are also present, but more frequently initial Thakali conversations evolve into longer discussions in Nepali.

Early in my research work, while staying in Kobang, I was invited to attend a meeting of the *tera mukiyā*, the thirteen headmen of Thaksatsae. I hesitated because I thought my Thakali would be insufficient to comprehend the meeting fully. My host laughed when I explained my hesitation and replied, "Our meetings are conducted in Nepali; you can't talk about anything important in Thakali." While I later learned that you could indeed talk about important things in Thakali, it has nevertheless been impressed on me that in many circumstances serious discussions among the Thakali must necessarily occur in Nepali. For example, at the meeting about Thakali culture in Kobang in 1993, one of the first invited speakers, a prominent Thakali woman from Kathmandu, began her talk in Thakali. Almost immediately, a large portion of the audience responded by shouting her down and insisting that she speak in Nepali, a language they could all understand. Somewhat reluctantly, she continued in Nepali.[1]

As I note at several points in this book, the work of researchers on the Thakali has been influenced by their social connections and their theoretical and geographical perspectives. In this respect, my work is no different, and readers should recognize that it reflects a decidedly contemporary view of the Thakali, one that includes migrants as well as those resident in Thaksatsae. Thus the vocabulary I use in this book best reflects their everyday discussions, which employ a mix of Thakali, Nepali, and Tibetan words. This also reflects the writing of the Thakali themselves, both in the official documents of the national Thakali Sewa Samiti, including the Mul Bandej, its constitution, and in publications like *Khāngalo*. To rely on the Thakali language alone would privilege the narrow perspective of one small portion of the contemporary Thakali population.

My aim was to employ a vocabulary that would generally make sense or be intelligible to all of my informants. Because I have dealt with a wide range of Thakali perspectives throughout the book, I have on occasion employed vocabulary that is not known to or well understood by members of all Thakali communities. In some cases, I use Thakali words to discuss concepts or rituals that are important even though younger members of migrant communities are not well informed about them. In other cases, I have elected to use Nepali words understood by all communities even though Thakali-speaking Thakali would prefer to see Thakali. (For instance, I refer to some ancestor rituals as *kul devtā puja* rather than *jho chuwa*).

Several incidents had significant bearing on the conduct of my research over the years. One was my formal incorporation in 1983 within the web of Thakali kinship as a fictive in-law by a large extended lineage of the Tulachan Jhongman *phobe* in Khani Khuwa (and by extension as a fictive brother by other Thakali lineages who had affinal ties to the first lineage.

These networks became richer and more complex in 1993 when I was incorporated as a fictive kin with the Sherchan Pompar *ghyu*. These ties provided privileged access to ritual and kin relationships, as well as some moments of mirth to my Thakali companions.[2]

Throughout my years of contact with the Thakali, beginning with the formation of the Thakali Sewa Samiti in 1983 and continuing through the involvement of the Thakali with the Janajati Mahasang (Nepal Federation of Nationalities) in the 1990s, my research has been influenced by and benefited from a high level of Thakali group consciousness. In the early years of my work, my own movements from settlement to settlement were incorporated into the efficient network of communication that flowed among Thakali communities. This worked to my advantage: as a courier for the Central Committee of the national Thakali association and the community associations of Khani Khuwa, I easily gained access to individuals and associations I might not otherwise been able to approach so quickly.

Names of places are accurately reported, but names of some individuals have been changed to protect the privacy of my friends and informants.

Acknowledgments

Over the years I have conducted research among the Thakali I have accumulated many social and intellectual debts.

I am indebted to many members of Thakali communities in Nepal and around the world for both insights and hospitality. These include the late Sher Bahadur Sherchan and his family of Darbang; Tetindra Gauchan of Darbang; the late Tejab Gauchan of Galkot; Dirga Narayan Bhattachan of Ruma; Ramesh Gauchan, Hikmat Gauchan, Krishna Prakash Gauchan, and the Burtibang Thakali Samaj; Pradam Bahadur Gauchan of Pokhara and Sauru; Jahendra Tuluachan, Debindra Gauchan, and Lachim Prasad Sherchan of Kasauli; Basanta Sherchan, Devi Lal Sherchan, Prabatkar Sherchan, and the late Komal Bahadur Sherchan of Bhairawa; Bhadri Lal Sherchan of Tansen; Basanta Bhattachan, Bijaya Sherchan, Jyoti Man Sherchan, and the late Indra Man Sherchan of Kathmandu; Anil Gauchan of Tatopani; Lil Prasad Bhattachan; the late Govinda Man Sherchan, Shankar Man Sherchan, and Takur Prasad Tulachan of Tukche; Shyam Prasad Sherchan and the late Jaya Prasad Sherchan of Kobang; Purna Prasad Gauchan of Naphrakot; and Govinda Narsingh Bhattachan of Jomsom. I am also grateful to many, many others—in Darbang, Burtibang, Beni, Baglung, Galkot, Kobang, Larjung, Tukche, Ghsa, Tatopani, Dana, Bhairawa, Kasauli, Pokhara, Kathmandu, and many other places along the trail—who took the time to talk, teach, listen to my interpretations, and respond, I owe special thanks to Jyoti Sherchan and the *dājyu-bhāi* and *celi* of the Pompar Gyupa, who have welcomed me to all their events and treated me with exceptional hospitality, and to Ganga Tulachan and all the descendants and in-laws of the late Jagat Bahadur Tulachan of Darbang, who warmly accepted me as one of their own. I thank all the people of Darbang who have long provided a refuge of good humor and quiet affection to which I have returned both physically and in my mind many times and that I will never forget; to them I owe a debt I can never fully repay.

Other scholars of Nepal have offered advice and insights in the field, including Dor Bahadur Bista, Prayag Raj Sharma, Michael Vinding, Don Messerschmidt, Andrew Manzardo, Kanat Dixit, Bruce Owens, and Gabrielle Tautscher. I thank David Holmberg, James Fisher, Owen Lynch, Bruce Owens, Gabrielle Tautscher, Mark Turin, Theodore Riccardi, the late Robert Murphy, the late Morton Fried, Alexander Alland Jr., and Ainslie Embree for reading all or part of the manuscript.

Fieldwork was supported at different times by a Fulbright-Hays Doctoral Dissertation Research Award, Columbia University Traveling Fellowship, the Social Science Research Council, the American Council of Learned Societies, Columbia University's South Asian Institute, and Harvard University's Clark Fund. I also acknowledge the assistance of His Majesty's Government of Nepal, the Research Division of Tribhuvan University, the Center for Nepal and Asian Studies, and the United States Educational Foundation in Nepal.

I am also grateful to Janet C. Fisher for the maps, John Michel and the staff at Columbia University Press for their patience and support, and Bruce McCoy Owens for more sundry support over the past twenty years than he would ever admit.

Finally, I thank the lovely and witty Tad Kenney, who shared many of the early experiences on which this work is based, and the insightful and good-humored Jarvis Fisher, who wishes he had.

Fluid Boundaries

1   Introduction: Thakali Again for the Very First Time

It is only because things are so confused in practice that we must make our distinctions clear in theory.
— Max Weber

Meeting at the Crossroads

Jostling for vantage points among the crowds of adulators, we scrambled for spots along the stone walls lining the footpaths from which to observe the approach of the processions of priests and clan gods. Shaking and prancing like a yak, jingling the large bells wrapped around his body, the *pāre* (a clan priest) of the Bhattachan clan approached the crossroads from the north in the midst of a throng, delivering the decorated yak skull that represents the Bhattachan clan deity, Lha Yhāwā Rāngjyung (the self-made yak). A second procession approached from the south, descending from Nakhung temple. The lead drummer was followed by three men carrying the wooden heads or masks that represent the Gauchan, Sherchan, and Tulachan clan deities: Lha Lāngbā Nhurbu (the jeweled elephant), Lha Ghāngla Singi Karmo (the white lioness of the glacier), and Lha Chyurin Gyālmo (the queen crocodile), respectively—followed by the three clan *pāre*. Each priest was dressed in his clan's color: Gauchan red, Tulachan green, Sherchan white, and Bhattachan black.

United at the crossroads, *pāres*, drummers, mask bearers, and their attendant processions pressed through an opening in the stone wall into a nearby field where the platforms that were to serve as the bodies of the four clan deities had been prepared. On each of the four-by-five-feet platforms was mounted a wooden frame covered with a cloth in one of the clan colors. After the masks were mounted on the frames, male clan members lifted the deities on long wooden poles: first, Gauchan, then Tulachan, Sherchan, and Bhattachan. Shouting exuberantly, the men carried the deities high over their heads three times around the field; dust stirred up by their stomping feet obscured the view and choked the hundreds of adulators who crowded around. After the third circuit, the deities were replaced on the ground, and the large number of Thakali and observers from neighboring areas sought the deities' blessings by touching their foreheads to the heads of the deities.

The scene described above occurred in the village of Larjung in central Nepal on January 5, 1993 (Poush 21, 2049 V.S.), the tenth day of the seventeen-day Thakali festival, Lha Phewa (T: literally, "the appearance of the gods").[1] In the days that followed, the deities were similarly lifted and moved with equal fanfare along a path that simulates and recalls the stories of the original migration of the ancestors and deities of the four Thakali clans from disparate places of origin to the Thak Khola Valley in central Nepal.[2] This tradition is based on the four clan *rhabs*, or histories, that are read aloud by the clan priests during the unfolding of the Lha Phewa celebration.[3]

Lha Phewa, or the Bāra Barsa Kumbha Melā (N: the twelve-year festival), is performed every twelve years, in the year of the monkey (T: *prelo*), by the Thakali of Thaksatsae, who comprise four clans: Sherchan, Gauchan, Tulachan, and Bhattachan.[4] The sentiment expressed in the *rhabs* — "Although our birthplace is not the same, we should have the feeling that we have been born in the same place so that we may have good feelings when we gather" — seems as appropriate for the now widely scattered Thakali as it would have when the ancestors first gathered in this spot after migrating from different points of origin. For seventeen days every twelve years, the Thakali descend on the valley, returning to the Thakali homeland from all over Nepal to renew their connections with the land, the deities, and their fellow clan members. In 1993 many of those attending the festival were coming to the valley for the first time in their lives; others were returning after absences of many years. They came from Kathmandu, Pokhara, Bhairawa, and other urban areas to which Thakali families have migrated in large numbers in the past three decades. They came from rural areas of Baglung and Myagdi Districts, an area colloquially referred to as Khani Khuwa, where Thakali communities have been established since the early nineteenth century and where the Thakali are well integrated into ethnically plural communities.[5] And they came from other far-flung places, including Nepalgunj and Chitwan in southern Nepal near the Indian border. A majority of those in attendance, including almost all of those from Khani Khuwa and most of those less than twenty-five years of age who were born outside of the Thak Khola, did not speak or understand the Thakali language, and many readily expressed their conviction that they were poorly acquainted with Thakali culture and tradition. They came seeking connections with other Thakalis and affirmation of their identity as Thakali.

Searching for Culture in the Past

Throughout the years I have been studying the Thakali,[6] they have been searching for a Thakali identity and seeking to clarify their culture and history. Although united in the process of this search, the Thakali are divided by the variety of answers that they have proposed. Since the early 1980s, attempts to revitalize Thakali culture have taken many forms, including the advocation of a Sanskritization or Hinduization of Thakali religious practices, the promotion of Tibetan Buddhist practices, and the revival of practices associated with the Thakali *dhoms*, or shamans. Attempts to clarify Thakali culture have all anchored their claims to authenticity in a traditional past, but these claims are disparate in form and content, and the validity of each has been repeatedly challenged by many of the Thakali themselves. Issues of identity, culture, and historical precedent have been the cause of public confrontations among the Thakali during the past two decades. Shortly after I began research among the Thakali in 1982, Thakali ethnic self-consciousness was raised to a high level by the events preceding and following the formation of the Thakali Sewa Samiti, a nationwide Thakali association.[7]

Squeezed among fifty-two other men and women, including some of the most successful entrepreneurs, contractors, shopkeepers, and traders in central Nepal, I sat in a modern *cementi* building under a corrugated steel roof on the hot and dusty afternoon of April 27, 1983 (Baisakh 14, 2040 V.S.), in the central Nepal *bazār* town of Pokhara. There are times and places in the plains and lower valleys of Nepal when heat and dust hang so heavy in the air that they seem to affect the judgment and good humor of everyone around, when one yearns for rain and one's mind desperately focuses on memories of the brisk air and cool water of high Himalayan valleys like Thak Khola. Pokhara in April 1983 was such a time and place.

Years of preliminary negotiations had brought together these delegates from Thakali communities throughout Nepal to form a national association. Charged with agreeing on a set of bylaws for a new nationwide Thakali association and a codification of Thakali cultural practices, the delegates had been engaged in five days of vigorous and sometimes acrimonious debate about what it meant to be Thakali. In the course of discussing line by line the drafted bylaws proposed by a fifteen-member ad hoc planning committee, debates and disagreements returned again and again to the nature and substance of Thakali cultural practices. This small community hall became a stage on which the complex, interwoven tensions of Thakali society were dramatically played out.

A wide variety of strongly held views concerning Thakali tradition were expressed. Some parties held that the Thakali should embrace Hinduism because it was the religion of their putative high-caste Thakuri forefathers; others that their forefathers were not Thakuri but Bhote or Tibetans and they should thus readopt Tibetan Buddhist practices; and yet others that they had never systematically followed Buddhist practices and now was not the time to start. Some speakers took the less doctrinal view that they should restore pure Thakali tradition, whatever that might be (an opinion often expressed with the qualification that the speaker himself was not professing to know what, exactly, Thakali tradition was). Other speakers urged that they stop arguing about religion (*dharma*) and agree to leave the matter up to individuals.

On this humid afternoon tempers were particularly short, and the tension in the room had grown to a palpable level as a speaker dramatically recounted his version of the history of the Thakali. The Thakali, he said, were descended from the Hansa Raja, a high-caste Thakuri prince who was said to be the son of the Hindu ruler of the Malla kingdom in Jumla. After the Hansa Raja and his followers migrated to central Nepal, the difficult environment forced them to give up the symbols and practices of their high Hindu status: they stopped wearing the sacred cord, because it was difficult to ritually bathe as frequently as necessary, and they drank alcohol and ate yak meat to survive. It is true, he acknowledged, that in the past the Thakali have followed some Buddhist practices, but this was not their original religion, and, he argued, it was never fully adopted by the Thakali. He further argued that the tradition of the indigenous Thakali ritual specialist, the *dhom*, always had a limited role in ritual and cultural life and that the *dhom* was never the sole religious practitioner in Thakali communities. As this speaker finally reached the end of his long tale, he began to state his conclusion and recommendations. "Thus," he began, "without a clear tradition to which to return, we ought to embrace Hinduism because it is the dharma of our forefathers and because it is the most practical dharma for our future."

Like a clap of thunder, loud voices interrupted his presentation, and the room erupted into almost immediate bedlam as delegates leapt to their feet to voice their objections. As the impassioned delegates vocalized their convictions, each more loudly than his or her neighbor, while ignoring the chairman's calls for order, it seemed for a moment that the shouting would escalate endlessly. Suddenly, a hailstorm of unusual intensity hurled ice against the corrugated metal roof above them, making such a clatter that the delegates were swiftly and completely silenced. For a few minutes they stood transfixed, and then, one by one or in small groups, they left the building in search of quieter shelter.

Imagining Thakali

The issues that perplex Thakali themselves become no clearer when we turn to the scholars, historians, and anthropologists who have written about them.[8] Assessments of the Thakali by the earliest scholars in central Nepal are intriguingly contradictory. For example, Giuseppe Tucci in 1951 found signs of both Hindu and Buddhist practices and saw Buddhism gaining in strength. One year later, David Snellgrove felt that Buddhist culture was in decline and only practiced by old women. In the following year, 1953, a Japanese scholar, Jiro Kawakita, observed that Thakalis "don't adhere much to either Hinduism or Lamaism," but he saw what he felt was a revivalism of Thakali "shamanistic" practices (1957:92). In 1958 Shigeru Iijima saw Hinduism gaining in strength and argued that the shaman's practice was reduced by the process of Hinduization. In 1962 Fürer-Haimendorf described what he observed to be a process of secularization camouflaged as Hinduization.[9]

Curiously, then, within the first decade of anthropological research in Nepal, from 1952 to 1962, scholars observed among the Thakali a gaining in strength of Buddhism, an increased emphasis on their original "shamanistic" cult, a conversion toward Hinduism, and a secularization camouflaged

as Hinduization. While it is possible to imagine these religious revivals occurring simultaneously (indeed, I think it likely that they were so occurring,
a point I will return to in latter discussions), they were not perceived that
way by scholars: in the view of all analysts, with the exception of Tucci, the
occurrence of each of these religious revivals was necessarily at the expense
of practices associated with the others. How, within a single decade of anthropological research and with access to almost identical ethnographic evidence, did scholars who agreed that Thakali culture was in the process of a
major transformation interpret that transformation so differently?

Emergent from these many views is a dominant story of the Thakali
that relies on the two aspects of the Thakali situation that have attracted
the greatest attention from scholars and travelers. The first of these is the
Thakalis' fame for making their way into the history of Nepal through the
monopolization of the salt-for-grain trade by means of an important north-
south route transversing the Himalayas from the lowlands of the Gangetic
plains to the Tibetan plateau. Their subsequent rise to regional political
power is widely regarded as unique and unprecedented in Nepal.[10] The
second aspect of the Thakali situation is the apparent cultural metamor-
phosis that is said to have followed their initial economic and political
success: they are characterized as a people who "purposefully and unilat-
erally" (Fürer-Haimendorf 1978) altered their social and religious behavior
and values to conform more closely to high-caste Hindu norms (see, for
example, Messerschmidt 1984:266).

An overemphasis on the first aspect of the Thakali situation has distorted
our understanding of the second: that is, the emphasis on one historical
era—the trading monopoly of 1862–1928, one select group of Thakali, and
one economic strategy—trade[11]—distorts our understanding of Thakali cultural change and continuity.[12] It is not an unusual phenomenon in scholarship that the single historical moment at which the scholar enters the scene
becomes privileged in his or her account(s), whether he or she enters the
scene literally, arriving with porters and notebooks, or metaphorically,
through the discovery of particular written records. Thus, while examining
and sorting out the processes and influence of culture and change on various
elements of Thakali society, this study includes a reexamination of the observations of previous scholars.

The literature on the Thakali emphasizes cultural change and frequently
alleges that the Thakali consciously abandoned old traditions in favor of
Hindu customs in order to justify their claim to high-caste Thakuri status.

The Thakali have often been characterized as a non-Hindu "tribe" or "tribal" group that, through the acceptance of Hindu values and beliefs, became a caste. Characterizations that portray the Thakali as a people purposefully altering their religious orientation and creating a new identity rely on two dichotomies that recur in the anthropological literature on Nepal: (1) tribe and caste; and (2) Hindu and non-Hindu. The emphasis place here on continuity, however, should not be taken to imply that the Thakali rise to regional prominence was not dramatic or without significant consequences for the community. My aim is to account for both change and continuity: to sort out the processes and influences of continuity and change in various elements of Thakali society.

Borderlands

Historically, the Thakali have long occupied a niche in Thak Khola that lies along the upper Kali Gandaki river valley in central Nepal, an region that has been a true geographic, cultural, and political border area. Geographically, the area sits on a major trade route that cuts through a gorge in the Himalayan range, providing a route from the lowlands to the Tibetan plateau. Culturally, it lies in an area where Tibetan Buddhist and Hindu cultural influences have long overlapped. Politically, it has been on the periphery of areas of political control that at various times have extended into the region from the north, west, and south. Living on a major trade route and yet remote from political centers, the Thakali have historically demonstrated an ability to adapt, at least outwardly, to a great variety of cultural and political forms.

This condition of being on so many kinds of borders, both literally and figuratively, has had profound repercussions for the Thakali and requires careful attention. In the context of the wide interactions entailed by their straddling of numerous borders, Thakali identity is necessarily defended by various kinds of boundaries, boundaries that must be flexible enough to adapt to a variety of changing contexts. Anna Tsing has noted that "borders are a particular kind of margin; they have an imagined other side. The image of the border turns attention to the creative projects of self-definition of those at the margins." Highlighting the perspective of actors who are in a position to imagine and act on multiple possibilities "raises issues of agency without neglecting the constraints of power and knowledge" (1993:21). The Thakali are an excellent example of a border people who have found ways to act creatively within the constraints imposed by externally based systems of power and knowledge. Renato Rosaldo's characterization of "border cross-ings" as "sites of creative production" (1989:208) is especially appropriate for the Thakali, many of whom pride themselves on their ability to function equally well on both sides of their "borders." We cannot understand the complexity of their case until we shift our focus from the merely local to include the broader context within which the local operates and how the local is both peripheral to and integrated with larger political entities. Fluent in several languages and conversant in several religious and cultural tradi-tions, the Thakali have demonstrated mastery of the multiple character of their borderland and have been able to move in and out of a variety of situations adroitly. They continued to demonstrate these adaptive skills when they migrated out of the upper Kali Gandaki region into strikingly diverse communities and socioeconomic contexts.

The wide variety of sociocultural contexts within which the migrant Thakali communities now reside further complicates the issue of group iden-tity and solidarity among the Thakali. Over the past two centuries, beginning before their nineteenth-century rise to regional prominence, the Thakali had begun to migrate from Thak Khola, their homeland in central Nepal, into areas in the middle hills, where they still maintain considerable political and economic influence. This movement brought them into increasing con-tact with populations with different cultural traditions, including some heavily influenced by Hindu traditions of the subcontinent. In the past four decades, following the reduction in trade over the Nepal-Tibet border, in-creasing numbers of Thakalis have migrated from Thak Khola and settled in the major urban and commercial areas throughout Nepal—Pokhara, Kathmandu, Bhairawa, Butwal-Kasauli, Nepalgunj—as well as in many smaller market towns located throughout the central hills. No more than 20 percent of the total Thakali population currently resides permanently in Thak Khola. While the significance of these migrated communities has been discussed and the need for a study of them noted, only my work in the 1980s has considered the particular dynamics involved in the patterns of Thakali migration and the adaptation of identity to particular socioeconomic con-texts.[13]

A basic proposition underlying this study is that since migration has played such a key role in Thakali economic and social history, to understand different groups' claims to be Thakali one must consider the Thakali both in relation to the contexts within which they operate and in contexts where members of these groups interact with members of other groups. Migrant Thakali populations come under both local and national pressures to adjust their cultural beliefs and practices. Not surprisingly, as migration out of the Thak Khola increased and Thakali families became well established elsewhere in Nepal and adapted to different socioeconomic contexts, their different interpretations of Thakali tradition have become more apparent. Yet despite, or perhaps because of, this dispersion and these differences in interpretation, there is a strong motivation to maintain or rekindle Thakali identity.

This book's concern with boundaries considers both the efforts of the Thakali themselves to search for a "true" culture and history and the tendency of scholars to describe changes in Thakali cultural practices as unilineal, absolute, and irreversible.

Tourists in Their Own Land

Earlier in the day described at the beginning of this chapter, on which the clan deities were first lifted and carried on their symbolic journey, I went across the Kali Gandaki River to explore some relatively obscure ritual sites with several Thakali friends, two of whom had returned to the valley for the first time in twenty-five years. These two were intellectuals in their forties—a computer engineer and a professor of political science—and intensely interested in discovering things about their own culture. To travel with them and to see Thak Khola remembered and rediscovered through their eyes was to view it in a way I had not done before. They were, in the most positive sense, tourists in their own homeland; they took pleasure in each new discovery and showed intense interest in every oddity they discovered along the way.

During this trip they confirmed that they had been successful in arranging for a public meeting that would be sponsored by the Lha Phewa organizing committee. Seventeen speakers were to address the topic of Thakali culture, and I was to be among them. Given the Thakalis' enormous interest in discovering their history, culture, and identity, it was not surprising that at a large gathering of Thakalis dedicated to reconstructing a mythic story of the past and rereading the clan *rhabs*, or histories, some individuals would seize the opportunity to organize a seminar on the topic of Thakali culture. It should be equally unsurprising that while I saw this as a welcome opportunity to share my thoughts with the Thakali, I was also wary. The list of participants included many of my friends and informants, whose views were at odds with one another. For an earlier workshop, held in Kathmandu in 1983, the organizers had invited a number of foreign scholars to address the Thakali community. Two had accepted. Recollection of the frank conclusions of one of these scholars was still enough to rouse heated responses among the Thakali.[14]

While participation in a workshop organized to address the question "Who are the Thakali?" would be equally appropriate for both Thakali and those who have conducted research among them, there is a fundamental difference between answering this question from the perspective of "Who are we?" and answering it from the perspective of "Who are you?" This difference is not readily apparent to those Thakali and researchers who see the question as an empirical one with a discoverable, definitive answer. But for those scholars who approach identity not as a discoverable thing but as an ongoing process of conflict and negotiation, the difference is critical. Any speaker acknowledged as Thakali has a right to address the question "Who are we?" however much his or her answer may be rejected by others. As a non-Thakali participating in a public discussion about culture when Thakali culture was already heavily politicized, I faced several challenges. Scheduled to participate with sixteen members of the Thakali community, many of whom were among the most knowledgeable of the informants I had relied on over the past decade, I was keenly aware of these challenges. Any answer was bound to offend some members of the community, and the appropriateness of my participation was certain to be challenged by those who would disagree with my conclusions. This was not a straightforward issue where I could take refuge in just speaking the "truth."

Part of my challenge was the need to explain the difference between my research agenda and the Thakali concern with culture. Throughout my years of research, I often encountered individual Thakali, sometimes in the most unlikely places—shopping for yoghurt in Kathmandu, sipping tea along the trails in Baglung District, cooling my heels in the Myagdi River—who exhorted me to address my research efforts to answering the question that most troubled them. They repeatedly argued that while my concerns with cultural complexities and historical processes might be interesting to foreign scholars, my real task, from their perspective, should be discovering the true history and culture of the Thakali.

Now I found myself invited to enter into a public debate I had always observed but within which I had not yet publicly participated. Not only was

I asked to participate as an outsider in what I considered to be an internal process of negotiation but also to do so on par with those who were the most knowledgeable members of the Thakali community. Despite my concerns, however, I did not hesitate to accept the invitation. My acceptance of the invitation to speak on the question of Thakali culture to the Thakali community as a scholar who had conducted research among the Thakali was consistent with a promise I had made to the Thakali Sewa Samiti in April 1983 to share my work with the Thakali community. The challenge was to address tactfully the gap between the question they wanted to address (what is our true tradition?) and the question I found most compelling (how does culture practice evolve over time and under specific circumstances?). I had to negotiate a balance among conveying my concerns, remaining faithful to the intent of the workshop's organizers, not offending my friends and principal informants, and not publicly privileging any one of their views over the others.

The differences among the approaches to history and culture favored by the Thakali, by earlier scholars of the Thakali, and me turn on core concepts of anthropological discourse, in particular, history, structure, agency, community, and power. I wanted my answer to the Thakali to illustrate the essential interdependence of anthropology and history in the study of social systems, to demonstrate the inadequacy of synchronic models that presuppose the perpetuation or reproduction of existing sociocultural structures, to challenge teleological models that make simplistic projections about the nature and direction of processes of change, and to refute a set of stubborn dichotomies in the legacy of South Asian studies. All this, of course, had to be done in a nonspecialized discourse, in the vocabulary available in Nepali, and in a manner accessible to an audience with widely divergent educational backgrounds and interests.

My answer had to take into consideration three important issues. First, history and culture were central concerns to both the Thakali and me, but the notions of history and culture commonly held by the Thakali were in contrast with the notions of history and culture as ongoing and conflicted processes that informed my research and this book. Second, during my decade of research on the Thakali, their society had been characterized by a very high level of group consciousness and public debate about Thakali culture, tradition, history, and identity. The politicization of this public debate was but the most recent manifestation of the construction and recreation of Thakali culture. This process of constructing Thakali society has never occurred in a vacuum but has been embedded in changing local,

regional, and national political and economic contexts. Third, in my judgment, the difficulty of articulating and presenting aspects of Thakali cultural
practices to themselves and to others is due in part to the inappropriateness,
arbitrariness, and rigidity of the categories and conceptual boundaries available to them.

Reclaiming Culture

While the Thakali readily acknowledge that their current practices are
heterogeneous—and, many would argue, hybridized—and while many of
the Thakali would defer to the authority of unspecified others on the subject
of Thakali culture, they commonly hold that (1) the Thakali did have a
culture, in the sense of an essential, identifiable set of specific practices and
beliefs inextricably linked to their historical origins; and (2) while they had
lost sight of their culture sometime in the past, it was still possible to redis-
cover and reclaim it. This prevalent view of culture as a discoverable thing
contrasted with the view of culture as process that I carried into the field,
with the emphasis on the importance of people as agents in the formation,
maintenance, and transformation of their own culture, and with the concern
I had for the Thakalis' role in constructing their own histories. Along with
other contemporary scholars, I view the practice of making culture—the
production and reproduction of collectively held dispositions and understandings—as problematic. As Foster says, it as a process of multiple contests
informed by a diversity of historically specific actions and intentions
(1991:235).

The Thakali perception of culture as a thing, the true nature of which
could be recovered despite the mutations and mutilations it has suffered
through migration and cultural contact, contrasted with my own concerns with the historical processes leading to the expression of a form of
Thakali identity by specific groups at particular points in time. At the
same time, their own actions over the previous decade had been a dem-
onstration of cultural production as an ongoing activity coincident with
the process of social life.[15] I argue in the chapters that follow that Thakali
culture is not composed of rigid institutional and cognitive pieces that
form stable and static structures; it is instead flexible, permeable, and
malleable, with fluid boundaries. It is continually reinvented and modified without being totally transformed. Cultures in general, and Thakali

culture in particular, have always just become what they always already are; they are formed and reformed as individuals and groups confront their world and create their own histories.

Agency/Action/Practice

Cultures are not simply in the process of being constructed; they are being constructed by someone. Attention to the agents through whom and by whom culture is constructed, created, and re-created avoids the assumption that cultures and social groups are coterminous, homogeneous, and undifferentiated. Individuals have different access to resources and knowledge, and they live under varying circumstances. Thus we expect that, at least in some ways, the meaning of being Thakali for someone in Thak Khola is different from that experience for someone who grew up in Khani Khuwa or Kathmandu. Being a person the "Thakali way" varies as people attempt to reproduce a way of life during a time in which local, national, and global events alter the experience of life in profound ways.

For example, Thakali culture and identity are reproduced in the context of the social networks, families, and villages within which individuals are raised and reside. Within these contexts, individuals learn—what it is to be Thakali, Nepalese, Bhote, Khuwale, male—at a time when to be any of these things is changing. These identities are learned within the context of changing institutions—families, schools, lineages—each of which has its own (changing) form of discourse for talking about the world. Ideas about tradition, nation, caste, and gender are conditioned by practice and interpreted in terms of a discourse that emphasizes certain values. In this process, talking about new practices with old language stretches that language and develops new meanings, often in contention with the old.

To question the degree to which culture is a coherent interconnected system is not to postulate that culture is naught but a historical accident, an aggregate of separable parts. If culture is an assemblage—a metaphor used by Moore (1989:38)—it is one within which rearrangements and recompositions are inevitable and continuous. We must go beyond the identification of paradoxes to discover how disjunctions and contradictions are continually generated and restructured. That is, in addressing the issue of Thakali culture we need to ask questions about change and continuity simultaneously.

The Thakali case illustrates the simultaneous independence and inter-dependence of culture with ongoing sociopolitical processes of wider societal contexts. The formation of Thakali identity is and has been a process of interaction and definition of collective self in opposition to others; thus there are two aspects to it: a determining of what and who "we" are not and of what "we" are, do, and believe. This dual process occurs within the context of being a part of and yet somehow separate from larger wholes, such as the state. This process of identification is ongoing as both these elements change and are redefined over time.

Many of the events described in this book—Lha Phewa, the formation of the Thakali Sewa Samiti, Thakali disagreements about ritual practice—are not to be understood as exemplary examples of Thakali symbolic or social order. On the contrary, they provide windows that open on to the interactions between structure and practice, revealing these interactions to be ongoing processes in which structure and practice are constantly being shaped, re-produced, and transformed through negotiation and activity.[16]

Anthropologists and historians have been widely criticized for their complicity in the formulation of ethnic projects defining and reifying bounded communities. While early studies in Nepal tended to analytically isolate ethnic groups and thus inadvertently contribute to the perception of them as bounded and timeless entities,[17] more recent studies in Nepal have recognized that ethnic boundaries emerged in tandem with the development of the Nepali state and that these boundaries were and remain fluid (see, for instance, Levine 1988; Holmberg 1989; Guneratne 1994; Fisher 1987).

From the Thakali case emerges a picture in which conflicting discourses and patterns of practice pose both problems and possibilities for actors. Culture does not operate as a static, homogeneous force working on the actors but "in and through its varying relations with various actors" (Ortner 1989:14). The Thakali comprise actors culturally constructed in different historical eras and contexts interacting over time. As they forge their own lives under circumstances not of their own choosing, they encounter and struggle with the constraints of their varying social, political, and material contexts. While in many other cases, anthropologists focus on how constrained actors ever come to transform the conditions of their existence, in the Thakali case we might also wonder how actors who are products of so many differing forces and contexts maintain a sense of identity based on a dynamic and contested structure.

I take ethnicity to be a social construction and not a simple cultural given defined by primordial evidence such as language, dress, social organization, religion, and the like. Individuals have access to numerous dimensions of identity—for example, those based on class, kinship, locality, or religion—some of which become more important at certain times. Historically in Nepal, as is true elsewhere, it has been moments of political or economic crisis that have often been the catalyst that brings forth aspects of group and individual identity. Looked at over time, the interactions within and between groups and the conflicts between national identity and other identities reveal a changing set of relationships. Ethnicity is not an ad hoc or random social construction but a re-creation using the past (albeit partially or wholly imagined) to construct a present with an eye toward the future.

Ethnic boundaries are fluid and flexible but not indefinitely so.[18] They move in response to economic and political opportunities and constraints and vary within the community depending on such factors as age, gender, locale, occupation, education, and so forth (see also Williams, Foster). In Nepal, as elsewhere, these constraints are and have been affected by the constraints set in play by the emerging and changing nature of the state.

The current process of Thakali cultural contestation and reform is the contemporary manifestation of an ongoing process. Identity is relational and thus dynamic, constantly changing, emerging over time through interaction with other groups and with the state. Thakali identity, in particular, emerged or solidified after the consolidation of the state in the eighteenth century and the codification of the Muluki Ain, the legal code of 1854. The period 1779–1846, particularly the years following the death of Prithvi Narayan Shah[19] in 1775, was marked by wars and overall political instability. Jang Bahadur's 1854 Muluki Ain was both a product and a means of implementation of an emerging political consolidation. Höfer has described the Muluki Ain as an attempt to "re-legitimate the identity of Nepal and to motivate the solidarity of her citizens" by integrating three historically and regionally distinct caste systems—those of the Newar, the Parbatiya, and the plains peoples—as well as a variety of loosely defined groups in the middle hills, into one national hierarchy (1979a:40). This code and its emphasis on ascribed status characterize the period of secular rule by the Rana prime ministers from 1846 to 1951. In the Nepali case, group identity emerged as an effect of the project of state formation, a project that produced hierarchized forms of conceiving and treating people by assigning categories of people varying degrees of social status and privileges. The Muluki Ain of 1854 and King Mahendra's new legal code of 1964, which cleared the way for a competitive society and placed an emphasis on achieved status, both mark significant turning points in Nepalese history, and, as I will discuss in the ensuing chapters, each had an influence on the evolution of Thakali ethnic identity, their interactions with other Nepalese *jāts*, and attempts to improve their relative *jāt* status.

Addressing Thakali and scholarly concerns about the character of Thakali culture and history must consider why, when, and to whom the Thakali feel the need to answer questions about their identity, their *jāt*, and their culture. Their answers emerge within contexts of changing conditions, opportunities, and constraints. Only by examining these multiple contexts can we come to understand how interrelated sets of artificers have been and are forging histories: the Thakali, high-caste Hindus, and anthropologists have all contributed to the forging of histories in central Nepal.

Recent dramatic changes in central Nepal — particularly the overthrow of the partyless *panchayat* system and the establishment of a constitutional monarchy in 1990 and the ensuing debate about caste, national culture, and discrimination — have underscored the fluid and malleable character of the discourse underlying the artifice of the nation of Nepal and drawn our attention to the always ongoing process of forming and transforming societies. The issue of Nepal's cultural diversity became especially heated during the writing of Nepal's new democratic constitution. Conflict emerged between the desire of elites to describe and encourage a unified and homogeneous national culture based on the values of high-caste Hindu hill society and the demand that the government treat the multiple languages, cultures, and religions of Nepal equally. Non-Hindu populations in particular argued for more varied representation on the constitutional committee. In response to numerous queries by foreigners and Nepalese alike as to how the committee intended to ensure that the new constitution represented the will of all the people, members of the largely urban, male, high-caste Hindu committee replied that the previous political system had been overthrown by the will of the people, that they represented these people, and that they would thus act in the interest of all the people. Some members went so far as to insist (inaccurately) that the rural non-Hindus in Nepal were largely illiterate and thus incapable of participating in the process. In response to inquiries concerning the equally heated issue of whether Nepal should be a Hindu or secular state, a Brahmin representative professed to see no problem, saying, "In Nepal, Buddhism has always been accepted as a version of Hinduism, and only now they are trying to claim that Buddhism is a separate religion."[20] This conflict pits those who are striving to introduce democracy while maintaining the hegemony of a national culture based on high-caste Hindu values and practices against those who are attempting to use the differences once highlighted and encouraged by the Muluki Ain to establish a more democratic and equitable access to power.

Fluid Boundaries

I pondered all these things as I crossed back from the Sauru side of the Kali Gandaki River to Kobang. During this season the river is relatively easy to cross. The riverbed is particularly wide, and the current cuts its way in numerous separate streams through the loose gray and black gravel. Among these stones are found ammonite fossils (*shāligrams*), which are regarded as sacred by Hindu pilgrims to the shrine of Muktinath. Some of the streams are narrow enough to be leapt across; the wider ones are crossed on logs. From time to time these logs are washed away and then replaced. The flow of the river changes during the course of a day, from season to season, and from year to year, with the main current meandering from side to side. As it flows down from Tibet, the river sometimes divides into a number of major strands; some will connect and then redivide. Crossing the river in other seasons can be a real challenge, requiring one to assess the depth of the various channels, the force of the flow, and the rise and fall of the river during the day as it increases from forces outside the immediate area, largely from glacial runoff far upstream.

I stood in the middle of the riverbed and considered anew how complex the relationship of this place was to the Thakali: to those who still lived there, to those who were born here and now rarely return, and even to those born elsewhere who had never visited. More than a merely physical place, it provided the symbolic material for a whole set of complex and shifting relationships. As Rafael has observed of the "local," "Rather than a static place, [it] turns out to have shifting partial and temporal boundaries; a nexus of asymmetrical exchanges, conflictual interests, and multiple histories" (1993:xiii).

The river valley had been a main trade route linking the middle hills of Nepal with the high plateau of Tibet via an easy pass north of the town of Mustang. I stood in a valley, at the twenty-ninth parallel between 83°5′ and 84 longitude east, 30 kilometers long, hemmed in by the Annapurna range of the Himalaya and the eastern slopes of Dhaulagiri. The distance between the Annapurna massif and Dhaulagiri is 35 kilometers. In the west,

FIGURE 1.1 The Bhattachan clan priest, shaking and prancing like a yak with large bells wrapped around his body approaching the crossroads from the north during Lha Phewa.

Dhaulagiri rises abruptly from the valley floor of 2,500 meters to 8,172 meters. On the eastern side the slopes rise more gradually to alpine pasture at an altitude of 4,000 meters before reaching the peak of Annapurna I at 8,080 meters. The area that was immediately around me is called Thaksatsae (*Thāksātsae*, lit. "the seven hundred Thāk") by the Thakali; to the immediate north lies an area known as Panchgaon (*pāchgāũ*, N, lit. "five villages"), whose inhabitants identify themselves as Thakali but who are not acknowl-

FIGURE 1.2 Thaksatsae looking north toward Tukche

edged by the Thaksatsae Thakali as members of the same group. And though some attend and even play a role in the twelve-year festival, they do not participate as members of one of the clans whose deities are being propitiated.

While this place is important to the Thakali, its significance varies. For some, the actual land, the local deities, and the ongoing boundary disputes are part of the real substance of everyday life. For others, the area's importance is more abstract: it provides a sense of belonging to a place, even though one migrates from it and never returns until after death. Above the villages in front of me I could see the gleaming white *khimi*s (ossuaries) of the subclans, or lineages, in which a small piece of bone of each deceased lineage member ought to be deposited.

It was the river that gave me an analogy to use to convey my thoughts to the Thakali, a river whose peculiarities would be obvious to all of them. Thakali culture, I said in part, is like the Kali Gandaki River. It flows in a wide riverbed that allows it to break up into several meandering streams that merge again downstream. These separations and mergings vary unpredictably over time, but the separated channels always rejoin further downstream.

If you ask me which channel is the main channel, how could I answer? I could tell you which stream was the strongest one today, but I could not tell you which channel was the original or true channel of the river. The flow of the river changes from one season to the next, from one year to the next. We can describe it as we encounter it at a particular moment. Other individuals viewing the river in another year or in another season and comparing it to our description would recognize it to be the same river by its general location and by the general boundaries of the riverbed hemmed in by the mountains, but they would find the specifics of our description inadequate, even inaccurate. The river changes over time. Sometimes it flows peacefully and at other times with great turbulence. At any specific time it may be deeper, shallower, stronger, or weaker than at others. It may run in one channel or in five. But it is nevertheless the same river.

Similarly, any description of Thakali culture is at best a representation of a moment in an ongoing cultural process. The difficulty of locating cultural coherence does not mean that Thakali culture has broken down or that it is in a transitional phase between one coherent structure and another. It merely reflects the process in which Thakali culture has been continually renewed.

Fluid Boundaries examines the relationship of social practice, historical processes, and culture in a Nepali society. Specifically, the book addresses the changing conditions, opportunities, and constraints under which sets of agents forge histories, visions, and procedures for organizing, and it examines the conflict that arises as people construct their identities and communities through innovation and accommodation. It asks why claims to status and identity are expressed in particular ways at particular times and explores the contexts within which these claims become critical issues. This study of the Thakali of west-central Nepal analyzes the way identity and culture are defined and acted on over time within the highly differentiated, relatively rigid, plural society of Nepal; my concern is with the myriad processes—social, political, economic, and cultural—whereby the Thakali define themselves and are defined by others as a specific group within various regional contexts and within Nepalese society at large.

The book concludes that the process of constructing boundaries is an ongoing one in which boundaries, rather than being rigidly constructed, remain fluid. This process is engaged in simultaneously by the Thakali and by those who encounter them: their neighbors, agents of the state, anthropologists, travelers, and so forth. It is a contribution to academic discussions of the relationships among the structures of society and culture, human action, and political economy. My account stresses the specificity of experiences, institutions, and discourses, and it is in this sense an ethnographic account. But the emphasis on specificity does not presume that the relationship between "cultures" and their adherents are perfectly contiguous. More than contiguity, the examination reveals permeable cultural boundaries that reflect control and abandonment, selective recollection and forgetting, exclusion and sharing, all taking place within larger regional, national, and global processes (see Said 1989). The project involves the study of intersecting discursive fields in which social identities are created and maintained, the contexts within which and the methods by which the Thakali have sought to define and redefine themselves and their relationships to other groups and categories of people in Nepal. The intersection of processes within which identity in Nepal is shaped—state formation and rule, the emergence and transformation of regional and ethnic identities—reverberate with asymmetry, inequality, and domination, reflecting a world that is politically charged.

This book is, in part, an account of my attempt to understand the Thakali attempt to understand what it means to be Thakali.[21] Specifically, it takes as its focus attempts by the Thaksatsae Thakali to define their identity more precisely and to unify and codify their cultural practices. The events leading up to and following the founding of the nationwide Thakali association in April 1983 and the subsequent yearly meetings of that organization's general assembly exposed deep divisions among the Thaksatsae Thakali and revealed the ways in which religious identity reflects political and social status both within the group and in Nepalese society at large. By unpacking the conflicts, tensions, and factions intertwined in and exposed by attempts to discover and use Thakali culture and history as the basis of a new group unity, the book explores the ways in which the Thakali respond to and transform social contexts in various locales and at various historical moments.

Ironically, the attempts by the Thakali over the past two decades to define their identity and clarify their practices reveal that to return to tradition they must first re-create it, but this process of re-creation establishes tradition in a way in which it has never existed before. That is, to return to tradition—to become Thakali again—is, in a way, to become Thakali for the very first time.

2 Drawing Lines: On Constructing and Contesting Boundaries

Here the boundaries meet and all contradictions exist
side by side.
— Dostoyevski, *The Brothers Karamazov*

I wish to pose the question of the bord, the edge, the border. . . .
The question of the borderline precedes, as it were, the determination of all the
dividing lines.
— Jacques Derrida

After Lha Phewa in January 1993, while my friends and I were walking north along the Kali Gandaki river valley to reach the hard, packed grazing land that now serves as an airport for small eighteen-seat planes at Jomsom, my friends tried once more to convince me that as part of my research I should get to the bottom of the dispute over the land where the Larjung Hotel now stands. During the course of Lha Phewa celebrations this issue had been the subject of several emotional meetings and many private discussions among the Thakali. Nor was this the first time the issue had arisen: it had been discussed at the previous twelve-year festival in 1981 and had resurfaced numerous times during the years between. "This land is sacred," my friend Lal repeated. "On the thirteenth day of the festival the clan deities should rest right on the site of that building. That land belongs to the village, and no one should ever have been allowed to build there. The Larjung headman should never have given permission to that family." This comment started my friends on a long discussion of the lamentable failure of some headmen to meet their responsibilities to their families, their villages, and the Thakali community as a whole, the changes they perceived to have resulted from the declining attention of the Thakali to culture and history, and the likely future of a people whose leaders now seem to put individual personal profit ahead of the preservation of sacred sites. As Thakali educated and residing outside the valley, my friends felt it was incumbent on those remaining there to uphold what they considered to be the noble traditions of the past. The dispute over the boundaries of the sacred sites of Lha Phewa served as a means to debate and reenforce appropriate social and political behavior.

North of the village of Tukche we quickly reached the *chorten* (Tib.: religious construction) at a site called Dhocho Kang. This *chorten* marks the southern boundary of a disputed area. The residents of the villages to the north argue that it marks the boundary between Thaksatsae and Panchgaon. The Thakali from Thaksatsae acknowledge that this was once the border, but they insist that it was later moved north to the river Dhon by the order of the king of Parbat. The entire region between these two points is currently a desolate land where no one is allowed to build. As we walked the two-mile stretch toward the Dhon River, my friends turned their conversation to the border dispute with Panchgaon. As they talked, they recalled parts of the oral traditions of the Thakali, including the story of the Hansa Raja and the land given by the Thini Raja on the marriage of the Hansa Raja and Nhima Rani, the daughter of the Thini Raja. They recalled the eighteenth-century influence of the Parbat Raja and his moving of the border north to the Dhon River.[1] Their talk became more and more animated as they discussed the relative arguments made by the Panchgaonle to the north and the Thakali from Thaksatsae to the south, other disputes between the two groups, and differences in culture, history, and status. Here, as in their discussion of the Larjung case, the recollection of a boundary dispute about land quickly evolved into a discussion about cultural and social boundaries. This time, as I found myself listening to another variation on a debate I had heard so many times before, it became clearer to me that one outcome of these discussions is less resolution of the disputes than the development of narratives useful for the reexamination of history, culture, and difference.

The Terms of Boundary Disputes

There are essential disagreements involving the use of the terms *Thakali* and *Thak Khola*, both of which have been inconsistently applied by scholars and Nepalese alike. There are, however, general parameters within which these terms are applied. The term *Thakali*, in its broadest use, refers to peoples residing in or claiming a connection to the upper Kali Gandaki valley, which lies between the Himalayan ranges of Annapurna and Dhaulagiri.

The term *Thak Khola* refers to part of the upper Kali Gandaki valley, though not to an area with exact geographical boundaries.[2] Some argue that the term *Thak Khola* literally designates the river valley inhabited by the Thak or Thakali people, while others define Thakali as referring to a native of the district of Thak in Nepal.[3] Whether the river valley is named for the people or the people for the valley is unclear, but, in any case, the terms do suggest a close association between a particular place and a people. The boundaries that both circumscribe and delineate the place and the people, however, are actively contested, and even when theoretically delineated, they turn out to be fluid in practice. In this chapter, I examine the problematic of drawing boundary lines—lines of both inclusion and exclusion—whether they are drawn by schematizing scholars or by the populations themselves. As Ortega y Gasset has observed, "Only when elementary things are subdued can we advance toward the more complex" (1961:87). This chapter begins by subduing the entangled and apparently contradictory use of the terms *Thak Khola* and *Thakali* in a process of circumscribing and extending identity claims.

Thak Khola

The names Thak, Thag, or Thak Khola refer to an area of the upper Kali Gandaki that lies between the Himalayan peaks of Dhaulagiri (8,167 meters) and Annapurna I (8,078 meters) (see map 3). Some writers and cartographers have adopted the term to indicate all the upper Kali Gandaki valley south of Lo (Tib.: *glo*).[4] Its southern border is generally agreed to be Ghāsa, the first village of consequence situated directly north of the narrow canyon that which leads from the south into the upper Kali Gandaki valley. Its northern border is variously placed at Tukche, Jomsom, Kagbeni, or just below Lo: for example, Snellgrove has used "T'hak" to refer to the area south of Jomsom (1961:174 n); Jest referred to "Thak" as the area between "Ghasa" and "Tukucha" (1964/65:25); Vinding has called Thak Khola the area of "Thaksatsai" stretching from Ghāsā to Tukche and Panchgaon the area extending north from Tukche to Jomsom (1984).[5] Jackson has observed that in its conventional use as a geographical name, Thak Khola designates an area that includes a heterogeneous collection of Thakali and non-Thakali communities. There is no equivalent name for the whole area in the available Tibetan language texts (Jackson 1978:196).[6] A number of scholars have suggested that Thak Khola can be divided into two parts, the southern portion correlating with the areas of Panchgaon and Thāksātsae and the northern portion consisting primarily of the area commonly called Baragaon (N: *bāragāū*, "the twelve villages").[7]

The valley and the trade route running south from the Tibetan border through the valley and on to the market towns of Riri and Butwal in the south were first described in the early nineteenth century by Kirkpatrick and Hamilton (1811:287; [1819] 1971:273–74).[8] Hodgson later referred to the Thakoras of Nepal's northern border ([1874] 1971, 2:13). The earliest first-hand account of the valley was included in a report issued by then lieutenant-colonel Thomas George Montgomerie, recounting the journey of one of his *pundits* in the fall of 1875 crossing into Nepal from Kumaon.[9] This agent arrived in Thak Khola during an attempted journey to Tibet. While in Lo, Montgomerie's agent observed Thakali and described them as "a class of traders of mixed origins, who have the privilege of going to Lhasa, and they even go to Calcutta for the purchase of goods" (Montgomerie 1875:358). This account provides a description of the upper Kali Gandaki valley and the trade route to Riri *bazār*.

While there is no clear agreement (among the residents of the valley, those residing elsewhere who are referred to as Thakali, Nepalese, or scholars) as to the use of the terms *Thak Khola* and *Thakali*, generally those who narrowly interpret one term will invariably interpret the other equally narrowly. Thus a restricted application of the term *Thakali* usually entails a narrow definition for the area Thak or Thak Khola, while a broad interpretation of *Thak Khola* implies a broader application of the term *Thakali*. In this text I use the terms *Thak*, *Thaksatsae*, and *Thasang* interchangeably to refer to the area from the village of Ghāsā in the south to Tukche in the north. I follow current colloquial use in applying the term *Thak Khola* to a wide stretch of the upper Kali Gandaki reaching approximately from Ghāsā to Jomsom.

The upper Kali Gandaki valley falls within the administrative district of Mustang in Dhaulagiri Zone (see map 3). The distance from Ghāsā in the south to Jomsom in the north is approximately 32 kilometers, with the major villages situated at altitudes ranging from 1,900 meters to 2,700 meters above sea level. Higher elevations ranging up to 4,000 meters on the ridges lining the valley are used for pasturage. Villages in the upper Kali Gandaki valley are nuclear settlements situated close to the valley floor, usually where tributaries join the Kali Gandaki. The largest villages are Marpha, Jomsom,

Tukche, Syang, and Thini, each with around one hundred houses. These villages are occupied by a number of related yet distinct endogamous clan-based populations, many of whom identify themselves to outsiders as Thakali, but not all of whom would agree that the others are entitled to the use of the label.

The Term *Thakali*

The designation *Thakali* is a term more relevant to the interactions of Thak Khola residents with nonresidents or putative Thakali with non-Thakali than it is to interactions among the various groups who call themselves or are referred to by others as Thakali. One cannot say precisely how long the Nepali term has been employed for or by residents of Thak Khola. There is no equivalent term among the Tibeto-Burmese dialects of the groups who reside in Thak Khola.[10]

Among the people who call themselves Thakali, three distinct clan-based groups make significant efforts to mark their exclusivity. Those who are the principle subject of this book belong to the largest and best known of these groups.[11] They derive from the area that its members call Thāksātsae.[12] The people of Thāksātsae insist that only their area can rightly be called Thāk Kholā.

As I noted in chapter 1, some contemporary scholars refer to this group as the Tamang Thakali.[13] Many members of this group object vociferously to this form of address, arguing that they are not a *type* of Thakali, but *the* Thakali. These protesters argue further that if a qualifier is needed to distinguish them from other groups to the north, more appropriate terms would be the *Thāksātsae Thakali* or the *chan Thakali*.[14] In deference to the sentiments of my informants, I do not use the term *Tamang Thakali* in this book. Instead, I generally refer to them as they refer to themselves, as Thakali, except in instances where to distinguish them from other so-called Thakali groups I refer to them as Thaksatsae Thakali and to the northern groups as Panchgaonle.[15]

The Thaksatsae Thakali are the most exclusive of the groups in the upper Kali Gandaki valley, and most of them insist that of all the groups resident in this area, they, and only they, are Thakali: most vocal in this regard have generally been those descended from the Tukche merchant families. Members of this group call themselves Thakali when speaking with people from outside Thak Khola.

It was members of these families who, through a contract with the central government, controlled the salt trade through the valley from 1860 until the middle of the twentieth century.[16] The Thaksatsae Thakali are an autocephalous, ideally endogamous group composed of four named, strictly exogamous, patrilineal clans: Bhattachan (T: Bhurgi), Sherchan (T: Ḍhimchen), Tulachan (T: Salgi), and Gauchan (T: Chyogi).[17] The clans are further divided into named, exogamous, corporate segments called *ghyupa* or *phobe* (see table 2.1).[18] There has been some confusion in the literature concerning the nature of the clans and their subsections, a confusion increased by the Thaksatsae Thakalis' inconsistent use of terms such as *ghyu, ghyupa, ghyuwa, thar,* and *phobe*.[19] For consistency, I adhere to the use of the term clan for the four major descent groups of Thaksatsae Thakali society and employ the Thakali term *phobe* or the English *subclans* for the segments of the clans, which have been variously termed "subclans," "lineages," and "patrilineages" by other writers. I use the term *lineage* to refer to the unnamed subdivisions of the *phobe*.[20] The descent system of the Thaksatsae Thakali is discussed in greater detail below.

The Thaksatsae Thakali, while they refer to themselves as Thakali, now rarely use the name Thakali as a surname, by and large preferring to use the appropriate clan names as surnames.[21] Outsiders (scholars, travelers, and other Nepalese, etc.) always refer to the Thaksatsae Thakali as Thakali but are inconsistent in their application of the nomenclature to the other groups resident in Thak Khola.

Contesting Boundaries

As I have already noted, the geographical, cultural, and social boundaries between the Thakali of Thaksatsae and their neighbors are and have been aggressively contested. Immediately to the north of Thaksatsae lies an area known as Panchgaon in Nepali or Yhulnghā in Thakali.[22] Originally there were five villages—Thini or Thinang, Syang, Marpha, Chimang, and Chairo—but today there are several more. The inhabitants of these villages are often referred to collectively as Panchgaonle (i.e., the inhabitants of Panchgaon), but they consist of two distinct endogamous groups.

One endogamous group occupies the village Marpha (N).[23] This group comprises four named, exogamous, patrilineal clans: *Gumli thowa phobe* (N: Juharchan), *Gumli chyangpa phobe* (Panachan), *Puta phobe* (Hirachan),

TABLE 2.1 Thakali *Phobe*, or Subclans[1]

Gauchan	Bhattachan
Bhalamtan	Bharā dhorche
Chen	Cyāng mhirki
Ḍhom phobe[2]	Dyātan (2)
a. Bhlentan	Dyātan (1)[5]
b. Sapratan	Khunerā
c. Nakhungtan cyāng	Lama
Dyātan	Lhapu cyāng
Ghai mhirki	Mhi cyāng
Gharle	Ngha cyāng mhirki
Ghera	Tepalsāng mhirki
Ghocetan	
Khal kyu	
Lama	
Mharatsi	
Mhiti cyāng[3]	
Sonam mhirki	
Tancang[4]	

1. Over time, some *phobe* or *ghyu* have divided and separated. Lineages have sometimes broken away and taken new names, often constructing a separate mortuary shrine (*khimi*). This chart lists each named group. If groups with different names share a *khimi*, then they are listed as subgroups. Where groups have divided and created a separate *khimi*, they are listed as separate groups.
2. Dhom phobe has three named subdivisions, but all three share one mortuary shrine and have a single subclan gathering.
3. This is the subclan of the Gauchan *pāre*, or clan ritual specialists.
4. According to Vinding (1981:209), Tancang *phobe* originally included five lineages: Larā, Saicyāng, Bhuicyāng, Sānke dhorche, and Ghera. Ghera *phobe* is now a separate *phobe* called Ghera or Lāra Ghera. Some of Vinding's informants referred to this group as Tanchaang. The original group is alternatively called Tancāng, Tanang, or Larā *phobe*. Jest (cited in Manzardo 1978) listed these as three separate groups. All three names are still in use, but only two clearly distinct groups now exist.
5. Dyātan *ghyu* has been separated for several generations. Households of one branch now reside in Beni and Kathmandu; households of the other reside in villages in Khani Khuwa.

TABLE 2.1 *(continued)*

Sherchan	Tulachan[13]
Dhom (1)[6]	Chen
Dhom (2)	Chyakpa
Dhom (3)	Dyātan
Dyātan[7]	Jhongman
Gyonten chyoki	Kangtan
Kāngtān	Lama
Lha khāng dhunge[8]	
Paira	
Paisarā	
Baucyāng	
Singe cyāng	
Lhementan lhemencyāng[9]	
Mhar dhunge[10]	
Norje phobe	
Pakerā	
Pompar[11] (Manit cyāng)	
Sakeke palteng cyāng	
Sartan[12]	
Tāchā	

6. Dhom *phobe* divided because of differences of opinion. There are now three branches: Dhom (1) is centered in Kobang and Bhairawa; Dhom (2) is in Pokhara and Kathmandu; Dhom (3) is in Khani Khuwa.

7. The Sherchan Dyātan *ghyu* is the only *phobe* known to have completely died out.

8. These five named subgroups share the same *khimi* but maintain separate subclan gatherings. This is a particularly large *phobe*, and size is often cited as the cause of the subdivisions.

9. These two groups are often listed separately but share the same *khimi*.

10. In the early 1980s Mhar dhunge and Manetan rejoined as one *phobe* known as Mhar dhunge.

11. These two groups, Pompar and Manit cyāng, rejoined in 1982 and renovated their original *khimi* in 1992.

12. Sartan and Pakerā split because of a feud many generations ago. They maintain separate *khimi*.

13. Vinding (1998) mentions the Tulachan subclan Dhungpa. Fürer-Haimendorf (1981b:8) indicates that Lama and Dhungpa are two names for the same subclan. Vinding's informants say they are separate. I have no information suggesting they maintain separate *khimi* and have thus not listed them as separate subclans.

and *Rhoten phobe* (Lalchan).[24] The four clans consist of eighteen patrilineages that are the most important descent groups among the Mhowatan Thakali. Only a few of these groups are named. According to Michael Vinding, the form and function of the eighteen Marphali lineage groups are similar to the *phobe*, or subclans, of the Thaksatsae Thakali.

Depending on the circumstances, the inhabitants of Marpha might refer to themselves or be referred to as Marphali, Mawatan, Panchgaonle, or Thakali. They would generally refer to themselves as Mawatan (Mhatan or Mhowatan) when speaking Thakali with other Thakali language speakers. They will often refer to themselves as Thakali when speaking Nepali with people from outside the valley and often use the surname Thakali outside the valley. They are sometimes referred to as Marphali (the term *Mawatan* is not used outside of Thak Khola) by non-Thakali speakers, though very often they are referred to by the broader terms of Panchgaonle or Thakali.[25]

A second endogamous group of Panchgaonle comprises the descendants of the original residents of three other villages of Panchgaon: Thinang, Syang, and Chimang.[26] Members of this group refer to themselves and are referred to by the other groups in the valley as Thinel, Syangtani, or Chimtani, depending on their village of residence. Like the other groups resident in the upper Kali Gandaki valley, the residents of these villages use the surname Thakali and refer to themselves as Thakali when speaking with outsiders. Nowadays, they are generally referred to by outsiders as Panchgaonle or Thakali.[27]

This endogamous group is also composed of numerous exogamous patrilineal clans.[28] Among these there are two kinds of patrilineal descent groups.[29] Vinding considers some of these descent groups (what he calls "the high level") to be analogous to the Thaksatsae Thakali clans and others ("the lower level") to be analogous to the Thaksatsae Thakali subclan, or *phobes*. It is said that all the patrilineages originated in Thini village except for three that originated in Syang.[30]

In addition to these three groups (Thaksatsae Thakali, Marphali, and Yulngasumpa), other, more loosely defined groups reside in the upper Kali Gandaki valley, the members of which sometimes refer to themselves as Thakali. These include Kampachans, the descendants of traders from southwestern Tibet,[31] and the descendants of servants, many of whom moved to the valley several generations before from villages to the north; these last are disparagingly called *arānsi karānsi* by the groups in Thaksatsae and Panchgaon.[32] Individuals who fall into these categories commonly refer to themselves as Thakali and use the term as a surname. These two categories of people reside principally in Tukche, where they have lived for generations. In 1993, because of the emigration of Thakali merchant families, individuals who fall into these social categories constituted approximately 85 percent of the population of Tukche. Though they participate, to a small degree, in the social life of the Thakali, the Kampachans and *arānsi karānsi* are not part of any Thakali endogamous group. These two categories include a heterogeneous collection of families, and their interactions and identification with Panchgaon, Baragaon, and other areas to the north have yet to be adequately investigated.

Membership and Status, Groups and Categories

The concept retains merely the outline of the object. Now, in a scheme, we possess only the limits of the object. These limits mean only the relationship in which any object finds itself with respect to other objects.
—Ortega y Gasset

That there is a great deal at stake when different groups claim to be Thakali is discerned from the high emotion displayed in discussions of the issue. The claim to be Thakali means different things to different people, just as the application of the nomenclature by outsiders—by non-Thakalis—indicates different things to different scholars.[33] The claim to be Thakali of each of the three principal endogamous groups resident in Thak Khola and the claim of the Thakali of Thaksatsae to be the only Thakali become clearer if we bear in mind that the claim to be Thakali means different things to different groups. What Thaksatsae Thakali mean when they say they are Thakali and what Panchgaonle mean, for example, is different. Often confused in these disagreements are issues concerning group membership, cultural similarities, status within the Nepalese caste hierarchy and identity.

While there are claims by disparate groups and individuals to the use of the term *Thakali*, none of these claims is intended to imply that all those groups self-identified as Thakali are members of a single ethnic group; that is, no one argues that the Thakali groups (here I refer to Thaksatsae Thakali, Marphali, and Thinel, Syangtani, and Chimtani) collectively share a subjective identity, are conscious of a shared group solidarity, or coordinate activities in advancing common interests.

The Thaksatsae Thakali, however, do manifest the common character-istics of an ethnic group: first and most important, their claim to be the only Thakali reflects their emphasis on their identity as a distinct group with a subjective identity and as an endogamous group with its own gods and cul-tural traditions. They also claim a specific and unique history that includes historical connections to the Hansa Raja, the Thakali *subbas*, and events that have an important place in the narratives they tell about themselves and to which they attribute some credit for the current high status the social category "Thakali" enjoys in Nepali society. Furthermore, throughout the past 150 years, efforts to advance their common interests have focused on the Thakali of Thaksatsae and excluded all other self-declared Thakali.

Unlike the Thaksatsae Thakali claim, the villagers of Marpha, Thini, Chimang, and Syang do not claim group membership but category status. This is an important distinction. The claim of the northern groups arises from the fact that they are also residents of the region (Thak Khola in its broad sense) and from their contemporary contention that they are of equal status to the Thakali of Thaksatsae. In the context of Nepal, this is a claim to be of the same *jāt*,[34] or category of people, and to share the same social status within Nepalese society. It is not, however, a claim to be of the same descent group or of a shared subjective identity. Similarly, the Panchgaonle assertion that they, too, are Thakali is not a claim to be of the same endog-amous group as the Thakali of Thaksatsae, nor is it even a claim to be of the same culturally distinct group as the Thaksatsae Thakali. It is a claim to a category status based primarily on residence within the valley. For the Panchgaonle, the claim to be Thakali is a claim to a social status operative within the context of Nepalese society, while for the Thaksatsae Thakalis it is a assertion of identity, a claim of membership to a bounded group.

Fürer-Haimendorf (1966) argued that by the 1960s the Thakali (by which he meant the Thakali of Thaksatsae) had become (or were becoming) a caste because they think of themselves as a caste, that is, as representing a specific status group within the Hindu-derived status hierarchy of Nepal. Fürer-Haimendorf was particularly concerned with explaining the ways in which he saw the Thakali of Thaksatsae interacting with other groups in Thak Khola, such as the Panchgaonle and the Baragaonle. He speculated that previously these groups had been of equal status, and he reported that at the time of his research, the Thakali of Thaksatsae considered themselves of higher status than the Baragaonle while, in the opinion of some Bara-gaonle informants, the Thakali had previously been of lower status than they.

Fürer-Haimendorf's analysis draws on actions of a small subset of the Thaksatsae Thakali, particularly the merchants of Tukche, who attempted to use the wealth and political power gained through their domination of the salt trade in the late nineteenth and early twentieth centuries to effect a relatively higher status for the Thakali vis-à-vis the five categories of the caste hierarchy established by the Muluki Ain of 1854. As the Tukche merchants established important economic ties with the Hindu elite in Kathmandu, they sought to disassociate themselves from those populations classified as Bhote by the legal code and to identify themselves as descendants of high-caste Thakuris.[35]

While the merchants sought to establish new behavioral patterns for the four Thakali clans of Thaksatsae through their domination of the council of thirteen headmen,[36] the council banned the consumption of yak meat, decreed that dress be changed from the Tibetan style to the Nepali style, banned the sale of brewed alcohol, prohibited the performance of elaborate Tibetan Buddhist funeral rites, and forbade the use of the Thakali language outside Thak Khola.[37] These would appear to be dramatic reforms, but they meant a lot more on paper than they did in practice: not all segments of Thakali society were equally pleased with these initiatives, and many of the reforms were ignored by a major portion of the population. Individual headmen, particularly in the agriculturally oriented villages, made little effort to enforce them, and many of the reforms proved to be superficial: yak meat and alcohol, for example, continued to be consumed regularly, and Buddhist funeral rites were (and are) performed, if in a reduced style. The more elaborate Buddhist funerary feasts that were effectively banned at this time had usually been sponsored only by wealthy merchant families, and so this ban had little significance for most Thaksatsae Thakali families. Ritual practices in the more conservative agricultural villages remained virtually unchanged.[38] The reforms, when they were followed at all, were respected principally by the merchant families of Tukche. All in all, they affected less of the population than has been assumed: Thakali migrants in Khani Khuwa, in particular, who are descended from migrants who left Thak Khola before the reforms, appear to have been unaware of many of them. A great deal has been made of this attempt at cultural reform, by scholars and by some Thakalis, but on closer examination one can seriously question whether the few changes that did take hold signal a substantial or imminent "Sanskritization" or "Hinduization" of Thakali culture.

What the reforms did do was allow the Thakali merchants to make a case in the capital that the Thakali had banned inappropriate practices and to demonstrate through their own practice the legitimacy of their claim to high-caste Thakuri status. The reforms also allowed the Thaksatsae Thakali to create social distance between the Thakali of Thaksatsae and the populations of Panchgaon and Baragaon.[39] In fact, however, relative local status appears to have been more greatly affected by the emergence of an uneven economic relationship than it was by the later emulation of Hindu ideas by some Tukche merchants.

Within the last four decades, many wealthy merchants have emigrated from the valley, thus opening up economic and political opportunities for those who remain behind, including the residents of Panchgaon. Within Thaksatsae, those Thakali who remained behind were primarily agricultur-alists and pastoralists, since those involved in trade departed for the oppor-tunities provided by the urban areas of Kathmandu, Pokhara, and Bhairawa. The result has been growing animosity among traditional Thakali agricul-turalists, the *subba* lineage, other traders, and the Panchgaonle. With the subsequent improvement in the political and economic status of the groups resident in the upper Kali Gandaki valley (Panchgaonle and Baragaonle, etc.), there has been a leveling in status, both within the Thaksatsae Thakali community and among the various populations resident in Thak Khola. Panchgaonle, for example, have been successful in improving their eco-nomic condition and have aggressively voiced their resentment over the decades of Thaksatsae supremacy and asserted the claim that they are of equal status to the Thakali of Thaksatsae.

A process within Thak Khola that is directly related to the success of the Tukche merchants' efforts to improve the relative status of the Thakali through the insistence on the alleged connection with the Thakuri *jāt* and the subsequent attempts at behavioral reform has been the imitation of as-pects of Thaksatsae Thakali culture by the other groups in Thak Khola.[40] This process, observed by scholars and vehemently denied by the Panch-gaonle themselves,[41] illustrates the relativity of cultural boundaries in a con-tinual state of redefinition: as one shifts, another changes. It is apparent that in recent years the Panchgaon groups have made cultural and economic adaptations that mirror those made earlier by the Thaksatsae Thakali and that these adaptations have fueled the renewed claims of the Panchgaon groups to be of equal status to the Thakali of Thaksatsae (and thus by exten-sion to reap the benefits of the relatively high status commonly assigned to the Thakali *jāt*). This process is similar to the Rajputization process described by Sinha and called "secondary Rajputization" by Kulke, wherein social mobility achieved by part of a *jāt* (*jāt* is used here to indicate a cultural unit, not a political one) that has dissociated itself from the rest of the *jāt* and claimed high-caste status is followed by an attempt by the rest of the *jāt* to reassociate themselves with those who have improved their status (Sinha 1965; Kulke 1986). In the Thakali case, the Tukche merchants initiated the dissociation of the Thaksatsae Thakali from the other Thakali groups and claimed Thakuri status in the early twentieth century, and the Panchgaonle have recently begun to reassociate themselves with the Thakali of Thaksatsae by asserting their equal claim to Thakali status.

Among the Thaksatsae Thakali:
Ties That Bind, Lines That Divide

While the social boundaries of the Thakali of Thaksatsae seem to be clearly linked to endogamy, there are many areas of ambiguity. Simply stated, to be Thakali is to be a member of one of the four clans—Sherchan, Gauchan, Tulachan, Bhattachan[42]—but many internal divisions within Thaksatsae Thakali society have a bearing on an individual's status as Thakali, divisions that derive from descent, residence, class, and notions of ritual purity. So many divisions exist, in fact, that it is apparent that what often looked like a coherent, upwardly mobile group and was interpreted as such by many outside observers was, in many ways, a heterogeneous population. This heterogeneity of the Thaksatsae Thakali community deserves further consideration. Some differences arise because migration has placed the Thakali in widely separate geographical and social contexts, others because of differences in religious affiliation, and still others from differences in wealth. Some of these divisions have great significance for migrant communities; others have significance only in Thaksatsae. I argue that the emergence of the contemporary form of Thakali ethnicity was by no means inevitable. Historical circumstances played a determining role in stressing descent and endogamy as the central symbols of identity that led to the crystallization of the Thaksatsae clans as the Thakali.

One of the most striking features of Thakali social organization is its emphasis on descent. Kinship and descent organize Thakali society on a number of levels encompassing groups as small as nuclear families and as large as the entire Thakali population. In descending order of size, Thakali descent groups include: (1) the four named clans; (2) the *phobe*, the named subdivisions of each clan; (3) unnamed lineages; and (4) households, ranging in complexity from simple nuclear families to complex extended families.

Membership in a clan and in a *phobe* is acquired by birth. Clans and *phobe* are exogamous, and a woman changes clan and *phobe* membership when she passes from the clan of her father into the clan of her husband. If widowed, she remains a member of her husband's clan; if divorced, she returns to her father's.

Marriage is prohibited between members of the same clans, between individuals who can trace a common ancestry through successive generations of same-sex categorical siblings, and between members of any one of the four Dyatan *phobe*. The last is an interesting feature of the Thakali marital exchange rules. It effectively creates an exogamous group consisting of the four Dyatan *phobe*, though they are otherwise divided among the four exogamous clans (only three remain, the Sherchan Dyatan *phobe* has died out). Thus members of one Dyatan *phobe* may not marry members of another Dyatan *phobe* even if they are of different clans.[43] Some informants argue that these lineages derive their ancestry from the youngest sons of the ancestors of each of the four clans. A more convincing account suggests that the four lineages represent the original inhabitants of the Thaksatsae area before the arrival of the Thakali ancestors in the region. Each of the Dyatan lineages is linked to unique ritual sites on the east bank of the Kali Gandaki, where only they can make offerings to local spirits.

Preferred marriage partners are categorical cross-cousins (matrilateral cross-cousins usually preferred over patrilateral cross-cousins). Some writers have noted that the exchange of cross-cousins among the Thakali reflects a tendency toward restricted marital exchanges that results in close reciprocal marital exchange relations between two *phobes* over several generations. Bista, for example, has noted vaguely that "the preferred cross-cousin marriage system had led to a regular relationship between pairs of clans" (1971:56). More specifically, it led to regular relationships between pairs of *phobe* in different clans—one well-known example is the Sherchan Lha Khang Dhungi *phobe* and the Tulachan Dyachan *phobe*—but with the dispersion caused by migration these exchange patterns are breaking down.

As noted earlier, Thakali society is ideally endogamous; marriage with non-Thakalis does occur, but the social status of the offspring of these mixed marriages is ambiguous, and the circumstances under which these offspring are accepted as fully Thakali depend on a number of factors. In some ways, they are both Thakali and not-Thakali, and while they are excluded from some interactions because of their alleged impurity, they still possess the potential to produce "pure" Thakali descendants.

Clans are composed of from six to fourteen named *phobe* or *ghyupa*, the names of which are usually associated with a specific locality or ancestor. The subdivisions of the clans are more actively structured than the clans and, in many respects, are the most important patrilineal descent groups among the Thakali. A *phobe* comprises from three to fifty households. While some can trace all their members to a common ancestor, this is unusual, especially since the common ancestor of many lineages in the same *phobe* often dates back ten generations or more. Each *phobe* maintains a stone reliquary or ossuary (T: *khimi*) in Thaksatsae where a bone fragment (N: *astu*) of each deceased member is placed.

Narratives of common descent continue to hold together the different segments of Thakali society, while challenges to the purity of that descent blur the boundaries around the group. Similarly, as calculations of common descent provide the basis for subdivisions within Thakali society, there is broader solidarity embedded within the symmetry of the system: a Thakali is Thakali by virtue of his or her membership within a specific lineage, *phobe*, and clan. In other words, it is only by being a member of a recognized division of the Thaksatsae Thakali that one can be Thakali.

Cutting Across Descent

Although the Thakali of Thaksatsae ostensibly form one endogamous group in which an individual is a member by virtue of being a socially recognized offspring of parents who belong to one of the four Thakali clans, and a member of any one of the four clans can marry any eligible member of the other three (with the exception of the Dyatan subclans, as noted earlier), additional cross-cutting qualities that can affect the desirableness of potential marriage partners.

My friend Mahen is a Thakali of pure status who often discussed with me the difficulties of finding a suitable match for his oldest son. They were Sherchans and so that automatically eliminated all eligible women from the Sherchan clan, the most populous among the four Thaksatsae clans. One day, drawing on my knowledge of eligible women from my own kinship charts, which included information on thousands of Thakalis, I suggested possible matches. Invariably, these were deemed inappropriate because of inherited status imperfections.

A large number were dismissed as *celang melang* (T) or *khaccar* (N), terms used to refer to those individuals who are the offspring of mixed marriages: Thakali with non-Thakali.[44] These are not polite terms, and this status is not usually discussed publicly. In many instances, potential matches are dismissed as *celang melang* or *khaccar* when the speaker is not fully acquainted with an individual's kinship details. This is especially true for families from Khani Khuwa, who are all considered to be of mixed backgrounds by many Thak Khole. Technically, *celang melang* is a status that can be removed from a family only after three generations of intermarriage with pure Thakali.[45] But even in some instances where my charts demonstrated the pure status of Khani Khuwa Thakali, my friend Mahen remained unconvinced.

Another set of potential mates was rejected by Mahen as *pumi*, a term applied to suspected witches or their descendants.[46] A single *pumi* ancestor is sometimes sufficient to taint an entire lineage. Some informants report that the *pumi* form (or formed) an endogamous group.[47] If so, it seems likely that this was not endogamy by choice but because other Thakali are so reluctant to marry suspected witches or, by extension, their daughters. Numerous exceptions to this marriage restriction are reported as scandals, and informants, including Mahen, usually attribute these aberrations to the attempts of wealthy *pumi* families to improve their status by marrying into purer Thakali families.

Mahen also rejected otherwise eligible partners because they came from families he considered to be affected by *mang* status. *Mang* status is a similar but less dangerous affliction than *pumi*. Like *pumi* status, it usually applies to women and affects their descendants. Those who are *mang* are said to turn beer sour if they happen to look at it while it is fermenting. Informants state that *mang*, like *pumi*, ideally form, or formed, an endogamous group. It is believed that the qualities of *mang* and *pumi* are passed from generation to generation.

These status distinctions are not generally discussed publicly; their relevance arises when arranging marriages, when it comes time to place the bone fragment of the deceased in the ossuary of the appropriate lineage, and during the performance of some rituals. They also matter more to individuals in some communities more than others: for instance, they enter into the marriage calculations of informants in Khani Khuwa less frequently than they do in Thak Khola, Kathmandu, Bhairawa, and Pokhara.

Some informants mention other status differentiations, like that between the residents of the villages of Tukche, Sauru, Khanti, Narjhong, Nakhung, Naphrungkung, Sirkung and Dhumpu, on the one hand, and the people of the rest of the villages of Thaksatsae on the other.[48] Informants from the first group claim to be of a purer status than those of the other villages and formerly formed an endogamous group (Gauchan and Vinding 1977:131 n. 35). This is not currently active, however, and the nature of this status in the past is still disputed.

Other distinctions, including those based on religious orientation, occupation, wealth, geographic contexts, and purity and pollution, cut across the ties of descent and result in considerable heterogeneity in Thakali society. Migration, access to trade in the Thak Khola, and economic, political, and social alliances with the *subba* family have resulted in disparate levels of wealth and economic interests. Class differences among the Thakali have often been overlooked by analysts focused on the economic success of the Thakali traders and entrepreneurs. Nevertheless, among both those who have emigrated from and those who have remained in Thak Khola there are poor as well as comparatively well-off households and wealthy families. Occupation and wealth are also the basis for divisions among agriculturalists, landowning entrepreneurs from Khani Khuwa, prominent businessmen, contractors, shopkeepers, smugglers, and innkeepers. Additionally, there is lingering resentment in some communities of what were perceived as arrogance and high-handed practices by individuals of the *subba* lineage, which can still engender oppositional relationships between those of the *subba* lineage and everyone else.

Many of the currently relevant divisions evolved during the past few decades. The decline of the salt trade in the 1950s coincided with the modernization and development of Nepal, which moved into the international post–World War II economy with the end of the Rana regime in 1951. Thakali entrepreneurs and merchants moved to urban areas where they had already established economic connections, and in these areas they soon formed regionally based social organizations that organized community activities and set guidelines for Thakali behavior.[49]

In short, the Thakali form a heterogeneous society characterized by lingering schisms between rich and poor, Hindu and Buddhist, Khani Khuwa

Thakali and Thak Khole, urban and rural, traders and farmers, young and old. Clearly, some of the most significant and problematic social divisions are a result of the series of migrations from Thaksatsae. This migration has placed the Thakali in contexts where the construction of boundaries varies significantly from those constructed and contested in the upper Kali Gandaki valley. Ironically, in many ways, the internal divisions among the Thaksatsae Thakali are greater than the differences between the Thakali still resident in Thaksatsae and the Panchgaonle.

Khuwale and Thak Khole

More than 80 percent of the Thakali population now lives outside Thaksatsae.[50] Yet Thaksatsae remains symbolically important, and migrants draw distinctions between those who were born there and those who were not, between those who still own land there and those who do not, and between those who still speak the language and those who do not.

One of the most significant differences among contemporary Thakali is between those who consider themselves to be Thak Khole (that is, either resident in or a first-generation migrant from Thak) and those identified by as Khuwale (those resident in or migrants from the areas the Thakali refer to as Khani Khuwa) or *pho khāne* (those who can not speak Thakali, often used interchangeably with Khuwale). In the early nineteenth century a number of Thakali moved southwest from Thak Khola to the area now known as Khani Khuwa, where they took advantage of economic opportunities provided by copper mining in the region. More than 40 percent of the total current population of Thaksatsae Thakali now reside in, or have recently migrated from, this area, but, because most of those in Khani Khuwa no longer speak the Thakali language, the Thakali from Thak Khola often declare that it is difficult to distinguish a Khuwale Thakali from members of other ethnic groups in Khani Khuwa.[51]

Thak Khole and Khuwale are ideal types that play on questions of language, culture, and genetic purity. Indeed, the slang terms used to refer to the Thakali from this region highlight both differences in descent (*khaccar*) and culture (*pho khāne*).

In Khani Khuwa, the question of who is, and who is not, Thakali is less complicated than it is in other parts of Nepal, if only because there are fewer claimants to the category. Here, to be Thakali means to be a member of one of the four Thakali clans from Thaksatsae. Among the Thakali in Khani

Khuwa, there is little notice taken of the categories of ritual purity: *mang*, *pumi*, and *celang melang* are less important distinctions within these parts. Members of non-Thakali *jāts* in Baglung and Myagdi districts use only the term *Thakali*, and non-Thakalis know few of the internal distinctions among the Thakali. Asked to name the Thakali clans, few non-Thakalis can do so, some are not aware that there are four and only four clans, and others will name Hirachan, the best-known of the Marphali clans, as a Thakali clan.[52] A Thakali resident in Khani Khuwa will also refer to individual Marphalis as Thakali, but it should be emphasized that this is rarely an issue. There are no Panchgaonle in the immediate area, and most Thakali have no occasion to know one.

The status of Thakalis in Myagdi and Baglung districts is heavily dependent on economic wealth; indeed, social status and economic class are not clearly distinct in this area. In the middle hills of Nepal, belonging to a non-Hindu ethnic group does not necessarily imply a concomitant degradation in social or secular terms acted out in the daily village life. Wealth and power bring social prestige to a member of any ethnic group in the area and command a respectful form of address even from the high-status *jāts*. In Khani Khuwa, the Thakalis make no explicit claim to higher ritual status, and there is no apparent conflict between the status of high-caste Brahmans and Chetris and the economic status of wealthy Thakalis; instead, there appears to be accommodation between one realm and the other. The accommodation of Thakalis to Hindu notions of caste hierarchy has been a critical point of the argument offered by scholars that the Thakalis have "Sanskritized" or "Hinduized" their culture, and Fürer-Haimendorf (1966:145) has suggested that this accommodation has been especially pronounced in migrant areas. In Khani Khuwa, however, Thakalis appear to have accommodated less and not more to social restrictions imposed by caste.[53]

More troubling than the relations of so-called Khuwale Thakali with co-residents of Myagdi and Baglung districts are their relations with other Thakalis, particularly nonmigrants or recent migrants from Thak Khola who disparage the Khuwale Thakali because of the alleged frequency of their sexual and marital congress with non-Thakali women. Thakalis from Thak Khola often express uncertainties about the purity of descent of the Thakalis from Khani Khuwa and allege that the Thakalis in Khani Khuwa are casual about forming sexual alliances with non-Thakalis in this area and often treat the offspring of these relationships as if they were pure Thakalis. The ambiguousness of status attributed to the category of *celang melang* is sometimes extended impersonally to include the whole category of Khani Khuwa Thakalis. In fact, the Thakali from Thaksatsae sometimes explain their reluctance to marry with the Thakali in Khani Khuwa on this basis; that is, unless they are sure of the pedigree, they consider Thakalis from Khani Khuwa to be *celang melang* and hence less desirable marriage partners. In interactions with Thak Khole Thakalis, Thakalis from Khani Khuwa are sometimes regarded as both Thakali and yet not-quite Thakali.

This widespread conception of the Thakali resident in Myagdi and Baglung districts as *celang melang*, of mixed or impure descent, has some serious implications. In Thak Khola, those who are *celang melang* and thus not fully Thakali are unable to participate in the important Thakali rituals of *kul puja* and have no access to the sacred hearth of the *thimten*.[54] Because Khuwale Thakalis are assumed by nonmigrants to be *celang melang*, there is a general reluctance to intermarry with them (though intermarriage between Thakalis from Myagdi and Baglung districts and Thakalis resident in other areas does take place, usually between families or *phobe* with existing affinal ties). Strictly speaking, the great majority of Thakalis in Myagdi and Baglung districts are not of mixed caste marriages, or *celang melang*, as the Thak Khole Thakali allege, but there are frequent relationships between Thakali men and Magar women, some of these relationships result in children, and some can accurately be described as marriages. In effect, Khuwale Thakali is a category usually applied only to those one has never met. The tension between Khuwale and Thak Khole Thakalis may be strongest in the Terai town of Kasauli, where the Thakali community is evenly divided between emigrants from Khani Khuwa and emigrants from Thak Khola.

In Khani Khuwa, Thakalis themselves emphasize that they prefer to marry Thakalis, and most do, at least the first time they marry. The second wives or lovers of Thakali men are frequently of another *jāt*, most frequently Magar, and it is unusual for the second wife or her children to be brought into the man's home. Most Thakali women, on the other hand, strongly stress that they will not marry a non-Thakali. Asked about a mixed-*jāt* marriage involving a Thakali woman in Burtibang, one Thakali woman from Darbang explained, "We Thakalis don't go with Chantels and Magars, but [in Burtibang] they do. That is disgusting. We Thakalis don't like to marry Magar women either, but if you get them pregnant, what can you do." The frequency of intercaste marriage varies from village to village in these districts, and it is always much more common for Thakali men than women.[55] One side effect of marriage with non-Thakalis is the strengthening of ties within Khani Khuwa and the weakening of ties with Thakalis outside of the area.[56]

Summary: Criss-Crossing Boundaries

Clearly, for every designated social boundary among the Thakali, for every line drawn, there are qualifications or conditions that blur these lines and create no-man's-lands of ambiguity. Lines are drawn based on putative descent, residence, cultural practices, and ritual purity, highlighting differences among clans, subclans, Khuwale and Thak Khole or marking differences like *mang, pumi,* and *khaccar.* These boundary markers operate within Thaksatsae Thakali society, as well as between Thakali and other related groups. No boundaries hold under all conditions and for all purposes. Difference is relative and, in the Thakali case, often emphasized in contradictory ways: the criteria used to mark some social boundaries are often contested. Moreover, as I will discuss in the next chapters, social boundaries drawn in theory are often transgressed in practice. Categories like Khuwale may be disparaged in general, while individual Khuwale are accepted without question. As I shall show, this ongoing construction, crossing, and disputing of boundaries leads neither to resolution nor to the clarification or fixing of the boundary but to creative adaptations to contemporary problems.

3 Forging Histories

The ancient history of the Nepaulians, like that of all other
nations which affect to trace their origins beyond the date of authentic records, is
clouded by mythological fables.
—Colonel W. Kirkpatrick (1811)

What is involved, then, in that finding of the "true story," that
discovery of the "real story" within or behind the events that come to us in the
chaotic form of "historical records"? What wish is enacted, what desire gratified,
by the fantasy that real events are properly represented when they can be shown
to display the formal coherency of a story?
—Hayden White (1992)

The Thakali can be said to have made history in two ways. First, they
forged their way through a series of constraints and opportunities that arose
in the years of state formation after the Gurkha conquest. In particular, they
made history through their control of the salt trade and their rise to remarkable economic and political prominence in central Nepal in the early part
of the twentieth century.

Second, and in a very different sense, the Thakali made—or forged—
history through their shaping of historical narratives about themselves. This
shaping of narratives was a part of their strategy of adaptation within a changing sociopolitical environment. Since the 1950s Thakali narratives about
themselves have also been affected by the narratives scholars tell about them.
Understanding the Thakali forging of histories requires us to examine the
interrelatedness of the specific social, economic, and political circumstances
that confronted them, the narratives available to them, the various agents
involved in the forging of history and the telling of narratives, and, finally,
the influence of outsiders on the telling of these narratives.

Historical Narrative(s)

Not all narratives are equal. This inequality arises in different ways: they appeal to different audiences; they adhere in varying degree to the so-called facts; some are more persuasive than others; and some are more widely recognized as "coherent." Over time, some narratives about and by the Thakali have had more play and have been privileged over others. In the twentieth century two stories in particular have been widely circulated: the story of the Hansa Raja and the story of the *subba* domination of the salt trade. These two represent different types of "real stories" but share the characteristic of formal coherence. Who tells these stories and for what purposes? Which Thakali find the Hansa Raja story so appealing? Why do most scholars react skeptically to the narrative of the Hansa Raja while some find the story of the salt monopoly and ensuing instrumental cultural change so appealing? How do these narratives fit with the known or verifiable history of the Thakali? To answer such questions this chapter considers why, how, where, and by whom certain narratives of the Thakali have been privileged over others. The relationships of the events within these narratives with known historical events and the specific historical conditions within which the narratives gained prominence are considered against other possible narratives and interpretations of the Thakali.

The process of forming the Nepali state in the nineteenth and twentieth centuries provided the context within which one small subgroup of the Thakali from Thaksatsae first gained and then eventually lost the ability to manipulate the image of the Thakali held by ruling elites and foreigners — that is, to have their story accepted to a significant extent as the real story — at critical points in history. As Hegel noted, the rise of the state provides a context within which family and clan stories enter history. The rise of the Nepali state provided a specific context and incentives motivating Thakalis to link their narratives to it in specific ways. The factors that enabled the hegemony of one (sub)group's narrative of the Thakali story emerge in the account of how this group gained access to elites in Kathmandu (and, later, to scholars), access that allowed them to narrate their family history in a way that was consistent with the emerging narrative of the nation.

This chapter does not attempt to construct a definitive unilinear meta-narrative into which all the pieces of the Thakali past can be placed. Rather, it first sketches the historical landscape within which Thakali contestations took place and then examines the effects of these narratives. It does not seek to resolve the issue of whether any of these narratives of the Thakali are more or less true in the sense of being more or less consistent with some historical events, that is, things as they actually happened.

Narratives by and about the Thakali have not been equally influential. Conflict over narratives central to a group's identity has the potential to be as productive as it is disorienting, at least to the extent that competing narratives provide the contexts or justifications for multiple adaptations within different social contexts. By highlighting the instrumental choices that helped privilege some narratives over others, I am not countenancing a simplistic counterattack on or rejection of the previously dominant interpretations. That one narrative may have been more useful in explaining identity to a particular group at a particular time is not evidence for either its truth or its falsity.

This chapter addresses the problematics of several kinds of interrelated historical narrations. First, it examines the various oral narratives available to the Thakali. Second, it considers how the Thakali entered the national history. To expand on the earlier metaphor of the Kali Gandaki used in chapter 1, this requires the consideration of alternative sources and streams of narratives as they meander across geographical, economic, and political fields, merging and dividing. Family stories allow the richness and diversity of real lives as lived to be rescued from the historical narrative that paradoxically both contextualizes (providing the riverbed without which the individual stream would have no distinct existence) and generalizes (thus obscuring the unique and individual). Third, the chapter considers how some Thakalis linked themselves with the elite of the emergent Nepali state by telling the right story at the right time to the right people. This requires examining how a single stream of narrative was recognized as if it were the main river of Thakali identity on a map of newly emerging state structures.

Finally, the chapter examines what happens when outsiders—scholars and anthropologists—who enter the scene at a particular time and place and maintain that the particular (historical or narrative) stream they see *is* the river and contrast that static present with a static past constructed from fragmented evidence. In this contrasting of the present with a pristine past where cultures were not hybrids and of which only one possible interpretation is imagined, the emphasis is often placed on change. In contrast, this examination of the forging of histories reveals a long history of contestation, marginality, and fluid cultural boundaries.

Thakali Narratives of the Past

There are nine and sixty ways of constructing tribal lays, and every one of them
is right.
— Rudyard Kipling, "In the Neolithic Age"

Thakali reconstructions of the past generally derive from local oral narratives and the *rhabs*, the clan histories or narratives that tell of the journey
of the ancestor of each clan and each clan deity.[1] Previously written in
Thakali using Tibetan script, new copies of three of the *rhabs* were made
approximately one hundred years ago using Devanagri script. The Sherchan
rhab was reportedly destroyed by fire in the middle of the twentieth century,
and the only copy of it now existent was rewritten by the Gauchan *gamba*.[2]
In its rewritten form its character is different from that of the other three
rhabs and attempts to reconcile the tales of the *rhabs* with other local oral
traditions, including the narrative of the Hansa Raja. The *rhabs* are read in
public every twelve years on the occasion of Lha Phewa.

The Choki *rhab*, the clan history of the Gauchans, tells of the travels of
Khe Ani Airam, the ancestor of the Gauchan clan, who was born in the
northwest.[3] According to the *rhab*, Khe Ani Airam was a member of the
Chan family. he migrated to Sinjapati, the capital of the Malla kingdom of
western Nepal, where he felled a sandalwood tree. Three birds emerged
from the tree: these birds were Lha Lāngbā Nhurbu, the Gauchan deity;
Lha Chyurin Gyālmo, the Tulachan deity; and Lha Ghāngla Singi Karmo,
the Sherchan deity. Ani Airam left Sinjapati and travelled east through what
is now Dolpo into the Kali Gandaki valley. He and his traveling companions
met up with Khe Pau Kuti, the ancestor of the Bhattachan clan in Ghya-
tobra, opposite present-day Tukche. Together, they proceeded to Tamo (Khe
Ani Airam refers to the inhabitants of this place as Thātan). Khe Ani Airam
and Khe Pau Kuti travel on to Taglung and then on down the valley to the
turnoff for the Ghorepani pass. Unenamored with this place, they turned
back to Thak Khola, where they settled.

The Sālgi rhab, the clan history of the Tulachans, tells the story of the
arrival in Thāsāng (Thaksatsae) of Lha Chyurin Gyālmo, who was established as the goddess of the Tulachan clan. It also tells of the slaughter of
all but one of the descendants of Khe Samledhen Samlechyāng, the Tulachan ancestor. According to the *rhab*, the goddess arrived at Dhocho in

Thak Khola and was recognized and worshiped by the eighteen ancestors of the eighteen houses of Dhocho. She stayed and blessed them, and they became very powerful. When the ancestors of Thātan saw the eighteen ancestors misusing their power, they vowed at a secret meeting to kill them by inviting them to a *lha chuwa* ritual and poisoning them. The ancestors of the eighteen houses of Dhocho accepted the invitation of their *mhā* (T; N: *juãi*, "in-laws," "wife receivers"), but on the way they were warned, and when served food and drink they fed it to the dogs, who died. Again, the ancestors of Thātan called a meeting and vowed to kill the Dhocho lineage by tricking them into placing their hands in the cleft of a cut tree trunk, removing the wedges holding the cleft open, and rolling the trunk and the ancestors down the hill. The youngest ancestor and his grandmother (T: *mom*), Lhasarphi of Dhocho, warned them not to go, but believing no one could harm them they went and were caught and killed as the ancestors of Thātan had planned. Mom Lhasarphi and her grandson Bhum fled the village and hid. The Thātan lineage returned celebrating their deed and searched the eighteen houses of Dhocho to discover how they had become so powerful. They found Lha Chyurin Gyālmo wrapped in cypress, and unable to pierce, break, or burn it, they threw it in the river. The goddess floated down the river and stopped at the gorge below the town of Ghāsā, thereby blocking the river and forcing it to flow northward. Seeking advice, the ancestors of Thātan were finally told by a lama that Lha Chyurin Gyālmo was blocking the river and needed her own people to worship her.

Discovering that two members of the Dhocho lineage still lived, the Thātan ancestors set out to find Mom Lhasarphi and Kāncha (youngest son) Bhum. A local astrologer determined that Khe Pau Kuti was best suited for the job. Pau Kuti traveled to Ipsang, where he discovered a fireplace under a tree. Mom Lhasarphi, hiding in a tree, saw him under the tree and realized that her relatives had been killed. Assuming that Pau Kuti had come to kill her and Kancha Bhum, she began to weep. Her tears fell on Khe Pau Kuti, and she was discovered. Pau Kuti begged Lhasarphi to come down and swore that he would not harm her or her grandson. He entreated her to return with him, and when she refused he explained to her what the ancestors of Thātan had done. She agreed to come if she was given the holy place of Ipsang. Pau Kuti also promised Lhasarphi that her clan would be the only one to wear the red turban and the silk turban.

When Lhasarphi returned to Dhocho, the ancestors of Thātan begged her to worship Lha Chyurin Gyālmo, but at first she refused because she was in mourning for her deceased relatives. Khe Pau Kuti (now called Khe Dhamchi Dhamru, "swearer of an oath," by Lhasarphi) promised that the ancestors of Thātan would mourn for the ancestors of Dhocho. Once Mom Lhasarphi and Kancha Bhum prayed to Lha Chyurin Gyālmo, the deity came out of the river and into Mom Lhasarphi's shawl.

The Bhurgi *rhab*, the history of the Bhattachan clan, tells the story of the god Lha Yhāwā Rāngjyung, the self-made yak. It relates his travels in Tibet and his meeting with the other Thakali ancestors and clan deities at the holy waterfall of Rupse (north of the village of Dana). After Khe Pau Kuti established Lha Yhāwā Rnāgjyung as his protector, the Bhattachan deity returned with the other deities and ancestors to the area of Thak Khola. The ancestors spoke with the headman of that place, saying the gods had sent them here and that they intended to settle here.

Lha Yhāwā Rāngjyung then spent three years in the high Dhaulagiri pastures above Thaksatsae. While there, the lord of the gods sent him to Shyasen forest above Marpha, saying this would be the place where Lha Yhāwā Rāngjyung would die. Lha Yhāwā Rāngjyung lived in this forest for three years without seeing or hearing a human. Namchya Gholtok from Marpha encountered him and tried to kill him with arrows but failed. Returning to Marpha, Namchya encouraged others to bring their guns and arrows and come with him to kill the yak. Gumtan Khe argued that the animal was a god and they should not try to kill it. But the next day the villagers went with Namchya Gholtok to Shyasen forest, where they surrounded the yak and tried to kill it. They failed: Lha Yāhwā Rāngjyung spewed flames from his mouth, shook the ground, and brought on a hailstorm that killed many of the hunters. Namchya Gholtok and the hunters repented their action and begged Lha Yāhwā Rāngjyung to stop the hailstorm. He did so, and Gumtan Khe asked the yak deity what they should do to make amends. He said they had to agree to obey him, and they responded that they would obey him until the day the Kali Gandaki River started to flow upward and the black crow turned white. Lha Yāhwā Rāngjyung then told them that he was an incarnation of the black protective deity and the guardian of Khe Pau Kuti. He said that he would die in the forest, and they must eat his flesh when he did so. He told them they must not break their promise or the clan deities of this world and the serpent deities of the underworld would destroy them. He ordered Gumtan Khe to give his flesh to the villagers and his head to Khunara, the son of Khe Pau Kuti. Then he went to the forest and died. Gumtan Khe took the head and kept it in a cave, where he worshiped it.

On the third day of the twelfth month, Khe Dhamchi Dhamru (Pau Kuti) came and worshiped Lha Yāhwā Rāngjyung. He and Khunara went north, where they met the daughter and son-in-law of Gumtan Khe. They went on to Marpha, and the people there begged forgiveness. They then went to the forest and retrieved the head of Lha Yāhwā Rāngjyung. On the way back a salt trader from Lo offered salt to the god and begged him to bless the salt route. A grain trader also made offerings and begged the deity's blessing. In Tukche hundreds of traders came to see him. Khen Dhamchi Dhamru and Khunara went on to the village of Khanti in Thaksatsae, where the ancestors of the other three clans—Khe Ani Airam, Khe Samledhen Samlechyāng, and Khe Dhakpa Gyalsang—were returning from a bath in the Mharsyang River.

Collectively, the *rhabs* narrate the migration of the clan ancestors and deities from different places of origin to a common place of meeting where they settled down to become one society. Despite the many uncertainties in the texts, a few themes are consistently repeated: (1) that the ancestors of the four clans came from different places; (2) that the ancestors joined together when they came to Thaksatsae; and (3) that the area of the Kali Gandaki valley where they settled was already inhabited when they arrived and some of these original inhabitants joined with the newcomers. Each of the *rhabs* end with prayers to the four gods and the four ancestors who had come together in this place; they all close with the appeal "although we could not meet at our birthplace let us meet at our gathering place."

Nevertheless, these narratives do not convincingly resolve questions about the origin of the Thakali, a topic that continues to be a disputed subject among scholars and among the Thakali themselves; instead, various interpretations of the narratives are cited to support different theories about Thakali origins. The difficult language of the *rhabs* and the uncertain referents of many place and family names lend themselves to multiple interpretations.

The Thakali tend to make selective use of information in the *rhabs* to construct coherent narratives. Many Thakali note that the *rhabs* make reference to the Chan family and draw a connection with the Thakuri Chand clan.[4] Some Thakali use this to support their claims that they should have a status in the Nepali caste hierarchy equal to that of the Thakuri. They explain that after they settled in Thāk (Thā) they became known as Thāchan or Thātan, the *chan* of Thaa. They also note that the *rhabs* make frequent reference to Sinjapati near Jumla as a place in which the ancestors resided or from which they originated. Sinjapati was the site of the capital of the Malla kingdom of Jumla and an important site for the Thakuri Chan clan.

In addition to the written clan narratives, local oral traditions relate tales of the Hansa Raja, which provide a different account of the origin of the Thakali. In some versions he is the son of the raja of Jumla in western Nepal, and this connection has been cited by some Thakalis to support their assertion that the Thakali are descended from high-caste Thakuris. In most versions the Hansa Raja married a daughter of the raja of Thini in Panchgaon, Nhima Rani, and was given all the lands of Thaksatsae.[5] In some versions, the offspring of the Nhima Rani and the Hansa Raja are said to have been the ancestors of the four clans of the Thakali.[6] In other versions, the Hansa Raja is said to be the ancestor of only some of the Thakali, usually the ancestor of the Sherchan Pompar *ghyu*.

According to Gauchan and Vinding (1977), the Ḍhimchen *rhab*, which tells the story of the arrival of the Sherchan god, Lha Ghāngla Singi Karmo, was rewritten by Narendra Gauchan as he thought "it ought to be." In its current form, this *rhab* includes several elements that do not appear in the other three *rhab*s. It is much more contemporary in tone and attempts to reconcile aspects of the oral tales of the Hansa Raja and Narijhowa (see chapter 8) as well as provide rationalizations for the establishment of Thakali marriage relationships, the worship of *Torongla*, and *shyopen lawa*. It is also the only *rhab* to append to the praise of the Thakali gathering place the pronouncement that "they would neither be friends with nor include in their society those persons who left Thātongkor and settled in other places. The ancestors of Thāchan said that in their marriage system they would not include those persons who left Thātongkor and settled in other places."

Scholarship and the Reconstruction of the Past

The efforts of the Thakali and of foreign scholars to construct narratives of the past have not generally been supportive of one another. Foreign scholars have generally been dismissive of Thakali attempts to use the story of the Hansa Raja to link the Thakali to a Thakuri past, and they have downplayed the importance of the clan *rhabs* as historical documents. With limited sources, scholars necessarily rely on a great deal of speculation.

Some scholars have sought to reconstruct the history of Thak Khola through other sources, relying primarily on Tibetan texts supplemented with a few local sources.[7] Unfortunately, these promising efforts have not yet been able to fill out the connection between the early history of the area and the contemporary population of Thaksatsae. They have added a great deal to our understanding of some events in the upper Kali Gandaki valley, but as yet it is extremely difficult to document any connection between the current residents of Thaksatsae and peoples referred to in Tibetan texts.

Scholars of Tibetan texts have tried to correlate textual references to areas called Lo and Serib in the texts with the kingdom of Lo in the upper Kali Gandaki valley and the present-day Baragaon, respectively.[8] A Tibetan text, the Dunhuang Annals, refers to the existence of areas called Lo and Serib in the seventh century, when they are said to have come under the influence of the Tibetan Yarlung dynasty.[9] David Jackson has suggested that the Lo kingdom in the upper Kali Gandaki valley is the Lo mentioned in the chronicle. Serib, he speculated, would then refer to the area to the south (Baragaon and perhaps Panchgaon).

The scholarly reconstruction makes it clear that, while Thak Khola lies in a relatively remote area of the Himalayas, inhabitants of this region were not as isolated from external influences as were many other similarly placed groups in the Himalayas. Over the centuries prior to the Gurkha conquest in the late eighteenth century, the upper Kali Gandaki valley apparently came under the influence of a number of regional powers: Ladakh and Jumla to the west, Lo to the north, Parbat to the south.[10] The ruins of forts in the area attest to a history of outside threats and changing fortunes.[11] Before the eighteenth century, however, there is little that can be taken to refer to either Thaksatsae or the Thakali.

According to the chronicles, Tibetan Buddhist and reformed Bon missionaries came to the area of Lo and Serib in the twelvth century (Jackson 1978:200).[12] One of the Bon missionaries was Lubra Tashi Gyaltshan, who is said to have founded a monastery in the village of Lubra in Baragaon around 1160 (Ramble 1983; Jackson 1978:204–5; and Vinding 1988:118 nn. 17, 18). Buddhism and Bon continued to have supporters in the following centuries, though there is little evidence to help us to determine the waxing and waning of their influences over time.[13] The oldest and southernmost local evidence of Buddhism in the present Thaksatsae is the temple Meki Lha Khāng, which appears to have been founded three hundred years later, in the early fifteenth century (Jackson 1978:218).

Jackson cites a suggestive line from *Gung thang gdung rabs* that refers to the construction of a fort in Mu-Khun for the domination of the "ta mang se mon" (1978:212).[14] Jackson (1978) concludes that the Ta-mang se mon were non-Bhote people living near the southern boundary of Lo.[15] It is not ascertainable, however, to whom this term referred.

From the sixteenth century through the middle of the eighteenth century there were struggles among the kingdoms of Lo, Jumla, and Ladakh.[16] In the 1500s both Ladakh and the Malla kingdom centered in Jumla had influence in the upper Kali Gandaki valley; by the late sixteenth century Jumla appeared poised to overpower the kingdom of Lo along the northernmost stretch of the Kali Gandaki (Jackson 1978:219). After the decline of the powerful Malla kingdom in Jumla, local rajas continued to rule over Jumla and its capital of Sinja (Semja), but the new rulers of Jumla had difficulty in asserting their authority over the marginal areas of their kingdoms, and tributary chieftains sprang up in various places (Fürer-Haimendorf 1975: 138–39).

While a history of early kingdoms in the areas neighboring Thaksatsae emerges from Tibetan texts, these include few references to the present Thaksatsae, and there is little additional evidence that helps to correlate the history of the surrounding areas with that of the Thakali or to identify clearly the entry of the Thakali into the history of the region. It is possible to date with some assurance the founding of the Lha Khang Temple in Kobang in Thaksatsae in the fifteenth century. This temple was considered by Tibetans to mark the southern boundary of Tibetan cultural influence.

The reliance of scholars on Tibetan texts to account for the period before the eighteenth century privileges the views of Tibetan Buddhist monks, many of whom were never within a hundred miles of the Kali Gandaki. Not surprisingly, their accounts concern the establishment of monasteries and temples and the achievements of missionaries and lamas and support the narratives of scholars within which Buddhism figures prominently. But the lack of other voices should not lead us to assume that the area was uniformly influenced by Buddhism.

Matching the references in the chronicles to actual events in the upper Kali Gandaki valley is no simple task since there is little concrete evidence to confirm the connection of this area with that mentioned in the Tibetan chronicles. Tibetan texts that deal with the early period are primarily concerned with the kingdom of Lo, several days' walk to the north of Tukche, the northernmost village of the Thaksatsae Thakali. In some instances, superimposing the history of the Lo and Serib of the chronicles on Mustang District or Thak Khola encourages a casual set of assertions about early history that confuses rather than clarifies understanding of the extent to which populations residing in this area were subject to external influences. Based on the existing evidence, it is premature to assume that the political boundaries of the contemporary regions correspond to those mentioned in the texts. Moreover, in view of the uneven pattern of influence contemporary events have had in the region, it seems likely that areas and peoples lying within what is now called Mustang District or Thak Khola were varyingly affected by the invasions and conquests of parts of the upper Kali Gandaki valley by the kingdoms of Gungthang, Yarlung, Ladakh, Jumla, or Parbat, the missionaries of Bon and Tibetan Buddhism, and local rulers in Lo, Serib, Thini, and Tukche.

What evidence does exist suggests that the southern stretch of the upper Kali Gandaki valley was less integrated into the Tibetan political and cultural sphere than were the areas just to the north. The area now known as Thak-satsae appears to have been a true border area, where goods from the plains were exchanged for goods from the north and south of which there were no Tibetan Buddhist temples.[17] It was clearly involved in and important to but also peripheral to both northern and southern influences and not central to the struggles among competing political powers.

The village records (bemchāg) of the five original villages of Panchgaon describe a different set of events and personages from those found in the Tibetan texts.[18] These records make no reference to Serib, and few of the named places and groups can be clearly linked to those currently existent in the Thak Khola.

By at least the eighteenth century, the kingdom of Parbat (Malebum), one of the more powerful of the twenty-four principalities to the south known collectively as the Chaubisi Raja, had some influence in the area.[19] A 1705 treaty signed by the rulers of Jumla, Lo, and Parbat, as well as by the head-men of Thak, Thini, and Marpha, regulated trade and relations among these areas (Schuh 1994:75). From the treaty one can infer that Parbat ruled as far north as the village of Dana and that Thak, Thini, and Marpha were autonomous. In 1719 the ruler of Lo asked Kirthi Bam Malla, the ruler of Parbat, to help him fight Jumla.[20] An alliance of Parbat and Doti ended Jumla's influence in the Thak Khola area. The raja of Parbat confirmed the rules of conduct of the monks and nuns of Meki Lha Khāng temple at Kobang in 1774 (Fürer-Haimendorf 1975:141).

While no complete picture emerges of the area before the Gurkha conquest, it is at least clear that in the centuries preceding the unification of Nepal many external influences on the upper Kali Gandaki area disrupted local powers and encouraged some population movements in and out of the valley. The coming of the Gurkhas meant the addition of yet another external influence, one that dramatically shifted the orientation of the region toward the south. The general events of this era and the varied impacts on the Thakali are relatively well documented and are summarized below.

The Formation of the Gurkhali State

Over several decades in the late eighteenth century, an army from the town of Gorkha, west of the Kathmandu valley, conquered the territory that was to become the present state of Nepal. The Gurkhalis were Hindus and claimed to be high-caste Thakuris, descended from the raja of Sinja, who in turn was believed to have been a descendant of the Rajputs who fled India during the Muslim invasions.

The conquest of the Chaubisi Raja, including the territory of Thak Khola, followed by two decades the Gurkha conquest of the Kathmandu Valley. Parbat, whose control of mines and a large area on the southern slopes of Dhaulagiri made it one of the strongest and most persistent opponents of the Gurkhalis, was defeated by the Gurkha ruler Bahadur Shah in October 1786. Bahadur Shah completed his conquest of the Chaubisi Raja west of the Kali Gandaki in six months, three of which his army spent in camp awaiting the end of the monsoon season (Stiller 1973:181). In the next three years he was to add twenty thousand square miles to the area controlled by the Gurkhalis. He began this phase of the Gurkha conquest by attacking Jumla through a northern route extending from Mustang. In traversing this route, he was retracing the route of migration described in the Gauchan *rhab*, the route many Thakali believed to have been taken by the Hansa Raja and his followers from Sinja to Thak Khola.[21] With the conquest of Jumla in 1789, the way was opened for the conquest of areas farther to the west.

In the years following the conquest, the Gurkhalis' ambition to make their kingdom a true Hindustan faced external challenges from the British and the Mughals and internal difficulties posed by geography and religious, ethnic, and political differences among their subjects. Over the ensuing decades, the political and administrative efforts to integrate the outlying areas, maintain a steady income for the central government, and forge a common nation out of diverse populations with different cultures, languages, and religions had profound effects on the Thakali.

The focus of scholars of the Thakali on the salt trade monopoly, which began only in 1862, has led many to date the modern history of the Thakali from the administrative reforms of Jang Bahadur Rana in the middle of the nineteenth century. But while these years are crucial to understanding the remarkable adaptation of some of the Thakali to changing conditions in the late nineteenth and early twentieth centuries, these changes were really set in motion in the years immediately following the Gurkha conquest. The changes in trade after the awarding of the salt monopoly in 1862 followed other changes in economic and political opportunities in the region.

Three main activities brought the Thakali into widening networks of contacts outside Thak Khola in the nineteenth century. These include the collection of taxes, the management of mines in the Khani Khuwa area, and the dominance of the salt trade along the Kali Gandaki River. As the following account will make clear, the importance of the salt trade in the history of the Thakali has been overrated, and the central role played by migrant Thakali communities has been overlooked. Influences have been multiple, both simultaneous and sequential, and flowed in more than one direction.

Tax Collection

It took years before the central Gurkhali government exercised complete control in the conquered areas. After an area was first subdued, a *subba* was usually established in the place of each of the previous rajas, and affairs were conducted much as they had been by the former rulers.[22] Not closely watched by the central government, these individuals had considerable latitude for interpreting their power. Both Kirkpatrick and Hamilton stress that government in Nepal took its "colour" from "the character and temporary views of the ruling individual" (Kirkpatrick 1811:196; also cited in Hamilton [1819] 1971:101).

The Gurkha conquest brought relative peace to the conquered areas but also resulted in high and uneven taxes. In Parbat, as in many other former hill kingdoms, revenue collection was initially subcontracted to *ijaradars*.[23] Through the *ijara* system the government delegated to an individual the authority to collect taxes in a specific region or with respect to a specific source of revenue for a set period of time on payment of a stipulated amount in advance. The *ijaradar* was allowed to collect whatever he could: anything in excess of what he had paid was his profit; if he fell short it was his loss.

An alternate arrangement was the *amānat* system, within which revenue was collected by salaried employees of the government. These employees turned over whatever amount they had been able to collect rather than a set amount stipulated in advance. Because the government also had to pay costs out of the revenue collected, the net revenues were generally lower with the *amānat* system. The *ijara* system entailed little risk, no set expenditure, and no administrative complications. It was thus widely used for revenue collection, exploitation of mineral resources, lumbering, and management of trading monopolies. The *amānat* system was generally only used as a stopgap method when people complained about oppressive *ijaradars* or when no responsible *ijaradar* could be found.

One consequence of the *ijara* system was that it undermined the power of the central government; in the hills, where isolation was compounded by the nature of the geography, this gave the *ijaradar* great power. The *ijaradar* could also be at odds with other local men of wealth and importance.

High taxes apparently motivated a significant Thakali emigration from Thak Khola in the late eighteenth century: by 1798 many families had left Thak to escape the oppression of the *ijaradar*.[24] Some of these Thakali emigrants reportedly moved into Lamjung, Kaski, and other areas of the middle ranges. In 1798 the government appealed for emigrants to return home (Regmi 1972:140).

As the Gurkhali government continued to expand its hold over Himalayan territories in the early part of the nineteenth century, it increased its efforts to support this expansion through taxation. Over the nine years 1802–11, the central government made repeated attempts to increase the tax collected from Thak Khola. In 1802 the government shifted responsibility for revenue collection from the *ijaradar* to local Thakali headmen, *mukiyās* or *budhās*, in Thak.[25] The *ijara* system was reintroduced in 1807 in order to increase the tax revenue.[26] Despite local complaints of oppression and continuing emigration from the area, the settlement reached in 1811 represented an 88 percent increase over the sum provided in 1802.[27]

Among Thakali communities outside Thaksatsae, I found it difficult to find evidence confirming the alleged flight from high taxes in the eighteenth century. Instead, the descendants of early Thakali migrants into the middle hills traced their ancestors' motivations to opportunities that became available in the former areas of the Parbat and Baglung rajas. In light of these family accounts it appears that some Thakali were apparently quite active both in Thaksatsae and in the former regions of Parbat as *ijaradar*. Their move from Thaksatsae may be attributed less to the push of excessive taxes than to the pull of new economic opportunities.

Mining Contracts

The former principality of Parbat (Malebum) had amassed considerable wealth from its twenty-five copper mines before its conquest by the Gurkhas.[28] Mines continued to be an important source of government revenue for the Gurkhas in the nineteenth century: in the middle of the century they contributed about 7 percent of the kingdom's revenue.[29]

Mineral resources were state owned but exploited through individuals under tenurial arrangements: miners kept half the output and turned the other half over to the state. One of the two most important areas for copper mining was the area of Khani Khuwa in Baglung, Gulmi, and Myagdi districts (this included the mines of the former raja of Parbat). Demand for copper, lead, and iron had been fueled by the production of munitions beginning in 1793 and continuing into the nineteenth century.[30]

Copper was produced in these mines in excess of the quantities needed for munitions production. This excess was minted into coins in Beni, Baglung, and Tansen. These coins were used both within Nepal and in northern India. They were apparently so popular in India that in the mid-nineteenth century British coins had not replaced them.

Trade in copper was a government monopoly. As a consequence, the miners had to sell their portion of the production to the government at a rate fixed by the government. The need for an administrative network to procure and transport copper was met through recourse to the *ijara* system. Most of the metal extracted from mines in Nepal was done under the direction of two *ijaras*. One of these—in the Myagdi-Baglung-Gulmi area— was controlled by the Thakali during parts of the nineteenth century.[31] The mining *ijaradar* controlled both the trade in copper and the minting of coins. He also collected agrarian taxes and administered justice in the mining area. For these privileges, he paid a stipulated amount of money to the government or turned over a stipulated quantity of metal.

In the late eighteenth and early nineteenth centuries, Thakali emigrants began to move into the area referred to by the Thakali as Khani Khuwa, the mountainous mining region in what are now the administrative districts of

Baglung, Myagdi, and Gulmi. The term *Khani Khuwa* refers generally to the *bāis khāni* (N: lit. "twenty-two mines") area of what were the former principalities of Galkot and Parbat. The term is more metaphorical than geographically specific. Roughly speaking, the area in question lies southeast of the ridge marked by the passes to Dhorpatan, south of the Dhaulagiri massif, and west of the Kali Gandaki River. The area is encompassed by two drainage systems that flow into the Kali Gandaki River and a series of ridges that rise to altitudes exceeding eleven thousand feet (see map 4).

Hamilton mentioned the mines in Galkot in 1819, and informants' accounts indicate that Thakalis were resident in the area by at least 1845 (though evidence collected from current residents in that area may not reflect this, as apparently no descendants of the earliest migrants families still reside in Galkot). Many Thakali families in Khani Khuwa can trace back their residence in this area one hundred and sixty to one hundred and eighty years, to the early nineteenth century, 1820–1840, but of the ancestors of the current residents in Galkot, the earliest migrant appears to have arrived in the 1880s.[32] Manzardo has dated the Thakali migration to the Galkot area to 1915, which is only a decade or so before most of the mines in the area closed (1978:39, 208).[33] Manzardo's estimate is consistent with the information provided by some of the current residents in Galkot (relative latecomers to that area) and with the dates of migration for other migrant communities with which he was familiar.[34]

Mining opportunities increased throughout the nineteenth century as a result of the central government's need for increased copper production to offset the financial drain of the still-large Gurkhali standing army. As the territorial expansion of the Gurkhali empire slowed, the government was hard pressed to meet the expenses of the army from the existent territorial base.

By the middle of the nineteenth century, long before the era of the salt trade monopoly, the Thakali operated as agents for the central government in this region. Copper mining was an important economic draw for Thakalis, many of whom came to manage or supply the mining operations. The emigration from Thak Khola to Khani Khuwa may have had two distinct advantages for migrants: it took them out of the influence of greedy *ijaradars* in Thak Khola and toward the opportunities provided by trade and mining contracts in Khani Khuwa.

A competitive system was introduced into the mining contracts about this time: contracts were awarded to the highest bidders, usually for five-year terms.[35] This allowed the government to increase its revenue at little cost.

This system did not encourage long-term investment in the mines by the *ijaradars*, however, and over the course of the nineteenth century the mines suffered from mismanagement and the lack of technological advances. The mines were on ridges at elevations of about seven thousand feet, which meant they could not be worked during the winter. Monsoon rain further prevented work from June to September. This resulted in a mining season of only four months, from March to June.

The ranas made no significant change in the mining contract system after they came to power in the middle of the nineteenth century, and, as a consequence of general neglect and lack of investment, the overall production of the mines declined steadily over the second half of the nineteenth century. The government began importing copper and iron from India by the 1860s, and by the end of the century revenue from mines was less than a quarter of what it had been at the middle of the century.

As profits dropped, so did competition for the contracts; eventually, the government was lucky if it could renew contracts without a loss from term to term. In Khani Khuwa, mining administrative eventually shifted over to the *amānat* system managed from offices in Baglung, Beni, and Tansen.[36] Amānat officials responded to low production by putting pressure on the miners. The headman of Bahunga village reported this to the government, "Prabhu Narayan Thakali visited this area and compelled us to accept an undertaking to supply 55 dharnis of copper every year in spite of our protestations. Because we were not able to produce that quantity of copper, our oxen and household utensils were seized."[37] The *amānat* administrator was not amiss in thinking that the miners had metals they were not turning over to the government office. Prices paid by the government were so far below market prices that there was an extensive system of smuggling. So many miners were caught smuggling ore that *amānat* officials ran short of fetters to confine them.[38]

Control of the mines returned to the *ijara* system in 1885, when the contract went to Subba Ram Prasad Thakali,[39] but pressure on the miners did not abate. As the headman of Bahungau village related to the central government, "Krishna Dhoj Malea and Sarbajit Chand [sub-*ijaradars* to Subba Ram Prasad Thakali] came and demanded that we double the quantity of 55 *dhārnis* of copper yearly that we had previously been forced to stipulate. When we refused to do so, they put us in fetters and shackles and tortured and insulted us."[40]

Within a few years, control of the mines again returned to the *amānat* system. The resulting high administrative costs, combined with the lower productivity of the mines, resulted in a net revenue of only 1,867 rupees by the turn of the century. Government operation of mines in Khani Khuwa ended at that time, though independent mines run by small-scale *ijaradars* continued to operate in Khani Khuwa until the 1930s.

Trade and the Salt Contract

As the importance of mines diminished, the salt/grain trade through the Kali Gandaki gorge began to change with the establishment of a monopoly in the trade of salt. The story of the salt monopoly looms large in many narratives as the event that shaped the Thakali and largely determined the nature of their cultural adaptations in the late nineteenth and twentieth centuries. The monopoly was indeed an important historical influence on the Thakali, but it needs to be seen in perspective. Correcting for the misplaced emphasis on a single part of the historical narratives of the Thakali is possible by placing the sixty-year period of the salt monopoly in a wider context, examining alternative economic strategies undertaken by the Thakali before, during, and after the salt monopoly, and noting alternative sources of financing for the contract bidding.

For centuries, the trade route extending from the Tibet border through Thak Khola and south to the market of Butwal on the edge of the Terai has been a means by which the Thakali were exposed to a variety of cultural influences. The trade on this route included animals, wool, and salt from Tibet, grain from the middle hills, and clothes and industrial goods from Calcutta and the plains. One of the most significant aspects of this trade was the high volume of salt exchanged for grain from the middle hills. Differences in the local climate made the lower routes impassable during the summer monsoon rains, while the pass into Tibet was closed by snow during the winter. This made Thak Khola a logical middle entrepôt where goods could be traded and stored until they could be carried on to their destinations.

Because of goods traveling south along the Kali Gandaki River, the entrepôt of Butwal along the southern part of this trail was acknowledged as an important center of trade in the seventeenth century (Regmi 1972). Both Kirkpatrick, in 1793, and Hamilton, in 1802–3, commented on the trade route's importance (Kirkpatrick 1811:287; Hamilton [1819] 1971:272–74). In the early nineteenth century, Hamilton reported that Thak Khola (which he referred to as Thakakuti) was the chief market for the trade with Tibet through Mustang.[41] It appears that the Thakali controlled neither the trade nor the entrepôt of Tukche before the late nineteenth century[42] but instead shared the trade along this trail with other people in the region (see Snellgrove 1961:182).

Many rulers have seen this trans-Himalayan trade as an important source of revenue: for example, the raja of Parbat established a customs office in Dana in the eighteenth century, and the Gurkhalis continued to collect customs duty at Dana after their late-eighteenth-century conquest of Parbat and Mustang.

Changes in the customs system in the mid-nineteenth century had profound effects on trade and the history of the upper Kali Gandaki valley.[43] In the first half of the nineteenth century, customs duty was probably collected through *ijaras*, though the earliest record of this dates from 1853, when the contract cost 29,001 rupees (Regmi 1983:349). In 1853 the government shifted briefly from the *ijara* system to the *amānat* system. The supply of salt immediately declined, and the following year the government ordered the headmen of Panchgaon to supply salt to the Dana customshouse on a regular basis and at reasonable rates (Regmi 1977d:353–54). To ensure a steady flow of revenue the government almost immediately returned to the *ijara* system for the collection of customs duty.

In 1855 the war with Tibet disrupted trans-Himalayan trade and resulted in the suspension of the collection of customs on trade between Nepal and Tibet. In September 1855 Thakalis were recruited as soldiers and served in a regiment organized by Subba Balbir and Subba Dhansaram of Thak.[44] This is the first appearance of Balbir Thakali in the historical record, a man whose diplomatic talents and good relations with the ruling Rana family helped to establish his lineage as the richest and most powerful in Thak Khola.[45] Balbir served the Gurkhalis well during the war and was given a copy of the 108 volumes of the Kengyur, the Tibetan sacred text (Fürer-Haimendorf 1975:143–44).[46] His descendants, now known colloquially as the *subba* family, became the most influential family in the upper Kali Gandai region.

Bidding for the customs contract in 1860 was eventually won by Lieutenant Champa Singh Khadka Chetri, son of Captain Hem Karma Khadka Chetri, who subsequently recruited three Thakalis to work for him: Subba Balbir Thakali, Ramshankar Thakali, and Dhana Prasad Thakali. Chyalpa Thakali, who had lost out in the bidding, persuaded Ramshankar and Dhana Prasad to quit and in July 1860 devised a plan to disrupt the trade of salt for

TABLE 3.1 The Salt Contract in Thak Khola from 1862 to 1928[1]

	Contract Holder	Comments
1862–64	Hem Karma Khadka	The monopoly was abolished by the government briefly in 1863.[2]
1865–67	Lt. C. S. Khadka	
1868–70	Bal Bir (Kalu Ram) Sherchan[3]	
1871–73	Bal Bir Sherchan	
1874–76	Bal Bir Sherchan	The monopoly was abolished from 1874–76.[4]
1877–79	Kabi Ram Sherchan	The annual payment was 82,000 rupees.[5]
1880–82	Kabi Ram Sherchan	
1883–85	Ram Prasad Gauchan	
1886–89	Ram Prasad Gauchan	By 1886 the annual payment was 97,000 rupees. The monopoly was again briefly abolished in 1886.[6]
1889–91	Kabi Ram Sherchan	A customshouse was created in Tukche.[7]
1892–94	unknown (Harka Man Sherchan?)	
1895–97	Harka Man Sherchan	
1898–1900	Harka Man Sherchan[8]	

1. This information is collected from a variety of sources, and some of it is contradictory. Occasionally the Thakali listed the contract in the name of their children, thus the individual with the title was not always the one making the decisions. This chart indicates the individual with effective authority.

2. Regmi (1972:1).

3. In documents of the time Bal Bir is given the surname Thakali. In this chart, I identify Thakali *subbas* by their clan names. It was not common practice for Thakali to use their clan names as a surname (rather than the nomenclature Thakali) until the 1920s.

4. Regmi (1972:1).

5. Regmi (1972:1).

6. Regmi (1972:1).

7. Fürer-Haimendorf (1975:144) stated that the customhouse was first moved to Tukche in 1877. Regmi (1972:1) notes that it was in Dana in 1886. Vinding (1988:192 n. 121) notes that the Thakali *subba* established a branch office in Tukche for use in the summer and that it is this office that was moved by the Gurung *subba* to Chairo.

8. Kawaguchi ([1909] 1979:45). See also Fürer-Haimendorf (1975:144) and Vinding (1988:192 n. 113).

TABLE 3.1 *(continued)*

1902–3	Man Lal Gurung	The value of the contract reached 150,000 rupees per year.[9]
1903–4	Harka Man Sherchan	Harka Man died in 1903.
1905–7	Man Lal Gurung	Man Lal died in 1907.
1908–10	Narjang Gurung	
1911–13	Ganesh Man Sherchan	
1914–17	Ganesh Man Sherchan	
1918–20	Narjang Gurung	The Tukche customshouse was moved to Chairo.[10]
1920–22	Ganesh Man Sherchan	The customshouse was returned to Tukche.
1923–25	Hit Man Sherchan	
1926–28	Mohan Man Sherchan	The monopoly was abolished in early April 1928.

9. This was equivalent to 56 kilograms of gold (Vinding 1988:182; Regmi 1981d:116).
10. This office was not the formal customshouse that remained in Dana throughout this period.

grain. Balbir objected to his actions and helped to prevent a public meeting planned by Chyalpa, who sought the endorsement of the Thakali community for his scheme. In October 1860 Chyalpa and others filed suit against Balbir in the court at Baglung.[47] The court sent constables and Chyalpa to arrest Balbir, who was beaten and put in fetters without being told the charges against him. Somehow, Balbir escaped and made his way to Kathmandu, where he petitioned the prime minister, Jang Bahadur Rana, to intervene. Jang Bahadur subsequently ordered Lieutenant Champa Singh Khadka Chetri to arrest Chyalpa, Dhana Prasad, and their colleague, Prem Ranjan Thakali, for the unlawful arrest of Balbir.

In 1862 a delegation of Thakalis requested a reduction in the land revenue tax, which then amounted to 12,500 rupees assessed to the seven hundred households of Thaksatsae.[48] A deputation sent to Kathmandu to make the plea argued that the burden of the tax had motivated two hundred and sixteen households to leave Thaksatsae and settle in Kaski, Lamjung, and other parts of the middle ranges. As an alternative, the government proposed, and the Thakali agreed, to a system whereby free trade in salt and grain would be eliminated, customs duty would be charged on most commodities carried past the Dana customs post in either direction, and a monopoly on trade in salt would be granted to the customs collector. The contract was auctioned to the highest bidder, who, in addition to his rights as tax collector, was invested with the powers of a magistrate and called *subba*. The awarding of monopolies in the import trade with Tibet was widespread during the rule of Jang Bahadur Rana. This was a significant change in the way salt was traded along the Kali Gandaki valley, and as the system evolved over the next sixty-six years the customs contractor became the dominant political force in Thak Khola and the areas immediately surrounding it.

The period of the Kali Gandaki salt monopoly was marked by contests for power among rival groups. In response to the objections of other traders who were shut out of the trade by the monopoly, the government briefly rescinded the system in 1863, in 1874, and again in 1886, but each time the monopoly was quickly reestablished.

By 1869 the contract, which was usually auctioned for three-year periods, was held by Balbir Thakali (also known as Kalu Ram Thakali). Balbir's son, Kavi Ram, held the contract in 1876.[49] The contract was taken next by Pati Ram Sau (lit. Pati Ram, the rich), a Sherchan from Larjung of the Pompar *ghyu*, who had earned a fortune managing mines in Khani Khuwa. The contemporary tension between Khuwale and Thak Khole Thakalis may have been foreshadowed in the bidding competition between the Pompar Sherchans and the Lha Khang Dhungi Sherchans for the salt trade contract. Pati Ram acted as guarantor (he would be obliged to pay the government in case of contractual default) for his son-in-law, Subba Ram Prasad Thakali, when the latter bid successfully for the custom's contract in 1884 (at that time Ram Prasad was already the *ijaradar* for twenty-two mines in Khani Khuwa).[50] When Kavi Ram regained control of it, he reportedly moved the customs-house north to Tukche, where it was farther away from Khani Khuwa and Pati Ram's influence.[51]

After this move, but not necessarily because of it, Pati Ram and Ram Prasad apparently never again bid successfully for the contract. According to widely told stories, Pati Ram's considerable wealth was depleted during the later part of the nineteenth century. This is commonly attributed to his own arrogance and the frivolity of his son-in-law Ram Prasad Thakali.[52] These two were certainly at the height of their influence in the 1880s, when they controlled both the mining *ijara* in Khani Khuwa and the salt trade *ijara* in

FIGURE 3.1 Wall with Buddhist prayer wheels in Tukche

Thak Khola. Whether they overextended their reach by bidding too high for the contracts or lost their wealth through other mistakes or misfortunes we don't know, but neither they nor their relatives play a major role in the bidding for *ijaras* after 1890. Unlike the descendants of Balbir and Kavi Ram, who became the most powerful family in Thak Khola, are still referred to as the *subba* family, and still rank among the wealthiest families among the Thakali, the descendants of Pati Ram and Ram Prasad retained no significant wealth or honor from their terms as *subba*. Some of Pati Ram's descendants continued to reside in Larjung until the early 1980s, but the lineage is better

FIGURE 3.2 Partially crumbled subba family home in Tukche

represented in Khani Khuwa, where many of his descendants remained permanently and continued to be involved in mining for some years. Ram Prasad was the last Thakali from Khani Khuwa to make a serious bid for the salt contract. As the power of the Khuwale mining *ijaradars* faded in the late nineteenth and early twentieth centuries, the power of the salt contract *ijaradar* in Thak Khola soared.

As the *subba* family gained more control over the salt contract they also gained influence through positions as tax collectors in the northern villages of the Kali Gandaki valley—Baragaon and Panchgaon—and to the west in Dolpo. Their growing contacts in Kathmandu and their increasing wealth put them in a position to take advantage of many other opportunities. Also, in the early part of the twentieth century, they introduced through the council of thirteen headmen in Thaksatsae a series of cultural reforms that had the appearance of Sanskritizing Thakali cultural practices.

Though Pati Ram and Ram Prasad faded from the scene, Balbir's Lha Khang Dhungi lineage was not without competitors for the salt contract.

When Kavi Ram died the contract was worth about 50,000 rupees, and his widow voluntarily relinquished the monopoly. Man Lal Gurung (1857–1907) of Ghan Pokhara, who had a reputation as a reliable and successful customs contractor in Bhot Khola, successfully bid for the contract. This success led to a rivalry between Harkaman Sherchan (1860–1903) and his brother, Ganesh Man,[53] the sons of Kavi Ram, on one side, and Man Lal and his son, Narjang (1879–1941), on the other. The post was held alternatively by one group and then the other for about twelve years until it was permanently reclaimed by Balbir's descendants in 1919. During his tenure as *subba* from 1917–19, Narjang moved the customshouse three miles north to Tserok. In 1919 Ganesh Bahadur Sherchan, a grandson of Kavi Ram, ousted Narjang with what has been called "a combination of force and diplomacy" (Iijima 1960). From then until 1928 the post was held by descendants of Balbir. The salt monopoly era ended in 1928, when, at the request of the Thakali, the salt trade was freed from the control of the contractor.

Seasonal Migration

During the period of the salt contract system (1862–1928) Thakali emigration from Thaksatsae continued.[54] Based on household surveys and family accounts, Thakali migration to communities along the main trails in central Nepal appears to have increased significantly in the early part of the twentieth century.[55] An interesting aspect of this particular migration pattern is its fluidity: throughout the middle part of the twentieth century, the number of Thakali households situated along the main trails appears to have been fairly stable, but there was considerable turnover as one household would move on and another would move in to fill the economic niche within which the first family had been operating.

Migration into Khani Khuwa continued to be stimulated by the business opportunities provided by the mines until the 1930s, when many of the copper mines were closed. As the Khani Khuwa mines were played out and closed down in the 1920s and 1930s, some of the Thakalis within Baglung, Gulmi, and Myagdi Districts began to move down from the ridges where the mines had been located to help establish new market towns along the valley floors. The Thakali *bazār* of Darbang in Myagdi District was established at this time, for example, just across the river from the site where the old administrative center of the region had been buried in a landslide in 1929.

Mines, however, were not the only attraction for migrants in Myagdi District: rich agricultural land also attracted successful Thakali farmers from Thaksatsae. The availability of capital to invest may have been a factor that allowed Thakalis from Thak to buy winter fields farther down the Kali Gandaki, near Jhii, Rakhu, Sikha, Tatopani, Birethanti, and other towns along the Myagdi Khola and the Modi Khola. A pattern of seasonal migration was under way by the 1880s. This temporary migration did not include members of the *subba* lineage or their affines but, instead, was composed of Thakali farmers from more agriculturally dependent villages in Thak, Khanti, Kobang, and Sauru who purchased land along the Myagdi Khola and the lower Kali Gandaki, where they resided for half of the year. They usually stayed long enough to plant two crops before returning to Thak. Pastures above the fields in Myagdi also allowed them to bring animals back and forth.

In the early part of the nineteenth century, migrants maintained contacts with Thaksatsae. The first families to migrate into the Khani Khuwa area maintained close ties with their relatives in Thaksatsae through the early part of the twentieth century: they visited Thak Khola and received visitors from the area and often married Thakali from Thak Khola. Many migrants continued to hold land in Thak Khola, and often a relative remained on the property to manage it.

The Effects of Nation Building

As the brief foregoing review makes clear, the Thakali interacted with the agents of the Gurkhali government in many ways during the nineteenth century. These interactions preceded by decades the cultural reforms attempted in the early twentieth century by the salt monopoly *subbas*. The Hinduization of the Thakali attempted by the *subba* family evolved at the end of the salt monopoly period and in response to a number of changing aspects of the evolving state and the ruling elite. To understand the next phase of Thakali adaptations, one must first revisit earlier events in the formation of the state.

Following the Gurkha conquest, politically and administratively uniting the country proved to be a formidable task, and there were a series of wars, attempted coups, and general political instability at the center in the period

FIGURE 3.3 Looking east along the Myagdi valley from the market town of Darbang

preceding 1846. Better situated than their northern neighbors to take advantage of a political reorientation that connected Thak Khola with the south rather than the north, the Thakali responded ably to the new constraints and opportunities that arose during this period.

In addition to the creation of an institutional administration, however, state-building required the formation of a national ideology, a process that proved to be even more difficult. The attempt to forge a common nation out of diverse populations with different cultures, languages, and religions also affected the Thakali by changing the rules of the many social contexts within which they operated.

With the fall of other Hindu principalities in South Asia to the British, Gurkha saw itself as the only independent Hindu realm in the sacred land of the Hindus (Burghart 1984:106) and acted to preserve the purity of the realm (116). Within the possessions of the Gurkha kingdom were a wide array of social groups speaking more than forty distinct languages. The region included at least three historically and geographically distinct caste hierarchies, a number of loosely defined groups in the middle hills, and culturally distinct Tibeto-Burman-language–speaking populations along the northern border (Fisher 1987; Levine 1987; Höfer 1979a). Over the years, strategies employed to create a Hindu nation out of these disparate populations included persuading outlying populations to adopt some Hindu practices, broadening the definition of Hindu, and outlawing the conversion of Hindus to other religions.

Central control of the hinterlands increased in the middle of the nineteenth century after the Rana family took control of the government, reduced the king to a figurehead, and began a century of rule as hereditary prime ministers. The Ranas initiated a significant step in the process of state formation in 1854 with the codification of a national hierarchy that ascribed a status to each of the categories of social groups named in the legal code. This 1854 code, the Muluki Ain, was a Hindu model superimposed on a heterogeneous population. It served a dual purpose by distinguishing Nepal's society from foreign societies and cultures and justifying the placement of the rulers at the top of the hierarchy. This social amalgam ranked high Hindu castes at the top, followed by a wide array of non-Hindu hill groups, Bhotes, or Tibetan Buddhist groups from the mountains along the northern border, and, at the bottom, untouchables. The code put forth the country's laws on diverse social, religious, economic, and administrative matters in 163 categories in order to ensure that uniform punishment was meted out to all subjects according to their offenses and their statuses (Sharma 1977; Regmi 1976). It included legislation on commensality and physical contact and provided different groups with different sorts of land tenure and trading rights. Thus the code imbued these group labels with a significance they did not formerly have. Being able to claim membership in a named category was a matter of economic and political consequence and engendered a process whereby groups began to define or redefine themselves with respect to the legal hierarchy.

As a hegemonic discourse that asserted the authority of a ruling class, the code would seem to have set obligatory terms for anyone wanting access to power. As Raymond Williams, Foucault, Gramsci, and others have argued, hegemonies are never complete, and in this case, in fact, there were opportunities to resist, contest, or at least evade practices presented as obligatory in the Muluki Ain.

Ambiguities in the middle ranges of the hierarchy established by the Muluki Ain combined with the code's use of categories that did not, for the

most part, conform to precise groups of people to encourage creative presentations of identity. Strategies of genealogical reckoning designed to lay
claim to a higher status than assigned by the code were widespread and were
not beneath even the family of Jang Bahadur Rana, the ruler responsible for
the Muluki Ain. After he came to power in 1846, his Chetri family of Kun-
wars adopted the name Rana and had a new family genealogy written con-
necting the Rana lineage with the rajputs of Chitor (Gimlette 1927).

Narrowing ethnic boundaries the better to control the public image of a
group's cultural practices was one possible response to the unifying pressures
of the state. In other cases, like those of the Tamang and the Chetri, the
legal recognition of a new and higher category improved interactions with
the state and allowed those who were able to claim membership in the new
category to achieve a higher position than their former status (Höfer 1979a;
Holmberg 1989; Sharma 1977). The Chetri category, in particular, has been
subject to widespread infiltration from below by individuals of obscure and
nondescript social origins who were willing to improve their rank by emu-
lating Hindu norms (Sharma 1977). In other cases, like that of the Limbu,
broadening membership was advantageous in the struggle to maintain an
exclusive system of collective land tenure (Caplan 1970; Jones 1976).

While an assertion of Hindu ideology accompanied the formation of the
state and high-caste Hindus have been and remain the dominant political
elite of Nepal, these processes should not be read as a simple movement of
groups slowly undergoing the process of Hinduization or Sanskritization as
they progressively moved toward some standard Hindu model. While the
Muluki Ain may have been designed to create a homogeneous society, this
aspiration could not be satisfied. The Muluki Ain remained a projection
from above and represented a social order that was for a long time little
known and even less accepted in many areas of the high northern mountains
(Höfer 1979a:40). As in the Thakali case, there were many compromises
between the national and regional systems (147).[56]

Post–Salt Monopoly Adaptations

In the last decade of the salt monopoly, Thakali traders began to look
elsewhere for economic opportunities. This movement coincided with a
growing Hindu fundamentalism among the ruling elite in Kathmandu. After
the end of the salt contract system in 1928, large numbers of the Thakali

migrated all over Nepal, achieving economic and political prominence in most of the locales to which they migrated.[57] The decade following the end of the salt trade contract in 1928 resulted in a wide expansion of the Thakali network. At this time, many Thakalis joined the agents and relatives of the *subba* lineage in setting up as successful, independent merchants outside Thak Khola. Around that same time, wealthy Thakalis moved permanently to *bazārs* along the Kali Gandaki: Beni, Tatopani, Baglung, and so on. The wealthiest Thakali in Baglung, for example, moved there in the early 1940s.

Using a strategy of creative genealogical reckoning, some members of the *subba* lineage attempted to circumscribe more clearly the boundaries of the Thakali as a cultural group in the early twentieth century. The maintenance of powerful ties with the Hindu rulers in Kathmandu encouraged them to dissociate themselves from groups seen as low-status Bhotes and Tibetans. These traders adopted some Hindu practices and widely circulated a version of the Thakali origin myth that emphasized their descent from the Hansa Raja, described as a Thakuri from the Malla kingdom in Jumla and distantly descended from the Rajput ancestors of the king of Nepal. Through their political control of the Thaksatsae villages, they were able to present a coherent image of the Thakali in Kathmandu or to visitors in Tukche.

This strategy of elite emulation was not unlike the strategies adopted by other groups in Nepal with political or economic aspirations. Using the standards established by the Muluki Ain, many groups strove to improve their ties to power. The ambiguity of the categories and the flexibility of the application of the code enabled numerous strategies. In some cases, like that of the Thakali, where a small subgroup was in more direct contact with the ruling elite, it was able to narrow the application of the ethnic label and make the behavior of those identified as members of this category appear to be in conformity with Hindu norms. Mirroring the code's hegemonic discourse on a local level, the Thakali *subbas* established new behavioral patterns for the Thakali in the early part of the twentieth century, when the Thakali monopoly on the salt trade was eroding and they were looking elsewhere for economic opportunities. The eating of yak meat, which was associated with beef, was banned. Clan names were changed from Tibetan to Nepali. Tibetan clothes were replaced with those in the style of the hill people. Brewed alcohol was banned. And a prohibition was placed on the most elaborate Tibetan funeral rites. These changes solidified the *subbas'* relationships with the Ranas, but they were quietly ignored by most of the Thakali: yak and alcohol continued to be regularly consumed, and Buddhist funeral rites continued to be practiced (only wealthy traders had been able to afford the elaborate rites in any case). Then, as now, the story of the Hansa Raja was met with a variety of responses among the Thakali themselves: with open acceptance, with puzzlement, and with emphatic rejection.

At this time Thakalis began to move into the Terai, the rich flat plains area that runs along the lower third of Nepal.[58] In 1930 Hitman Subba's eldest son, Anagman Sherchan, was appointed as a treasury officer of the central government and assigned to the Terai, then associated in the minds of most Thakalis with malarial fever.[59] This move is credited with overcoming Thakali reluctance to reside in the area, and the presence of Hitman's son in the area encouraged other Thakalis to follow. Hitman and his brother Mohan Man both actively pursued varied economic interests in all parts of Nepal in the middle of the twentieth century.[60] In the 1940s Hitman helped to establish other relatives in permanent residences in the Terai towns of Nepalgunj, Butwal, and Bhairawa to look after the varied economic interests of the family. At the same time, his brother Mohan Man took a contract for timber near Janakpur in the Terai.[61] Hitman held timber contracts for several years in the late 1940s and gained the contract for the distribution of Indian cigarettes in western Nepal. Later, the brothers opened a rice mill and two stores in Bhairawa.

By the 1950s the availability of Indian salt had reduced the demand for the more expensive Tibetan salt, and the Chinese occupation of Tibet had made trading conditions more difficult than they had been. Emigration from Tukche, in particular, increased dramatically in the 1950s, led by the major trading families, who were motivated by the diminishing trade through the valley and the lure of increasing business opportunities in the Terai, Pokhara, and Kathmandu.

The *rhabs'* accounts of migrating deities and ancestors, the oral tales of the Hansa Raja's migration from Jumla, the movement to Khani Khuwa, the long-distance trade from Tibet to Calcutta, and the seasonal and permanent settlement along trade routes in Nepal make the history of the Thakali one of fluid population movements, both short and long term, to locales both near and far. This essential unrootedness, which over the long term could be seen as almost definitional of the group, contrasts sharply with the image of them as a local group with a homeland in the Thak Khola valley.

Enter the Anthropologists, Surmising

Every man takes the limit of his own field of vision for the limits of the world.
—Schopenhauer

The arrival of the first scholars at a transition point in Thakali history, their focus on Thaksatsae, their extensive interactions with the *subba* lineage, and their predispositions to assume that there was one "real" story and that stories unfolded in a unilinear and irreversible direction set the context within which they each mistook particular streams for the whole river of Thakali culture.

When anthropologists began arriving in Nepal in the 1950s, the Thakali were already well scattered throughout the districts of Nepal.[62] The Italian scholar Giuseppe Tucci commented on the extensive networks of the *subba* family in 1952:

Tukche is controlled by one family and its members or representatives travel from one end of Nepal to the other; they have agents at Baglung and Butwal and at Nautanwa, the terminal of the Indian railway on the southern frontier of Nepal. Their headquarters is in Kathmandu. They hold a monopoly of cigarettes and textiles; at Tukche and further north they control and direct the trade with Tibet; they import wool, salt, horses and turquoise, and send rice, fabrics, cigarettes and European manufactured goods to Tibet. So Tukche is a big trade centre, the houses are full of goods and trading is all wholesale.

([1953] 1982:49)

Kawakita, visiting Thak Khola in 1953, commented on the Thakali tendency to leave their homes and settle on lines of commerce (1957:92), observations that have been echoed by many other visitors to central Nepal.

The arrival of the first anthropologists coincided with the most dramatic migration of Thakali from Thak Khola, following the closing of the Tibet/Nepal border by the Chinese in 1960. During this period, the completion of roads from the Terai to Pokhara and from Kathmandu to Pokhara (the Siddhartha Rajmarga was completed in 1968 and the Pritvi Rajmarga in 1972) dramatically changed the flow of goods in the hills and altered the course of migration. Thakalis began to migrate to more distant areas than they had before. Most of the Thakali families who moved to the Terai town of Bhairawa, for instance, did so from 1960 to 1963. Manzardo dates the largest growth of the Thakali community in Pokhara to the period coinciding with the closing of the northern trade (Manzardo and Sharma 1975:28; Manzardo 1978:100).[63]

The ethnic labels of the Muluki Ain had taken root in the century before the beginning of anthropological research, and scholars first took these categories to represent bounded groups with some historical depth and cultural continuity. The early scholarship of Nepal, as in such work elsewhere, tended to essential categories and cultures, the scholars acting as coartificers with the people themselves. In the Thakali case, they did so by associating primarily with the *subba* lineage and by simplifying and polarizing differences through the use of totalizing dichotomies such as Hinduism/Buddhism and tribe/caste.

It was in this context that the story of the Thakali was told from the perspective of the prominent Tukche trading families, emphasizing economic success and deliberate cultural transformation. I examine these interpretations in more detail in chapters 7 and 8.

4 Separation and Integration: Community and Contestation

> Although our birthplace is not the same, we should have the feeling that we have been born in the same place so that we may have good feelings when we gather.
>
> —Cyogi *rhab*

Moving On

Wide migration created communication and adaptive problems for the Thakali and resulted in a community considerably more heterogeneous than it had been when the small Thakali community resided in the limited geographic area of Thak Khola. Years of migrations had put different groups of Thakali in various contexts and provided them with different networks, different opportunities, and different cultural constraints. Population movements have also had a significant and often overlooked effect on Thakali economic and cultural adaptations, their identity, and their narratives. These movements have been particularly diverse and involved increasing proportions of their population in the nineteenth and twentieth centuries: in the early part of the nineteenth century they migrated to avoid high taxes and to take advantage of economic opportunities in the former principality of Parbat; during the period of the salt monopoly traders cut out of the salt trade sought opportunities elsewhere; at the close of the salt monopoly period the wealthy traders began to look for new investment opportunities all over Nepal.

This chapter considers two sets of themes in light of this historical process of migration: the tension between the growing geographical separation of the Thakali and the attempts to keep the community integrated and the tension between internal competition and community solidarity.

Despite the close association of the name Thakali with a specific piece of real estate in central Nepal, movement has been frequent and recurrent in Thakali history. From the wanderings of Ani Airam, Samledhen Sam-lechyāng, Dhakpa Gyalsang, and Pau Kuti, the ancestors of the four Thakali clans, the widespread movements of the Thakali have since taken them to every corner of Nepal and around the globe. In the past century, Thakalis have been on the move to conduct trade, as pastoralists, to work on their own agricultural lands in different climatic zones, for education, and for wage labor. These movements have been for long and short periods; they have been both cyclical and permanent; they have sometimes involved a second (or third) home and sometimes required temporary quarters; and they have been both domestic and international. In the 1990s these travels expanded to include Japan, Korea, and the United States.

Despite the difficulty of travel, the movement of populations in the Him-alayas is not an isolated or recent phenomenon. In contemporary Nepal, the most common pattern of movement has been from the middle hills to lower altitudes in search of land or wage-labor opportunities. This movement has often been stimulated by environmental pressures resulting from the de-creased ratio of land per person resulting from overpopulation.[1] It also occurs as a side effect of climatic patterns that encourage or require cyclical popu-lation movements. Improved transportation and employment opportunities attract these population movements into the Terai (where malaria eradica-tion programs have opened up new areas for cultivation) and into urban areas, particularly the Kathmandu valley.

Thakali population movements do not fit the general pattern of migration in Nepal, where migration generally involves those at the extremes of society, that is, either the rich or the poor (Dahal, Rai, and Manzardo 1977).[2] The poor emigrate from areas lacking resources and job opportunities and immigrate to areas where they believe these exist. This is as true for poor Thakalis as for any other *jāt*. At the other end of the economic scale, wealthy rural families migrate to take advantage of improved standards of living and investment opportunities. Thakali movement, however, includes not just the extremes of society but individuals and families from every part of the economic spectrum.

Thakali movement stands as an exception to most typological systems used to explain and analyze population movements.[3] In existing studies, population movements are characterized by the length of time involved — seasonal or cyclical, permanent, temporary — or by the underlying economic cause—transhumance, the search for wage labor, agriculture, trade. Some categorizations consider the migrants' own intentions, such as whether they intend to return to their native villages, or the length of time for which they intend to migrate; others interpret action, such as whether migrants sell their lands and home in the native village, or whether the entire family migrates, and so on. The choice of categories often reveals the analyst's own concerns, whether it be the migration of a particular group or the movement into or out of a particular geographical area.[4] Unfortunately, these systems of characterization can be misleading, since the movement from one category to another is more fluid than is implied. The variables that must be considered by a comprehensive typology are numerous. This is particularly true of Thakali migration: migration may involve a single individual, a household, or a group of households; seasonal or temporary migrants may reside in temporary quarters or possess land or a second home, making the transition to the category of semipermanent or permanent migrant quite easy; ongoing seasonal migration may involve predictable, uneven, or steadily increasing periods of stay in one of the residences; movement in search of wage labor occurs irregularly, but it may also be a prelude to a more permanent move; and even migration classified as permanent, where the migrant household has sold its home and land in the original locale, has not proved irreversible in the Thakali case. Most important, in Thakali movement there are factors that cushion the potential difficulties of migration, such as preexisting social relations with Thakali settlers already established in other areas and contacts established during travel for trade.

Though Thakali migration has been ongoing, it may help to consider these population movements during five distinct historical periods: (1) from the unification of Nepal in the eighteenth century to the initiation of the salt contract system in 1862; (2) during the salt contract system (1862–1928); (3) from the end of the salt contract system to the closing of the Tibetan border (1928–1960); (4) from 1960–1980; (5) from 1980 to the present.

The previous chapter discussed the first three periods. Before the salt contract, Thakali had already moved to the mining areas of what are now Myagdi and Baglung Districts and established themselves along the major trade routes running down to the Terai. During the salt contract period, additional families moved into these areas. Following the salt contract, Thakali began moving from Thaksatsae into the Terai and into the towns of Pokhara, Bhairawa, and Kathmandu. Around the same time, many Thakali

TABLE 4.1 Thakali Population Distribution by District in 1984

District	Number of households	Percentage of total	Estimated population	Percentage of total
Mustang	290	19.2	1421	17.0
Kaski	121	8.0	672	8.0
Kathmandu	119	7.9	660	7.9
Rupandehi	157	10.4	870	10.4
Palpa	21	1.4	121	1.4
Baglung	253	16.8	1521	18.2
Myagdi	280	18.5	1596	19.1
Gulmi	53	3.5	297	3.5
Parbat	55	3.6	308	3.7
Syangja	27	1.8	151	1.8
Chitwan	20	1.3	112	1.3
Nepalgunj	12	.8	67	.8
Gorkha	12	.8	67	.8
Far West	10	.7	56	.7
Other	80	5.3	448	5.4
Totals	1510	100	8367	100

households moved down from the mining areas into *bazārs* and agricultural villages along the valleys of the Myagdi and Baglung Districts. In the early 1950s and 1960s many of the families involved in the seasonal migration between Thak Khola and Myagdi purchased lands near the growing market town of Pokhara, located in a large valley in the low hills of central Nepal, and their previous holdings in Myagdi were purchased and permanently settled by new Thakali migrants from Thak Khola.

Before the formation of the national organization in 1983, ties with Thak Khola had become increasingly extenuated. Marriage exchanges that had begun to break down at mid-century were almost nonexistent by 1980, most families had sold the land they owned in Thak Khola, and fewer and fewer members of the families made the trip to Thak Khola for *jho khane* feasts or Lha Phewa or to deposit bone pieces in the *khimi*.

A primary destination of migration during in the 1950s was the market town of Pokhara in central Nepal.[5] The migration to Pokhara continued through the 1960s as Thakali emigration from Thak Khola stepped up after the closing of the northern border with Tibet. Manzardo notes that from 1951 to 1971 Thakalis were the fourth largest immigrant group in Pokhara, accounting for 8.6 percent of the immigrant households in a random sample taken by Shrestha (1979), a remarkable figure given the amount of immigration to Pokhara during this period and the relatively small size of the total Thakali population in Nepal. By 1974 there were eighty-three households.[6] But even then immigration to Pokhara and emigration from Pokhara had not yet abated. While Thakali continued to move on to Kathmandu and elsewhere from Pokhara, additional families moved to the area from Thak Khola and, in increasing numbers, from Khani Khuwa. In 1983 there were one hundred and ten Thakali households in the area. By 2000 there were more than 200.

The fourth period of migration (1960–1980), following the effective closing of the Tibet-Nepal border by the Chinese in 1960, had the most dramatic effect on Thaksatsae. During this period, the completion of roads from the Terai to Pokhara and from Kathmandu to Pokhara dramatically changed the flow of goods in the hills and altered the course of migration. Thakali began to migrate to more distant areas than they had previously. Most of the Thakali households that moved to the Terai town of Bhairawa, for example, did so between 1960 and 1963.

The constant but slow out-migration of Thakali families had had little effect on Thaksatsae from 1860 until the early 1960s. When scholars first reached Tukche, in the early 1950s, twenty-five years after the abolition of the salt contract system, the *bazār* was still an active, bustling entrepôt with over one hundred houses employing hundreds of servants.[7] Tucci ([1953] 1982) reported that in 1952 Tukche was still "controlled" by the descendants of Kalu Ram Thakali.[8] Yet by the 1950s the *subba* lineage was well established outside Tukche. Tucci observed that the family's "members or representatives travel from one end of Nepal to the other; they have agents at Baglung and Butwal and at Nautanwa, the terminal of the Indian railway on the southern frontier of Nepal" ([1953] 1982:49). Members of the family had regularly made trips to Kathmandu since 1862; one family was permanently stationed there after 1920, and in 1954 a home was purchased in the Thamel section of the city. By the 1950s their headquarters had already been moved to Kathmandu, and at that time members of the lineage earned much more from contracts that had nothing to do with the salt trade: in western Nepal they held a contract providing them a monopoly on the distribution of cigarettes and textiles; in Tukche and further north they still controlled and directed trade with Tibet, from which they imported wool, salt, horses, and turquoise and to which they sent rice, fabrics, cigarettes, and European manufactured goods.

Within a few years, events elsewhere had a dramatic effect on life in Thak Khola. In 1962, when Bista and Fürer-Haimendorf arrived to stay, trade with Tibet had been drastically reduced, but the town was still an active market. Fürer-Haimendorf estimated the population at 495 and found that 64 of 92, or almost 70 percent, of the remaining households were from one of the four Thakali clans of Thaksatsae (1981a:177; 1975:203). By the end of the 1960s, Tukche was virtually vacated by the Thakali trading families. Since then the percentage of the Tukche population that is Thakali has remained largely unchanged. During his 1976 visit Fürer-Haimendorf found that only 33 of a total population of 223 were "true Thakalis" (1981b:177).[9] In 1977 Manzardo found that 18.7 percent of the households were Thakali.[10]

The emigration of relatively large numbers of Thakali families from Thak Khola changed the character of the area. While it lived on in the memories of migrants as the economic center of a thriving trade and the political center of the surrounding region, Thaksatsae became a largely agricultural area, no more nor less significant or central than its surrounding environs. By 1984 much of the older part of the town of Tukche was in ruins, the two largest *subba* homes had crumbled, and the Rani Gompa (a Buddhist temple), once described as located in the center of the town, lay on the outskirts of the remaining houses. Still intact were the large stately homes built for the children of the last true *subbas* along the new road, many of them open as hotels for trekking tourists. The actual number of Thakali households own-ing fields, houses, or plots in Tukche was difficult to determine, but it was clear that most homes were occupied and most fields cultivated by non-Thakali families, many of them servants or employees of the migrant mer-chant families.

Migrants from Tukche reported that they had at first continued to culti-vate the land and that they had tried to have at least one member of the extended family living on and managing the property. Beginning in the early 1980s, an increasing number of families had begun to visit Tukche from time to time, and members of some of these households had expressed plans to return for future visits or to stay.

By 1993 there were signs of revival. While most of the profitable tourist trade was catered to by non-Thakali households, other ventures—including apple orchards and brandy distilling—were attracting some of the Thakali to return. During the 1993 performance of Lha Phewa, many migrant Thak-ali reported a longing to return permanently to Thak Khola, but most of those who expressed these sentiments were over sixty years old, members of the generation that had emigrated from Thak Khola thirty years or so previously. Their children were ambivalent about Thak Khola, and most made negative about the lack of urban amenities.

The predominance of *arānsi karānsi* and other non-Thakali families in Tukche aroused a Thakali zeal to reestablish boundaries, both geographic and social. Even individuals who lived quite harmoniously elsewhere in multiethnic communities and whose ancestors lived peaceably amid cultural difference in Thak Khola wanted to purify Thaksatsae to bring it into line with the homeland of their memory.

The emigration from other villages in Thaksatsae, which has been considerable, was never as dramatic as the exodus from Tukche. In the 1980s there was still regular movement back and forth between the village of Sassadhara in Myagdi District and the village of Khanti in Thak Khola, but this was more irregular than in the past, and the homes and lands in each locale were owned by different households rather than residences being held in both locations by one household as they had been previously. In the 1990s this movement continued to decline. The standard of living may have gone down throughout Thaksatsae after 1960, but Fürer-Haimendorf, who visited right after the end of the trading era and again in 1976, declared the decline in living standards almost imperceptible (1981a:16). In the past two decades, different interests have widened the gap between migrants from Tukche and agriculturalists remaining in Thaksatsae (see Manzardo 1978:42).

By 1984 only 18 percent of the Thakali population resided permanently in Thaksatsae. Larger percentages were found in Baglung and Myagdi Districts, each of which held close to 20 percent of the total Thakali population (see table 4.1). Other areas with significant Thakali populations were Kathmandu (with 8.3 percent of the total Thakali population), Pokhara (with 6.5 percent), the area around the Terai towns of Butwal and Bhairawa (with 11 percent), Gulmi District (3.5 percent), Parbat District (3.7 percent), Syangja District (1.8 percent), Palpa District (1.4 percent), Chitwan District (1.3 percent), Gorkha District (.8 percent), and Nepalgunj (.8 percent). Twenty-seven percent lived in cities with populations greater than 15 percent, and their population was distributed across Nepal, with approximately 20 percent in the highlands, 14 percent in the Terai, and 65.8 percent in the middle hills.

By 1997 this relative population distribution had changed slightly, with the largest gains coming in Kathmandu and Pokhara. There was also a remarkable growth in the number of Thakali residing temporarily overseas.

Samaj

Despite their wide separation through migration, Thakali communities
are integrated through a variety of mechanisms. The term *samaj* connotes
a circle of social intercourse, social identity, life in association with others,
or a body of individuals and is used by the Thakali to refer to three levels of
social interaction and integration: (1) the local village or *gāū* (N) *samaj*;
(2) the local or regional Thakali *samaj*; and (3) the Thakali *jāt* or *samaj* as
a whole.[11] In the Thaksatsae area of Thak Khola, where the villages are
populated almost exclusively by Thakali,[12] the first two categories noted
above are almost identical, but migrant Thakalis live in multiethnic societies
or communities in which they represent only a small portion of the local
population.

Tensions between individuals' integration into or identity with the multiethnic villages in which they live and their identity as Thakali are often
difficult to resolve. The differences between the integration of migrant Thakalis into local multiethnic communities and the degree to which the Thakali,
as a community and as individuals, maintain ties with Thakalis in other
locales are great, and understanding the influence of the differences is crucial for an analysis of Thakali ethnic identity, social change, and adaptability.

These different levels of community interrelationships present several
problems for analysis. Neither the village (*gāū*) nor the community (*samaj*)
is an isolate to be analyzed as a bounded whole: each must be considered
in relation to the state, as well as *samaj* and communities in relation to each
other, extending the analysis to factors external to the *samaj* that nevertheless
account for transformations that have taken place within it. Each of the three
levels of community exhibits considerable flexibility. The first level, the local
samaj, is bounded to some extent by the political and geographic divisions
of the local area, that is, by the village or valley within which it is found,
but Thakalis tend to be more mobile than members of many other groups,
and their economic, political, and social interrelationships extend far beyond
local villages. The local Thakali community, or the Thakali *samaj*, the second level of integration, is usually loosely organized in migrant areas and
often has an influence over households spread across a wider geographical
area than that covered by the local village *samaj*; that is, the local Thakali
samaj is not equivalent to the sum of Thakali households within a single
village or neighborhood.[13] Cross-cutting ties of economics and kinship

stretch the boundaries of both local and regional Thakali communities and on occasion temporarily incorporate Thakalis from far afield into the *samaj*. As for the role and influence of the third level of social integration, Thakali society as a whole, it is extremely complex, both as a concept and as a political and social reality. The interrelationships of the Thakali communities, at both the local and national levels, was significantly affected by the formation of the national Thakali social organization in April 1983.

Thakalis residing in multiethnic communities as immigrants vary in the degree of their adaptation to the local communities, their interactions with other *jāts* and ethnic groups, and their social, economic, and political pursuits in migrant areas. Thakali communities in Khani Khuwa, Bhairawa, Kathmandu, Pokhara, and elsewhere all interact with one another and yet differ from one another: the pattern of Thakali migration to and adaptation in these areas vary; the twentieth-century reforms that were introduced in

FIGURE 4.1 Thakali family bidding farewell to family members departing from Darbang for Burtibang

FIGURE 4.2 Author in conversation with Thakalis in the hillside town of Lamela in Khani Khuwa

Thak Khola influenced the Thakali in each area differently from the way they affected the Thakalis who remained there; and the remoteness of some regions makes them respond differently to forces of modernization and urbanization.

Two tensions—the opposition of inter-*jāt* ties and interactions to ethnic or intra-*jāt* solidarity and the opposition of competition and cooperation among the Thakali—recur throughout the encounters among Thakali communities. These themes weave through fields of interactions conventionally characterized as economic, political, and religious.

The first tension—between integration within a multiethnic community and ethnic solidarity—underscores the conflicting pressures on individual Thakali simultaneously to adapt to specific multiethnic social environments and to adhere to a resurging and more visible Thakali identity. When, why, and to what extent the Thakali adopt local customs varies, as do the ways in which individual Thakali help maintain or create a shared Thakali identity.

Integration and Solidarity/Competition and Cooperation

An examination of these two recurrent tensions—competition versus co-operation and integration versus solidarity—must balance romantic portrayals of the Thakali that overemphasize cooperation and cohesion with a realistic view of the competition, dissension, and diversity within the group. As noted earlier, the Thakali from Thaksatsae have been repeatedly described as cohesive, homogeneous, and cooperative.[14] Not only is the claim for Thakali homogeneity a remarkable one to make about a group marked by divisions of ritual purity, residence, descent, class, and ethnic identity, but it is especially surprising given the heterogeneous conclusions about these factors arrived at by the various scholars of the Thakali. Cooperation among individual Thakali is tempered and countered by patterns of both intra- and intergroup competition, as Thakalis compete among themselves for political and economic influence within local, regional, and national contexts. Manzardo's argument (1978) that Thakali economic "success" is best attributed to their cooperation "as a group" ignores the political and economic competition that occurs among Thakalis within many areas of Nepal. Cooperation, though a significant feature of Thakali society, has been stressed to the exclusion of competition and discord, which have been neither acknowledged nor examined thoroughly.

Economic Strategies

It is appropriate to begin a discussion of Thakali cooperation and competition with a discussion of economic strategies because it is these that brought them fame and notoriety. Opportunities provided by copper mining and salt trading were the activities that first brought the Thakalis to local prominence, but, true to their reputation, the Thakali usually have their hands in every profit-making activity in the area. These include agriculture, shopkeeping, moneylending, trade, mills, carpentry factories, slate quarries, and contracting, and they bring the Thakalis, as individuals, into webs of interaction with other groups throughout Nepal. The Thakalis have a reputation among the Nepalese and among scholars as traders, shopkeepers, and hoteliers, and in these roles they are perhaps most visible.[15]

While this image of the Thakali as traders and hoteliers is not unwarranted, what often goes unnoted is the extent of their identification with and reliance on agriculture. Thakalis are relatively more involved with commerce than are many other groups. Nevertheless, more than 50 percent of the adult males responded to a survey conducted by the national *samaj* that their primary occupation was farming.[16] Since many who list agriculture as their occupation also have a second occupation, this is somewhat misleading. Because of the diversification of Thakali economic investments and activity, it is difficult to ascertain the extent of the investment involved in each of their various economic activities. Thakalis residing in Burtibang *bazār*, for instance, listed shopkeeping and trade as their principal occupations, but they also have considerable land holdings both around the *bazār* and in the villages where they resided before coming to Burtibang. On the other hand, the majority of those Thakalis who list farming as their primary employment are also involved in other economic activities. Frequently the economic occupation with which an individual Thakali identifies him- or herself is not the activity that occupies the majority of his or her time, nor is it necessarily the occupation that provides the largest profit. For example, in Darbang *bazār*, almost all the Thakalis indicated in response to the survey that their primary occupation was farming, but ten of them owned shops where they spent most of their daytime hours, while one individual was employed in full-time government service.

While farming does not provide large cash returns, it is important to understand that agriculture is the economic base for most Thakali families. This is as true in Thak Khola as it is in Myagdi and Baglung Districts. Though farming neither occupies most of the productive time of the Thakalis nor provides the largest percentage of their earned cash, it does provide Thakali families with an assured means of living, and many families use a large portion of their earned income—including money earned through moneylending, government service, or the British army, for example—to purchase additional fields. Wealth is most often held in the form of land, and it is only after a household possesses an adequate landholding that it invests substantial amounts of cash in other forms of wealth.

The strategies pursued by Thakali outside of Thak Khola, in particular, make them prominent as individuals and provide opportunities for extensive interactions with other *jāts* in the area. One strategy in particular, the operation of inns for travelers throughout central Nepal, provides a way for individual Thakali to come into frequent contact with travelers and the information they bring from other areas.

As men of wealth and influence in the villages of Khani Khuwa, many Thakalis have served as the principal source of loans. Traditionally, when a debtor could not repay a loan, he appealed to the *sau* who had loaned him the money, and all his possessions were priced. The lenders or lender then claimed what would serve in lieu of repayment; when lenders disagreed, they would draw lots. Perhaps not surprisingly, when the law was changed in 1962, many outstanding loans owed to Thakali moneylenders were defaulted. In recent years, moneylending has come under increasing regulation, and its importance has declined. The maximum interest rate is currently fixed by law at 10 percent (previously the rate was much higher: Molnar cites rates of 30 percent, half of which was paid at the time of the transaction), although some current modifications of the way interest is paid make the effective rate higher than the percentage allowed by law.[17] Members of other *jāts* often cite moneylending as the means that allowed Thakalis to come into possession of desirable lands.

In the past decade Thakalis have provided the funding for loans for individuals making trips overseas to engage in wage labor. This has been true both for individual Thakali who have made trips to Japan, Korea, and the United States as well as for individuals from lower castes making trips to the Middle East.

Overseas wage labor, including service in the British army, has also become a highly coveted path to economic stability and social status. This strategy would seem to be out of character with the image others have of the Thakali as independent entrepreneurs, but its financial attractiveness easily explains its current popularity. Salaries earned overseas exceed what can be earned by all but a very few through agriculture and business.

Thakali sons who went into the British army did not generally leave their natal households but contributed their earnings toward the household fund. The remaining family members pursued other economic activities, usually both commercial and agricultural, while the mercenary son(s) provided cash that permitted the purchase of additional lands, the building of new homes, the stocking of stores, and the bidding for construction contracts. One son in the British army provided a household financial security; two or more sons in the army could transform a struggling household into a well-off middle-class one.[18] Aside from its monetary benefits, service in the British army, when it continues until one has become an officer, also results in considerable social prestige that can be transformed into political currency within the community.[19] While most common in the Myagdi area, military service in the British army is also pursued by Thakalis in other communities (such as Thak Khola and Burtibang), although in those areas there is less prestige attached to this strategy and its pursuit is consequently less readily acknowledged. Other wage labor overseas is now actively pursued by both men and women alike, sometimes husbands and wives together and sometimes single men and women. These earnings are not usually pooled with households remaining behind in Nepal.

Dhikur: Rotating Credit

An important means of economic cooperation in these communities is a form of rotating credit association known throughout central Nepal as *dhikur* or *dhikuri*.[20] *Dhikur* is a salient example of the interplay of the themes of both cooperation/competition and ethnic interaction/solidarity.[21] Simply stated, a rotating credit association consists of a limited set of voluntary participants who make regular contributions to a fund that is given, in whole or in part, to each contributor in rotation.[22] They are distinguished from other mutual-help systems by the criteria of regular rotation and payment.

The complex networks of rotating credit associations, on the one hand, reinforce ties of solidarity and dependency, serve as a means to help less fortunate members of the *samaj*, and emphasize the value of cooperation over time and, on the other hand, provide a means by which Thakali factions compete against each other for influence within both the local multiethnic neighborhoods and the local Thakali *samajs* and a forum for keen economic competition among members to gain access to capital at opportune times. More than any other institution, *dhikur* may best exemplify the tension between cooperation and competition that characterizes Thakali society.

Several important functions of rotating credit associations are relevant to understanding migrant Thakali communities and *jāt* identity. As a financial institution, *dhikurs* encourage the formation and investment of capital. Rotating credit associations have social as well as financial functions and are a form of social welfare (see, for example, Manzardo 1978; Vinding 1984). Geertz has noted that the primary attraction of rotating credit associations in Indonesia was communal harmony and mutual assistance rather than financial benefit.[23] Social welfare is the aspect of *dhikurs* most frequently cited by Thakali: informants often described *dhikur* as a way of helping needy members of the community, and the contracts drawn up for each rotating credit association usually mention this as the credit associations raison d'être.[24]

HOW A DHIKUR WORKS

Briefly, a *dhikur* functions as follows: an individual or individuals in need of capital takes on the role of organizer or founder of the *dhikur* and invites relatives, friends, and acquaintances to join.[1] The organizer(s) generally take the first turn(s) with the *dhikur* fund.

The number of participants varies considerably.[2] Among Thakali traders and businessmen, *dhikurs* involve considerably more members than has been reported among other groups.[3] *Dhikurs* of more than thirty members are not at all unusual.[4] In describing participation in a *dhikur* I follow Messerschmidt and distinguish between members and shares. A share obliges its holder to contribute a predetermined amount to the fund in each rotation and entitles the holder to take the fund on one rotation. *Dhikurs* are divided into a fixed number of shares. Partnership in a share is permitted: shares are shared by as many as six members.[5]

Every *dhikur* has a manager, whose responsibilities include record keeping, calling and overseeing meetings, settling disputes that may arise, collecting the funds and distributing them to the proper people on time, and collecting fines from those who pay late.[6] Most *dhikurs* now require a guarantor for each share, who is financially liable in case his client defaults.[7]

---

1. In almost all reported cases, rotating credit associations are organized by the individual or individuals in need of cash.
2. Messerschmidt observed *dhikurs* composed of between ten and thirty members, noting that among the Gurung and other rural agricultural communities *dhikur* are generally small, with between ten and fifteen members (1978:144). Grain *dhikurs* (which are discussed in text note 25) are also small. Women's and children's *dhikurs* are the smallest. Gurung *dhikurs* also have only occasional partnerships.
3. Messerschmidt also noted that "contemporary Thakali monetary dhikurs are consistently the largest in terms of membership, number of shares, and size of funds" (1978:144). Vinding observed that in Thak Khola, a *dhikur* usually consists of no less than twenty-one people (1984:37). This is consistent with the information I collected elsewhere in Nepal.
4. Messerschmidt (1978) has also documented larger *dhikurs*, including one with 63 members (twenty-one shares, each divided again among three people) and another with 105 members (twenty-five shares, each divided among five people).
5. In *dhikurs* I observed, most shares were held by single individuals, and only a few were held by partnerships. These partnerships were not always equal. In addition, a member in a dhikur will occasionally hold more than one share, which he or she will exercise in the same way as if the shares were held by two separate members. Many Thakali *dhikurs* have more than twenty-five shares but few exceed 105 members.
6. In urban areas, the manager has been replaced by a chairman and a secretary-treasurer (Messerschmidt 1978:145).
7. Both parties, the member and the guarantor, sign a written contract to that effect. The guarantor may or may not be a member of the *dhikur*. He must be recognized by the manager as a man of means and responsibility. In some *dhikurs*, a man may be guarantor for only one shareholder at a time. In others, an individual may stand as guarantor for any number of shareholders. It is not uncommon for the guarantor to charge the shareholder a fee for this guarantee.

HOW A DHIKUR WORKS (*continued*)

The order of rotation in a *dhikur* is determined in any of a number of ways. The first turn(s) goes to the organizer(s) or someone designated by the organizer. After that, the order is determined in one of four ways: by the relative need of the shareholders, by lot, by an open bidding system, or by a closed bidding system.[8] Either open or closed bidding is the preferred method to determine the rotation for Thakali *dhikurs*.[9]

Dhikur payments are made in installments of a fixed amount paid at a predetermined frequency.[10] Interest is added by increments of a predetermined amount per one hundred rupees per year and added proportionally per rotation. *Dhikur* documents generally list the interest rate and include a chart indicating the amount to be paid in each rotation (see table 4.3 for an example of an interest payment chart). In older *dhikurs* ten rupees' interest per one hundred rupees installments per year was common.[11] Interest rates for newer *dhikurs* range from 10 percent to 15 percent. An interest rate of 12 percent for a *dhikur* that rotates every two months and requires payments of one thousand rupees per rotation will require six twenty-rupee increases of the interest payment per year.

---

8. Messerschmidt also mentions a method of casting dice to determine the order of rotation, but this system is not used in Baglung and Myagdi Districts. In fact, it is apparently never used by Thakalis.

9. In some areas, open bidding is consider the fairest and most equitable means of distributing the fund. Many participants asserted that the lottery system is unfair because one has no control over it and may not get the fund when one wants or needs it most, while under the closed bidding system the winning bid may be much higher than is needed to be to win. Evidence collected in communities where closed bids are common belies the fear that bidders may have to pay more than necessary to gain the turn. In *dhikurs* I have documented that used the closed bidding system, the winning bid was usually no more than a few percentage points higher than the next three or four bids.

10. In Myagdi and Baglung Districts, installments as high as one thousand rupees, payable every two months, are not uncommon. More usual are installments ranging from two hundred fifty to one thousand rupees. They can, of course, be of much smaller sums. The largest *dhikur* in Thak Khola cited by Vinding has installments of two thousand rupees payable two times a year (1984). In Myagdi and Baglung, installments are rarely that large, but faster rotations result in payments of up to six thousand rupess per year. Most recently formed *dhikurs* require installments of at least five hundred rupees.

11. Vinding (1984) says 10 percent interest is most common. Messerschmidt (1978) says that everywhere but in Tingaun interest was ten rupees per hundred per year.

The Thakali claim that *dhikurs* are a Thakali innovation, but the evidence for their origin is inconclusive.[25] Today *dhikurs* are formed throughout central Nepal and are participated in by members of many different *jāts*.[26] *Dhikurs* in Myagdi and Baglung function basically as Messerschmidt has described them, though the precise form of *dhikurs* varies from locale to locale and according to local economic conditions. *Dhikurs* among migrant Thakali communities provide all the benefits generally attributed to rotating credit associations: they are significant financial institutions, they strengthen communal ties, and they aid individuals in financial need. Depending on the circumstances, *dhikurs* can contribute both to groupwide cooperation among the Thakali and to the integration of the Thakali within the local community.[27]

The criteria qualifying an individual for membership, for example, are roughly the same for all *dhikurs* and in all locales. Membership is usually confined to men (and some women) who know each other well and are considered mutually trustworthy. There are no explicit bars related to age, sex, ethnic affiliation or caste, occupation, residence, status, education, and so on. In practice, participation in particular *dhikurs* is usually determined by economic class, though poorer or less-known individuals will be considered for membership if someone who is locally trusted vouches for them. In most areas of Khani Khuwa, for example, permanent local residence is not a requirement for participation in *dhikurs*.[28] This is not surprising in an area where many Thakali appear to be in the process of shifting permanent residence from one locale to another. Thakalis are often simultaneously involved in *dhikurs* in more than one locale, including their last place of residence and their new one.

Dhikurs in Khani Khuwa vary in some interesting ways from the reported patterns. Messerschmidt has asserted that membership in a *dhikur* is confined to the "dominant" ethnic group in a locality (1978:144). He cited *dhikurs* as an example of Thakali group cooperation, claiming that, with few exceptions, membership organized by Thakalis is limited to Thakalis (1978:ix). If true, this feature would have significant implications for the argument that Thakali economic success is built on intragroup cooperation,[29] but my data indicate that, at least in Myagdi and Baglung districts, these claims are not correct: membership there has not been limited to the "dominant" ethnic group, nor is the membership of *dhikurs* organized by Thakalis limited to Thakalis.[30] It appears that historically, as Thakali have competed among themselves, they have reached out to seek other *dhikur* players.[31]

While there are no longer ethnically exclusive *dhikurs* in Khani Khuwa, patterns suggest class distinctions. Poor, non-Thakali individuals generally form *dhikurs* among themselves with appropriately sized payments and rotation frequency. In the Khani Khuwa area it is common for prominent

Thakalis to be asked to join as shareholders: the manager of the *dhikur* is chosen from among these participants, and the *dhikur* then meets at the manager's house. An exception is that relatively poor Thakalis, if they need or desire to join a *dhikur*, join predominately Thakali *dhikurs* even when the other participants are of a substantially higher economic status. One might question whether this practice stems from status consciousness or personal ties. *Dhikurs* in Khani Khuwa are often dominated by a Thakali plurality or majority, but they characteristically include as members Chantels, Magars, Brahmans, Chetris, and Gurungs.

Dhikurs are always organized by the borrower, never by the lenders. They are structured so that those who urgently require the money effectively pay a high rate of interest, while the largest benefits accrue to those who can afford to wait until one of the last rotations for their turn. But this does not indicate that *dhikurs* are not beneficial to those who take earlier turns. Consequently, the terms of the *dhikur* must be sufficiently seductive to attract enough participants.

There have been few defaults in Thakali *dhikurs*.[32] If the terms are too strict for those who take the early turns and they are forced to default, there would be no profit for the investors. *Dhikur* provides a means for the wealthier members of a community to act as bankers to the more needy members, though this is not always how *dhikurs* work out. In many instances, wealthy members of the community take an early rotation because they need ready cash. In rural areas, a man's wealth may be tied up in land, loans, and other investments, and in this context a *dhikur* often proves to be the best way to gain cash to take advantage of immediate investment opportunities.

While defaults are rare, they do occur. As might be expected, they are more common in urban settings, where communities are more loosely bound than in the villages. In 1984 Thakalis in Kasauli cited several *dhikurs* that had recently failed because of defaults. As *dhikurs* increase in both the number of members and the price of a single share, as individuals are drawn into more and more *dhikurs* simultaneously in a number of geographic locales, and as *dhikurs* come to include individuals who are not subject to the social pressures of a local community, the sanctions for default have become more formalized and are one of the issues regularly taken up by the local *samaj* associations.

Even in areas of Nepal where banks have established a community role, *dhikurs* offer distinct advantages: they are less impersonal, money can be borrowed without collateral, and there is no need to explain one's intended

use of the fund. In Myagdi and Baglung, *dhikur*s are employed simultaneously with banking services and moneylenders.

Dhikur is an institution that supports cooperation as well as encouraging
competition among its members. On one hand, it is in each *dhikur* member's interest that the other members succeed with the investments that they
take from the *dhikur* fund and that this success not occur at the expense of
the other players. On the other, the very process of bidding for the fund
rotation ensures intense competition, and the success of some of the investors in a *dhikur* necessarily comes at the expense of the other players. But it
is a success that can only come if the *dhikur* is maintained and each player
remains able and willing to continue to make his or her contribution to the
fund through to the last rotation. The tension between competition and
cooperation in the institution of *dhikur* is thus well balanced. Relationships
among some players may be characterized by dislike, anger, or revenge, but
when these tensions reach the point of disrupting the cooperation necessary
for the operation of the *dhikur*, individuals at odds with one another cease
to participate in the same *dhikur*s and instead compete for influence within
the community through different sets of *dhikur*s.

*Dhikur*s certainly promote cooperation, but this is not an adaptive advantage exclusive to the Thakali. In Khani Khuwa, *dhikur* membership is not
jāt-exclusive; *dhikur*s also promote cooperation among members of the same
economic class and among members of local communities. The question is
whether *dhikur*s in Khani Khuwa promote cooperation among Thakalis exclusively or whether they also encourage cooperation between Thakalis and
non-Thakalis. In effect, the monetary demands of *dhikur* restrict its mem-
berships to those within a certain economic class. In Darbang *bazār*, for
instance, individuals with cash to invest are almost all Thakali, and *dhikur*s
requiring a payment above a certain monetary level thus effectively exclude
most non-Thakalis. In this area, *dhikur* funds are usually employed for conservative purposes: they provide cash for construction and marriages, for
example, and not venture capital. In the Burtibang area, on the other hand,
*dhikur*s provide venture capital, and as a consequence of the competitive
climate the cost of money is much higher in Burtibang than in other regions
where *dhikur*s are common.

It is noteworthy that *dhikur*s entail not just short-term but continuing
cooperation. The practice of playing more than one *dhikur* simultaneously
ensures that most individuals are always engaged in ongoing networks of
exchanges. In this way *dhikur*s help to maintain ties even among individuals

DHIKUR INNOVATIONS

Innovations in the way in which interest payments are calculated in *dhikur*s have been cited as evidence of a change in emphasis from concerns of social assistance to those of finance. Many informants claim that traditionally every shareholder paid equal installments with interest added at each rotation both before and after his or her turn with the fund. Now it is much more common to add interest only after a participant has taken a turn with the fund. The significance of this change is a matter of contention. Messerschmidt (1978) and Vinding (1984) have asserted that this change means that the shareholders who wait until the last few turns to claim the fund gain considerably more profit than they did under the previous system.[1] This contention is incorrect: in absolute terms, the profit does not increase in the revised system. In fact, the net profit gained by the member who takes the last rotation is exactly the same under the new system as the old. What does change is the amount that members are required to invest in the fund: because interest is not paid until after a rotation has been taken, the member who waits until the last turn in a new-style *dhikur* will make the same profit he would have made under the old system but will have made that profit on a smaller investment, giving him a relatively higher rate of return on his money.

This is the significance of the new system: that the same gain can be made with a smaller investment than before. But this reduction in the investment required is marginal. Under neither system is the full investment contributed at one time; instead, it is contributed incrementally over a set period of time, and, under the original system, the largest contributions—those including large interest payments— come toward the end of the investment period.

Real interest rates go up in the new system, but this increase is in line with contemporary calculations of the present value of future income in central Nepal. The actual rate of interest varies depending on the precise amount charged per rotation, so the frequency of the rotation period must be taken into consideration. This accounting does not include any calculation for inflation, which is extremely high in rural Nepal. The new system increases the percentage of actual interest paid by the middle bidders but not above the interest rate paid by the founders.

Evidence collected in Myagdi and Baglung Districts further indicates that criticism of this reform is premature and ignores the economic realities of contemporary Nepal. Actual *dhikur*s are more complex than the models used to project profits. For example, a *dhikur* in Burtibang in 1984 that recently finished its last rotation had thirty-nine equal shares of one thousand rupees held by fifty-seven members. Members included thirty Thakalis, twenty Magars, two Chantels, one Brahmans, three Chetri, and one Gurung. The interest due increased by increments of twenty rupees on every rotation and was paid only by members who had already had a turn with the fund. The fund rotated every two months for a total of six rotations per year, and it took six and a half years from start to finish. After the first two rounds, rotations were determined by closed bidding. Instead of an actual auxiliary fund, the winning bid was subtracted from the total fund, and each member's share was reduced proportionately (except for the organizers who continued to pay full shares for thirty-eight rotations). Table 4.2 shows the value of a share in each rotation, the amount of the winning bid, the total amount available before the bid, and the amount taken by the fund taker in that round.

The intense bidding for early rounds in the Burtibang area often resulted in extremely high effective rates of interest. Table 4.3 shows the net take for the fund taker in each round of this *dhikur*, the total amount paid over six and a half years by each fund taker, and each one's net profit or loss. The amount paid includes the sum of the thirty-eight shares paid plus interest due. This example is typical of the *dhikurs* recorded in the Burtibang area. Bids in this area were much higher than those recorded in *dhikurs* elsewhere. The effect of the bidding is to increase the cost of money to those in the early rounds and greatly increase the profit of those who wait until the latter rounds. This is consistent with what Messerschmidt and Vinding have observed, but it is important to note that the increased cost is due not to the innovation but to the intensity of the bidding in Burtibang: bids this high are not common to *dhikurs* in all areas.

It has been suggested by some scholars that wealthy Thakalis wait until the later rounds, and the needy are forced to take the early rounds. The pattern can not be described so simply where one common characteristic of membership for *dhikurs* is rough parity of economic status: those individuals who have relatively few resources would only play *dhikurs* as organizers, and the interest charged them under the new style is no higher than in the old. An examination of the bidding pattern for numerous *dhikurs* in Burtibang revealed that relatively well off individuals bid for and took early rounds of *dhikurs* as frequently as they waited for the last.[2]

What, then, is the explanation for such high bids? In the Burtibang area, few individuals had access to ready cash. The Thakali, many of them well off, hold wealth in terms of land, stock, debts owed to them, bank accounts with restricted access, and *dhikurs*. At the same time, the periodic need for large amounts of cash to take advantage of business opportunities is strong. *Dhikurs* in this area function as a means of providing venture capital for business opportunities that have a potentially high rate of return and a strong possibility of success. Interviews with individuals who took early rounds in the *dhikur* examples cited above indicate that they were able to invest the *dhikur* funds in ventures that provided enough return to pay the ensuing amounts due and still make a net profit.

Some *dhikur* systems include an auxiliary fund that accumulates from the amounts bid for the rotations. The amount of the winning bid is subtracted from the *dhikur* fund available in that round and is placed in the auxiliary fund. In Khani Khuwa, the organizers of the *dhikur* are often required to leave a fixed percentage of their rotations in the auxiliary fund. In one example, in which the organizers took the first four rounds, the amounts left in the auxiliary fund were 7.2 percent, 10

***DHIKUR* INNOVATIONS** (*continued*)

percent, 12.2 percent, and 15 percent of the total available, for the first through fourth rounds, respectively. In some cases where rotation is determined by bidding,the last two members who take the *dhikur* fund are obliged to leave a specified amount in the fund. This amount may range from 5 to 7 percent of the total capital. This same amount is occasionally specified for any round in which no one bids for the fund. The rotation for that round is then determined by lottery among the members who have not yet taken the fund. In some systems, the individual making the highest bid takes the auxiliary fund at that time and receives the *dhikur* fund in the following round. When he receives the main *dhikur* fund, he deducts from it the amount of the auxiliary he previously received, the interest on the auxiliary, and the amount of his or her bid. The deducted amount is then placed in the auxiliary fund. When the auxiliary is about to equal the *dhikur*, it is passed on to the second highest bidder as if it were the main *dhikur* fund. That participant's turn is then finished. In the final rotation, the auxiliary fund is divided equally among the shareholders.

My data indicate that the interest rates of *dhikurs* are not high enough to encourage most members to wait until the final round to take their profit. In socioeconomic contexts where there are few ways to invest cash, *dhikurs* are a creative and valuable way to keep money busy. Even with the increase in banking facilities in the hills, *dhikurs* remain an important source of capital and have a lower rate of default than moneylending. These benefits counter the fact that the rate of return is slightly lower.

---

1. Messerschmidt (1978:148–49) claims that the last fund taker receives, in absolute terms, a larger profit. This is not correct.
2. A close study of bidding patterns also indicates that Manzardo (1978) is mistaken in his contention that the Thakali members of *dhikurs* take advantage of non-Thakali members. The percentage of Thakali shareholders who took early rounds in the *dhikurs* I examined was no lower than those who took later ones.

who have migrated from a community. Intriguingly, *dhikurs* also encourage ties that cut across community, class, and caste ties: for instance, a *dhikur* with relatively smaller installments organized among the poorer households in an area strengthens ties between these poorer households and the Thakali men of influence who are usually approached to serve as managers for these *dhikurs*.

Dhikurs are but one example of the complex, ongoing social relations maintained by Thakali businessmen. Cooperation among businessmen in

TABLE 4.2 *Dhikur* with Competitive Bids*

Round	Share value of each round	Winning bid in rupees	Net amount taken	Gross available before bid is subtracted
1.	1,000	—	38,000	38,000
2.	1,000	—	38,020	38,020
3.	317.68	24,500	13,560	38,060
4.	247.50	26,730	10,950	38,120
5.	268.06	26,350	11,850	38,200
6.	261.81	26,575	11,825	38,300
7.	291.70	25,500	12,920	38,420
8.	302.80	25,100	13,460	38,560
9.	318.06	24,550	14,170	38,720
10.	416.70	21,000	17,900	38,900
11.	415.31	21,050	18,050	39,100
12.	408.34	21,300	18,020	39,320
13.	402.75	21,001	18,059	39,560
14.	444.39	20,005	19,815	39,820
15.	452.75	19,700	20,399	40,100
16.	451.36	19,751	20,649	40,400
17.	430.42	20,505	20,215	40,720
18.	428.48	20,575	20,485	41,060
19.	469.42	19,001	22,319	41,420
20.	499.86	18,005	23,795	41,800
21.	513.18	17,526.50	24,674.50	42,200
22.	486.10	18,501	24,119	42,620
23.	512.50	17,550	25,510	43,060
24.	540.20	16,553	26,967	43,520
25.	537.48	16,651	27,349	44,000
26.	652.78	12,500	32,000	44,500
27.	722.20	10,000	35,000	45,000
28.	734.02	9,575	35,965	45,540

TABLE 4.2 *(continued)*

29.	747.90	9,076	37,005	46,080
30.	745.07	9,177.50	37,522.50	46,700
31.	755.42	8,805	38,495	47,300
32.	802.64	7,105	40,815	47,920
33.	813.86	6,701	41,859	48,560
34.	861.08	5,001	44,219	49,220
35.	883.33	4,200	45,700	49,900
36.	888.86	4,001	46,599	50,600
37.	944.42	2,001	49,319	51,320
38.	944.44	2,000	50,060	52,060
39.	944.44	2,000	50,820	52,820

This table compares the amount taken in each round.

TABLE 4.3 *Dhikur* with Competitive Bids

	Amount available to player in each round	Total amount paid over 39 rounds	Percentage "interest" paid or earned	Rupees earned or lost
1.	38,000	52,820	39.0	(14,820)
2.	38,020	52,060	36.9	(14,040)
3.	13,560	35,859.63	164.5	(22,299.63)
4.	10,950	35,209.81	221.6	(24,259.81)
5.	11,410	34,489.25	202.3	(23,079.25)
6.	11,725	33,815.50	188.4	(22,090.50)
7.	12,920	33,125.61	156.4	(20,205.61)
8.	13,460	32,474.51	141.3	(19,014.51)
9.	14,170	31,839.25	124.7	(17,669.25)
10.	17,900	31,140.61	74	(13,240.61)

TABLE 4.3 *(continued)*

11.	18,050	30,562	69.3	(12,512)
12.	18,020	30,008.97	66.5	(11,988.97)
13.	18,059	29,474.56	63.2	(11,415.56)
14.	19,815	28,912.92	45.9	(9,097.92)
15.	20,399	28,404.56	39.2	(8,005.56)
16.	20,649	27,925.95	35.2	(7,276.95)
17.	20,215	27,486.89	36.0	(7,271.89)
18.	20,485	27,048.83	32.0	(6,563.83)
19.	22,319	26,587.89	19.1	(4,268.89)
20.	23,795	26,157.459	9.	(2,362.45)
21.	24,674.50	25,764.13	4.4	(1,089.63)
22.	24,119	25,431.21	5.4	(1,312.22)
23.	25,510	25,064.81	1.8	445.19
24.	26,967	24,717.11	9.1	2,249.89
25.	27,349	24,419.83	12.0	2,929.17
26.	32,000	24,024.53	33.2	7,975.47
27.	35,000	23,695.11	47.7	11,304.89
28.	35,965	23,443.29	53.4	12,521.71
29.	37,005	23,209.41	59.4	13,795.59
30.	37,522.50	23,012.24	63.1	14,510.26
31.	38,495	22,821.89	68.7	15,673.11
32.	40,815	22,614.67	80.5	18,200.33
33.	41,859	22,463.45	86.3	19,395.55
34.	44,219	22,296.23	98.3	21,922.77
35.	45,700	22,173.98	106.1	23,526.02
36.	46,599	22,088.45	111.0	24,510.55
37.	49,319	21,972.89	124.6	27,346.11
38.	50,060	21,932.87	128.2	28,127.13
39.	50,820	21,912.87	131.9	28,907.13

This table compares the amount taken in each round to the total amount paid by each shareholder over 39 rounds.

OLD-STYLE AND NEW-STYLE *DHIKUR*S COMPARED

An example will make the implications of the reform in the *dhikur* system clearer. An old-style dhikur of eleven shares that rotates once a year with payments of 1000 rupees and interest of 10 percent per annum paid by each member whether or not he or she has taken the fund would evolve as follows: in the first year, each member except the member whose turn it was to take the fund would pay 1,000 rupees, resulting in a fund of 10,000 rupees. The following year, each member would pay 1,000 rupees and an additional 100 rupees interest, resulting in a fund of 11,000 rupees. The following year each member would pay the 1,000-rupee installment plus 200 rupees in interest, resulting in a fund of 12,000 rupees. In the final round, each member will pay a total of 2,000 rupees each, for a fund totaling 20,000 rupees.

Table 4.4 indicates the net gain or cost to each member of the *dhikur* based on their order in the rotation. Over the ten-year period of the *dhikur*, the organizer (taking the first turn) pays 55 percent more in payments (total payments of 15,500 rupees) than he received in the initial fund (10,000 rupees). This payment of 55 percent interest over ten years represents a per annum rate of 7.6 percent, a relatively low rate of interest. With a final fund of 20,000 rupees, the last fund taker earns a 5,500-rupee profit on his investment of 14,500 rupes. This appears to be a profit of 37.9 percent, but again one must remember that the investment has been made in incrementally increasing installments over ten years. The real rate of return for the last fund taker is 5.8 percent.

Under the new system, the payments and the size of the fund would remain the same for the first fund taker but would be reduced for each following round (see table 4.5). In the second round, each member would pay a 1,000-rupee installment, but only the one previous fund taker would pay interest. The total fund would be 10,100 rupees. In the third round, the two previous fund takers would pay interest: the first fund taker would pay 200 rupees, and the second 100 rupees. The total fund would be 10,300 rupees. In the last round, the fund would reach a total of only 15,500 rupees. In this dhikur, the total paid by the organizer would amount to 15,500 rupees, 55 percent more than the original fund. There is, however, an increase in the return to the last fund taker. In this example, the last fund taker would receive a fund worth 15,500 rupees, 4,500 less than in the previous example. But this is earned on investments totaling only 10,000 rupees, or 5,500 less than in the previous example. The net profit is 55 percent, which represents a real rate of return of 7.6 percent. Contrary to the claims of other scholars, then, the last fund taker does not gain an absolute increase in profit.[1]

---

1. Messerschmidt assumed that the amount available to the final investor would be the same in the revised system as in the original, but this is not so. Because no one begins to pay interest until after he or she has taken the fund, the fund does not increase as rapidly as before.

TABLE 4.4 Old-Style *Dhikur*

	Take	Pay	Percentage of Interest	in Rupees
1.	10,000	15,500	-55.0	-5,500
2.	11,000	15,400	-40.0	-4,400
3.	12,000	15,300	-27.5	-3,300
4.	13,000	15,200	-16.9	-2,200
5.	14,000	15,100	-7.9	-1,100
6.	15,000	15,000	0	0
7.	16,000	14,900	7.4	1,100
8.	17,000	14,800	14.9	2,200
9.	18,000	14,700	22.4	3,300
10.	19,000	14,600	30.1	4,400
11.	20,000	14,500	37.9	5,500

TABLE 4.5 New-Style *Dhikur*

	Take	Pay	Interest (%)	Rupees
1.	10,000	15,500	-55.0	5,500
2.	10,100	14,500	-43.6	4,400
3.	10,300	13,600	-32.0	3,300
4.	10,600	12,800	-20.8	2,200
5.	11,000	12,100	-10.0	1,100
6.	11,500	11,500	0	0
7.	12,100	11,000	10.0	1,100
8.	12,800	10,600	20.8	2,200
9.	13,600	10,300	32.0	3,300
10.	14,500	10,100	43.5	4,400
11.	15,500	10,000	55	5,500

Myagdi and Baglung, some of whom belong to as many as ten or twelve *dhikurs* at once, involves cooperation with other businessmen regardless of *jāt*. For example, in Burtibang, merchants meet regularly to set prices and discuss problems of trade in the area. This cooperation includes *dhikurs*, price fixing, and cooperation in political campaigns; it frequently extends to social exchanges as well.

Politics

Perhaps even more significant than their interactions as economic middlemen has been the role played by many Thakalis as political mediators between local communities and the national government. Throughout the years of the *panchayat* system and continuing since the institution of a democratic party system in 1990, Thakalis have been very successful in attracting support and obtaining public office in the area. Paradoxically, Thakalis have been more successful in gaining political office in *panchayats* where their population is scattered among a large number of villages than they are in *panchayats* where they are prominent in the *bazārs*.

In the political arena, competition among and between Thakali candidates is common. Public competition in Khani Khuwa contrasts with the public cooperation common in Thak Khola. Manzardo, for example, describes an election for the Rastra *panchayat* seat from Mustang District wherein three Thakalis were contesting for the seat. The solution was arbitrated by the *subba* who chose the poorest man "in order to improve the man's social standing and financial welfare" (1978:144–45). Disagreements are, of course, no longer resolved by the arbitration of the *subba*, but cooperation is more common in Thak Khola and competition more common in Khani Khuwa. In the elections of 1982, 1986, 1991, and 1992, bitter campaigns for the seats from Myagdi and Baglung divided the Thakali communities in these districts. In general, Thakalis do not make political alliances on the basis of ethnic lines, and, in Myagdi and Baglung, in particular, class is more operative than caste.

The local political achievements of the Khuwale Thakali emerge from the respect they earn as men of influence. Thakalis in Khani Khuwa have remained independent of the political influence of both the council of thirteen headmen in Thak Khola and the *subba* lineage. Political success in this area is due as much if not more to the strength of each individual's connections in other *jāts*, that is, the ability to appeal beyond lines of caste or ethnicity. Unlike those in Thak Khola, they do not boost their status by telling the story of the Hansa Raja, claiming Thakuri status, or trading on the reputation of the Thak Khola *subba*.

In their capacity as mediators between nation and community, individual Thakalis become influential by controlling new ideas and technologies, intervening directly with government officers, and promoting economic development. Their control of knowledge and technology is both subtle and direct: they use their access to capital, political networks, and knowledge to encourage change, plan for it, and anticipate it, and as private contractors they play an active role in carrying out many of the construction projects in this area. These changes cover a wide range of technology and ideas and include the introduction of methane gas, the construction of gas-engine–powered and water-powered mills, the development of irrigation systems, and the introduction of piped-in water. Thakalis are also directly involved with the planning and implementation of a large USAID-funded project called the Resource Conservation and Utilization Project (RCUP) involving millions of rupees in contracts for construction, the supply of materials, furnishings, and labor.

The Thakali in Myagdi and Baglung Districts are regarded with a mixture of respect and resentment by members of other *jāts*. Because many of them are well off, influential, well educated, and sources of loans, advice, and guidance on a wide range of subjects, they are respected by many of those less well off than they and resented by those in economic and political competition with them. Frequently heard assertions include the view that the Thakali are excessively clever, that they cheat, and that they made most of their money through extortionist moneylending policies. It is perhaps not surprising that many of these criticisms are offered by socioeconomic peers of the Thakali, but it is also true that no other group of people is so vilified as a group. During the initial research period in 1982, a Chetri I did not know in the town of Galkot in Baglung District sought me out to convey the opinion that I should not research the Thakalis because they were thieves. He went on to say that in Galkot the Thakalis had come on a golden opportunity and had succeeded in exploiting it because the Chetris were weak. In Darbang, another Chetri shopkeeper claimed that the Thakalis would never admit how they had really come by their money, and she went on to detail the villainous economic tactics and loose morality of each Thakali she knew.[33]

Despite this resentment, the Thakali, at least as individuals, are widely respected for the same qualities for which they are resented—their hard work, their wealth, and influence—and for the most part their political prominence appears to owe more to respect than to fear. Interestingly, Thakalis are generally respected as individuals and resented as a type.

Political rivalries, whether they are within local villages, districts, or the Thakali *samaj* itself, lack the balancing elements of cooperation that characterize *dhikur*, and therefore they more frequently result in open dissension. Examples of Thakali political rivalries are numerous, and at both the district and local level, the competition among political factions in Baglung and Myagdi Districts, for example, has periodically resulted in the political defeat at the polls of one Thakali faction by another.

5   Ritual Landscapes

The various modes of worship, which prevailed in the Roman
world, were all considered by the people as equally true; by the philosopher, as
equally false; and by the magistrate, as equally useful.
— Edward Gibbon

In a scheme, we possess only the limits of the object, the outline
which encloses the matter, the real substance of the object. These limits mean
only the relationship in which any object finds itself with respect to all other
objects.
— Ortega y Gasset

In a long, crowded, windowless room with stale air and dim
light, I sit for hours cross-legged on the floor with no place to stretch out.
During a lull in the shaman's chanting and drumming, a man arrives with
a chicken and squats down in front of me near the shaman. The shaman
begins again to chant and beat his drum. Some in the room ignore him and
continue to talk, to yawn, to sleep. Several women weeping loudly and dramatically in the center of the room are ignored. People casually wander in
and out of the room. I strain to understand the shaman's flat-pitched chanting, hoping to discover deeper meaning, but realize at this point that he is
providing instructions to the man in front of me, telling him to pick up the
chicken and twist off its head. After a great deal of difficulty, the man succeeds, and the chicken's blood is drained off into a brass cup. When this is
finished, the shaman puts down his drum, turns to the chicken killer, and
loudly jests, to his embarrassment and everyone else's amusement, "What
kind of way was that to kill a chicken? A small boy could do it more quickly."
During the interval the weeping women depart and a *damai*,[1] a well-
known local character who has cheerfully overindulged in the hospitality
offered on the occasion, staggers in through the far doorway and loudly
announces that he knows all about Thakalis because he lived in Thak
Khola for twenty-five years. "There are four clans," he intones authorita-
tively, "Sherchan, Bhattachan, Tulachan, Gauchan, Bhattachan, Tulachan,

Sherchan. I know all about Thakalis and Thakali ritual. I can tell you how to do it right, I can tell you how they do it in Thak Khola." During this pronouncement, the shaman goes on about his work as if he doesn't hear the man, while a few people laugh uneasily at the *damai*'s antics in the doorway. Most people ignore him. After he leaves the room, one man suggests that the door be shut to keep him out, but this idea is quietly rejected, and the door is left open. The *damai* returns time and time again throughout the night to repeat the mantra of his knowledge: "I know all about the Thakali. There are four clans. . . . "

When the drumming starts again, eight men, one wearing a white turban, each holding a knife in a quivering hand, gather around the shaman. As the shaman's drumming and chanting become more intense, they periodically build up to crescendos punctuated by the crowd shouting loud, long "wooos." The man with the turban picks up a pot holding dough figurines painted with chicken blood and turns it upside down into a frying pan. At that very moment and without warning, a gun is discharged, the pot overturned, and all the knives and the gun pressed against the bottom of the pot. The figurines are mashed inside the skulls of a monkey, a dog, and a cat, which are also painted with chicken blood. The skulls are wrapped in cloth, taken outside, and buried in the road.

Later, I stand outside with my friend Bal Bahadur as he hovers by the fire and plucks the chicken that had been sacrificed earlier. "We Thakali are Buddhist," he volunteers as he absent-mindedly plucked at the chicken. Then he pauses. "Well," he begins again thoughtfully, while gesturing toward the half-plucked chicken, "I suppose this looks like Hinduism."

January 12, 1982

The Thakali ritual world contains a relatively constant core set within a wider field of eclectic pluralism. This core is embedded in rites that use putative descent to emphasize and reinforce sets of social relations. In practice, the performance or nonperformance of these rites fuels and derives from ongoing tensions between interpretations of identity based on descent and cultural practice. While ideally an individual's identity as Thakali derives from both descent and cultural practice, there are many instances where this is not the case. Thus ritual performances provide fora within which those of questioned descent may demonstrate an adherence to Thakali practices that distinguishes them from nonpracticing individuals of pure Thakali descent. This chapter is focused on a central set of practices within which these tensions come to the fore. As such, it is not meant to be a comprehensive treatment of Thakali ritual practices.

Lineage rituals like the one described above constitute the core of the complex, heterogeneous ritual world of the Thakali. Understanding the complexities of this world is facilitated by bearing in mind several important points. First, membership in descent-based groups among the Thakali is continually reinforced and contested through ritual: each level of kin organization engages in ritual performances that dramatize ties of descent. Second, Thakalis acknowledge these lineage rituals as essential for the maintenance of social organization and identity. Third, they disagree about the details of their performance and interpretation. Fourth, when residing within culturally plural communities, the Thakali often use the widely understood vocabulary of the major religious traditions of Hinduism and Buddhism to explain their ritual practices. Fifth, the widespread adherence to the complex of rituals that accent descent—Torongla, *kul devtā puja*, mortuary rites, and *khimi tapne*—stands in contrast to the heterogeneity of other beliefs and practices characteristic of Thakalis residing in different locales. Sixth, within the parameters of these rituals there is wide latitude for variation.[2] Seventh, some Thakali ritual practices are more highly politicized than others.

The rules governing these rites do not establish a set of rigid boundaries delineating the correct performance of rites but function instead like the parameters of a wide riverbed like the Kali Gandaki within which streams of ritual variations may meander. While the river, to return to my original metaphor, meanders from side to side, breaks up into numerous streams, reconverges, and occasionally overflows its banks, it nevertheless exists in a necessary and definitive relationship of containment to a specific conceptual category, a particular riverbed. To cross from the village of Kobang to Sauru, for example, a Thakali may never ford the same river twice, but he always fords the Kali Gandaki and not the Ganges. Similarly, the practice of some of these rituals may vary in different ways from time to time and from place to place, but their similarity and family resemblances remain recognizable.

Eclectic Ritual Pluralism

While ritual practices emphasizing membership in descent groups form the base of the Thakali ritual landscape, they occur in contexts of religious pluralism wherein only some areas of ritual practice are socially prescribed while other areas of ritual practice are entirely left to each individual Thakali. There is no religious consensus among Thakali communities, and neither can professed religious beliefs be used to predict actual practices accurately. Any specific individual Thakali may also perform or participate in rituals from a range of traditions, be they Buddhist, Hindu, animist, or related to a specific local deity or belief. Both the varied ritual practices of individuals and the group performance of rituals fuel the contestation over internal and external boundaries separating different Thakali populations from one another or the Thakali from other neighboring populations.

Any random selection of the ritual practices of individual Thakalis reveals a tremendous heterogeneity. Individual Thakalis hold a wide range of beliefs, and some individuals may consider themselves to be Hindu, Buddhist, Christian, scientific atheists, agnostics, or adherents of any of a number of South Asian sects. In many cases, however, individual Thakalis do not strictly follow a single religious tradition, and it is not at all uncommon to find individuals who regularly perform rituals from several religious traditions. For individual practitioners, inclusive religious practice is the only way to ensure that one has appealed to the appropriate spiritual power. This is particularly true at times of spiritual stress or for individuals facing hardships, who are likely to call on various ritual practitioners, the precise choices dictated by the availability of practitioners in the immediate area. Individuals who regularly move between one or more locations may well perform different rituals in each locations: for example, many of my informants, while residing in Pokhara or Kathmandu, make offerings at Hindu temples, but on returning to Thak Khola, where there are no Hindu temples, the same individuals make offerings at Buddhist temples. This reflects not so much a religious syncretism as it does an eclectic religious pluralism in which the rituals practiced, deities propitiated, and religious practitioners consulted vary depending on a variety of factors including the age, gender, level of education, occupation, site of primary residence, site of secondary residence, and lineage of the propitiator.

Location, in particular, strongly influences the ritual practices likely to be followed by individual Thakalis. Individuals in Thakali communities vary in the use of religious practitioners—Brahman priest, Tibetan lamas, or Thakali ḍhom—employed for the observance of rites that include traditional Thakali observances, Nepalese practices, and orthodox Hindu and Tibetan Buddhist practices. Differences in choice derive, at least in part, from the availability or lack of availability of particular practitioners: Hindu priests do not reside in Thak Khola and must be called in from outside, while Tibetan lamas and Thakali *dhoms* have traditionally been available in the area.[3] In Khani Khuwa, there are no Tibetan Buddhist priests, but Thakali *dhoms* (called by the Nepali term *jāhkri* in Khani Khuwa) are available in the region, as are Hindu priests. In Kathmandu, there have been no practicing *dhoms* but an abundance of both Tibetan lamas and Hindu priests, and both these have been employed by the Thakali.

Thakali religious eclecticism emerges from a coalescence of individual choice, convenience, and cultural flexibility. Within each migrant area, the Thakali generally follow some, but not all, of the religious practices common to other *jāts* within the area, as well as some religious practices that are not common to it. Thus not only do Thakali religious practices vary considerably from area to area, but in any single area there is often only a rough correlation between the general religious practices of that area and Thakali religious practices.

That the Thakali follow some of the practices common to their immediate areas of residence needs to be considered in light of the fact that in almost all cases there are some local practices they do not follow. Furthermore, in some areas, Thakali practices differ radically from those of their immediate neighbors. Thus, while at first glance the Thakali may seem to have simply adopted the religious practices of their neighbors, the facts are much more complex. A few examples will help to illustrate this complexity.

In the Terai town of Bhairawa, a strong Hindu community, Thakalis not only do not follow the Hindu religious practices of their immediate neighbors, but many individuals make it clear that they are not Hindu. These individuals are strong public advocates of the performance of non-Hindu Thakali religious practices. This emphasis allows members of the Bhairawa community to distinguish themselves from both Hindus in the area and Thakalis who follow what they consider to be the Sanskritized habits of the *subba* lineage. The Thakali community of Bhairawa, which includes among its members many wealthy merchants formerly from Tukche who disparage the adaptations to Hinduism advocated by the *subbas*, sees itself as the migrant Thakali community striving hardest to preserve aspects of traditional Thakali practices.

Thakali ritual practice in Khani Khuwa vividly illustrates the ritual pluralism typical of the middle hills. A few of the Thakali are active Hindus, others are converts to Indian sects, and still others profess no specific faith but nevertheless perform a potpourri of rituals that include practices common to Hinduism, Thakalis, and the local area. In general, the Thakali, like other groups in the area, make offerings to a number of Hindu-derived deities and local nature deities and observe national and regional holidays. Nature deities are propitiated by sacrificial offerings in an annual series of rites, and the effects of malevolent demons, witches, and ghosts are countered through the engagement of local *jhākri*, or shamans, on an as-needed basis. The Thakali also maintain and publicly practice mortuary and ancestor worship rites peculiar to the Thakali.

Major Hindu holidays such as Dasain, Tihar, Tij, and Holi are celebrated in Khani Khuwa by members of all *jāts*. These Hindu holidays have been celebrated less as religious than as national holidays and without a heavy religious overtone. Since 1992, however, there has been an attempt among national Janajāti leaders to identify Dasain, in particular, as a specifically Hindu (and not Janajati) holiday and thus not an appropriate national holiday. This movement has begun to catch on among various Janajati populations. The Thakali response has been ambivalent. Without taking an overt public stand, they have continued to follow the secular customs of socializing and feasting at Dasain while ignoring the religious nature of the holiday.

While the Thakali in Khani Khuwa observe some of the religious practices of their neighbors, at the same time they maintain a distinctive set of practices that focus on ancestor worship and require the participation of the Thakali *ḍhom*. These are practiced simultaneously with and not in substitution for other religious practices, including both so-called Hindu and Buddhist practices. Ancestor worship, or *lha chuji*, is performed in a series of household rituals. Thakali from Khani Khuwa actually follow a more complete set of Thakali rituals associated with the *ḍhom* than do more recent migrants from Thaksatsae.

Ritual pluralism fuels the politicization of ritual practice and the construction of cultural boundaries. For example, older members of wealthier Thakali families established in Kathmandu have stressed Hindu rites and want to continue to distinguish the Thaksatsae Thakali from other groups more influenced by Tibetan Buddhism who also claim Thakali status, and this distinction between groups is often made on the basis of religion and religious practices. Another strain on the social fabric is presented by the many Westernized young Thakalis who advocate a return to an idealized Thakali tradition that they never knew and that many members of the older generations insist never existed.

The difficulties encountered by scholars in categorizing and analyzing these practices are numerous, complicated by the fact that distinctions among Hindu, Buddhist, and animist traditions are rarely very clear in the minds of informants. But the practitioners do not perceive themselves or their practices as confused.

Ancestor Rituals: "We Don't Have Any Gods"

While the form and style of ritual performance are a matter of dispute, one clear effect of many of these rituals is the reflection and strengthening of descent group membership. This occurs through a set of rituals centered around the ossuary, or *khimi*, and ancestor worship that include *lha chuji* (T: also called *lha chuwa*; or N: *kul devtā puja*), *khimi chuji* (T: also *khimi chuwa*; or N: *khimi tapne*), Torongla, and a selection of mortuary rites. These rites require the involvement of a variety of relatives including patrilineally related men, their wives, and their male affines. A Thakali man has ritual relations with patrilineally related males (in the most extended sense this constitutes his *phobe*); patrilineally related females, whether married or unmarried (his *celi*); men who have received wives from his *phobe* (*juāi*); men of the *phobe* from which he received his wife; and the group of men married into the *phobe* from which he received his wife (*sādo bhāi*). These relations are articulated within a web of obligations related to ancestor worship rituals.[4]

Rites called *lha chuji*—the name implies the "worship of the gods" or the "feeding of the gods"—are often described by the Thakali as an act of respect toward the ancestors of the lineage. As one Thakali woman insisted to me early in my research, "We don't have any gods; we just do the ritual." Or as other friends and informants repeatedly stressed, "It doesn't matter if you believe, but to be Thakali you must do these rituals."

Some informants distinguished between two forms of the ritual, an elaborate version (T:*hilbu*) and a simple one (T: *shirbu*); in either case, it is an involved and expensive rite.[5] The rituals I have attended have lasted from two to four full days and nights. The actual series of rituals and sacrifices undertaken varies according to the tradition of the particular *phobe*, or lineage—the *kul puja* of the Tulachan Lama *ghyu*, for instance, lasts for five days and must be conducted by the Tulachan lama—and the particular Thakali ritual specialist performing the rite.

Whether it is the elaborate or simple version, the basic pattern remains the same. The ritual requires the participation of a Thakali ritual specialist, the agnatic kinsmen of the household, the *celi*, and the *juāi* (N: sons-in-law) of the household. The *juāi* do most of the ritual work, and they play the major role in the rite. The ceremonies begin in the evening, by which time all the principal participants should have arrived (participants often travel a long way on short notice to fulfill obligations in this ritual). On that first evening, the *dhom* constructs a small altar, a chicken is sacrificed, and initial offerings are made to the ancestors. The second day's rites begin when the *juāi* return from the forest with the appropriate plants. During the ensuing days, an elaborate altar is built using these plants, dough *torma* (T: ritual figures created from dough), and the head, heart, and feet of a ram sacrificed by pulling out its still-beating heart.

Thakalis and scholars often try to relate the components of the rituals to major religious traditions in the Himalayas: the animal sacrifice suggests Hinduism to some, the dough *tormas* remind others of Tibetan Buddhist rites, and the reliance on juniper as a sacred plant, which is characteristic of this and other Thakali ceremonies, is reminiscent of both Bon and Buddhism.[6] But beyond a superficial similarity, there is no clear relationship between any of these traditions and the rituals that are part of this ceremony.

Some scholars have suggested that this ceremony must be performed in the *thimtens* of Thaksatsae and cannot be performed outside Thaksatsae.[7] This is incorrect: the rite has been performed regularly outside of Thaksatsae for generations. The ritual objects may be separated and reestablished in new households as extended families break up and establish new households. The youngest son usually inherits the established shrine along with the house of his father, and the senior brothers must establish the shrine anew in their own homes. This is done by performing the full *lha chuji* ritual in the existing site using two sets of ritual objects; one set is then taken to the new site, and the ritual is performed again with the same participants.

Differences have evolved between the performance of *lha chuji* by the early migrants from Thak Khola, particularly those living in Khani Khuwa, and its performance by later migrants, particularly those leaving Thaksatsae after 1960. One difference is reflected in degrees of concern about purity and pollution. In well-to-do households in Thaksatsae, the rite is performed in the *thimten* of the house, the hearth established for this purpose. Restricted access to the hearth was an important issue at one time in Thak Khola: non-Thakalis and Thakalis who were *celang melang*, *pumi*, or *mang* were not allowed to enter this area during the performance of the ritual.[8] In migrant areas, there is less concern about the purity of the worshipers or the possibility of pollution by outsiders, and most Thakali homes outside of Thak

FIGURE 5.1 Altar constructed by *dhom* for a *lha chuji* rite in Khani Khuwa

Khola do not have a proper *thimten* (though some contain a hearth used only for ritual purposes). Instead, families will clear a space in a utility room constructed partly for the purpose of storing the sacred objects. And in Khani Khuwa, for example, no restrictions bar the presence of non-Thakalis at the hearth during the ceremony, though occasionally non-Thakalis will be requested not to enter the storage room where the empowered objects are placed.

There are other differences between the ways this rite is performed by earlier and later migrants. It is sometimes undertaken by lineages, sometimes by single households, and at other times by an extended lineage that can trace its descent back five generations to a common male ancestor. It is performed at yearly, triennial, and irregular intervals, depending on the particular group. In Khani Khuwa, Thakalis perform *kul devtā puja* regularly, usually yearly or triennially, while migrants in other areas perform the ritual only sporadically and in conjunction with a visit to Thak Khola.[9] The early migrants from Thak Khola who moved to Khani Khuwa performed the

FIGURE 5.2 *Dhom* before his altar

necessary ritual to obtain and move the ritual objects from the ancestral
homes in Thak Khola to their new homes in Myagdi and Baglung Districts,
while later migrants to the cities have generally not done so. Characteristic
are responses like this from one informant residing in Kathmandu: "I remember the ceremony being performed when I was a child living in Gulmi
District, but since my family moved to Kathmandu, we have not done the
rituals to move the ritual objects. I don't know why we haven't done it."

Within Khani Khuwa, the ritual objects are commonly moved each time
an extended household breaks up. Moving the objects to a new home is not
obligatory, however, and in some instances many generations of descendants
of a single ancestor come together to perform the ritual in the ancestral
home. In one instance in Myagdi District, this ritual is performed by the
Tulachan Jhongman lineage in a unique fashion by households related
through a great-great-grandfather: these households rotate their yearly performance of the ritual from one household to another. The most recent
performance of this ritual, in 1998, was recorded on videotape and sent to

family members living overseas who had been unable to attend.[10] Other
Thakalis in or from Khani Khuwa regularly separate and move their shrines
from place to place: in the 1980s and 1990s many households moved their
shrines from homes in Khani Khuwa to new homes in the metropolitan
areas of Kasauli and Bhairawa.

In general, the Khuwale Thakali migrants have maintained their regular
practice of *lha chuji*, while the migrant Thak Khole Thakalis have abandoned it. I know of no instance where a migrant who left Thak Khola after
1960 has established an appropriate shrine for the worship of *kul devtā puja*
outside of Thak Khola. The greater adherence of Khuwale Thakali to lineage
rituals may have originally stemmed from their nineteenth-century dispersion over a wide area amid an alien population. These performances helped
to maintain their ties with each other as well as with the Thakali population
in Thak Khola. Ironically, the regular practice by the Khuwale of these
rituals now makes the Khuwale appear to be more traditional or more Thakali than the migrant Thak Khole migrants who disparage them.

Mortuary Rites

Death ceremonies (N: *kiriya*) play an equally important role in emphasizing the social ties among the Thakali. These performances, however, vary
greatly, depending on location and the kind of ritual specialist engaged to
perform the ceremony. Under different circumstances, these ceremonies are
performed by a Thakali *ḍhom*, a Tibetan lama, or a Hindu priest. The choice
of ritual specialists depends in the first instance on availability: in Thak
Khola, where both Buddhist Lamas and Thakali *ḍhom*s are available, the
choice between these two is dependent on the age and status of the deceased,
the time of year, and the religious orientation of the deceased's family. In
Thak Khola, death ceremonies (performed either by a lama or *ḍhom*) share
similarities in purpose and structure, but there is considerable variation in
timing duration and style.[11] The main rite is usually held on the night of
the twelfth day after death and finishes on the morning of the thirteenth
day, but other factors must be taken into consideration; for instance, some
informants say that the rite must be completed within the month in which
death occurred, and others note that inauspiciousness of certain days of the
month or week will cause the ceremony to be performed a day earlier than
usual.

In Khani Khuwa, unlike in other areas where Thakalis reside, the performance of death ceremonies is fairly uniform: they are always performed by a Thakali *dhom*, the main ceremony always falls on the twelfth night after the death and is completed on the morning of the thirteenth day, and except for variations resulting from the different personal styles of various *dhoms*, the performance of mortuary ceremonies is identical in content and form. On the day of death the deceased is cremated; on the third day after death a small bone fragment from the skull (N: *astu*) is retrieved from the cremation site and placed in an effigy of the deceased called a *mhendo* (T). The *mhendo* is made in a bamboo basket or a copper bowl, which is wrapped in new cloth and decorated with the belongings of the deceased; if the deceased was a women, the effigy is decorated with her jewelry, and after the completion of the rites these items are given to her son's wife. Every morning and evening for twelve days the household cooks the food that the deceased liked and feeds it to the effigy on silver bowls. The food is actually eaten by a male in-law of the deceased (N: *mul jāui*, literally, the main son-in-law), who stays with the family throughout this period to perform the ritual chores. The family of the deceased encourages him to eat as if the food were being offered to the deceased to prepare him or her for a long journey.

The principal ceremony is performed on the twelfth night after the death, and at this time at least one member of every household related to the deceased comes to the deceased's home. The ceremony lasts throughout the night and includes the presentation of food to the deceased by the descendants, the consumption of this food by the male in-law, and ritual weeping by the women, who will often bring up social disagreements that may be troubling the deceased, and it culminates in a ceremony wherein the Thakali *dhom* banishes the soul from the house, preserves the sanctity of the household, and determines the form in which the deceased has been reincarnated. Following this, the male in-law and the *dhom* take the effigy to a place where two paths meet, dismantle it, and burn the remains, keeping only the bone fragment, which must be taken to the lineage ossuary in Thaksatsae. They then return to the house, where the members of the deceased's *phobe* are purified using juniper, ritually pure water, and white stones that have been heated in a fire. Simpler ceremonies are performed on the forty-ninth day after death and one year after the death, involving the same practitioner and the same attendees.

Elsewhere, there is more variation in the performance of these rites. In Bhairawa and Kasauli, for instance, the religious practitioner of choice is the

FIGURE 5.3 *Dhom* (*seated, center*) resting the morning after a mortuary ceremony

Thakali *ḍhom*, but for many years no *ḍhom* resided in these communities, and families have had to make do with alternative performances. Death ceremonies in Pokhara and Kathmandu show the greatest variation: neither community has a practicing *ḍhom* (though each has several retired *ḍhom*s), and though Pokhara is geographically close enough to other areas of Thakali residence to summon a *ḍhom* on occasion, the members of the Kathmandu community have learned, or prefer, to make do by employing the religious practitioners available in the city. In Kathmandu, the Thakali cremate their dead at Pashupati, a Hindu temple on the Bagmati River, and frequently arrange for both Hindu and Tibetan Buddhist ceremonies to be performed on the thirteenth day after the death.

Disagreements arise because deaths often affect direct descendants who reside in more than one locale, and the different branches of the family may insist that the death rites conform to the custom they feel is most appropriate or traditional. The ceremony is usually performed according to the custom common to the locale where the deceased resided, but this is not always the case. In one unusual instance where the place of the deceased's death was different from his place of residence, two death ceremonies were performed: one branch of the family—including the deceased's wife and the households of two of the deceased's brother's sons—had the body cremated in Kathmandu and held a *kiriya* conducted by a Brahman priest; simultaneously, another segment of the family—including the deceased's daughter's household and the household of the deceased's brother's third son—held a rite conducted by a Thakali *ḍhom* in the deceased's home. Because the deceased had no sons, his estate was contested by his daughters and his brother's sons. Two years after the death, the two branches of the family finally reconciled, split the inheritance, and jointly conducted an ancestor worship ceremony in the deceased's former home.

Marriages: *Khimi Tapne*

Thakali marriages may involve two separate set of social rituals. The first set involves social rituals that emphasize Thakali corporate entities. The most important ritual is called *khimi tapne* (N) or *khimi chuwa* (T) and involves the propitiation of the ancestors of the subclan (T: *phobe*). *Khimi chuwa* is only performed when both marriage partners are Thakali. Additional marriage ceremonies may follow the *khimi chuwa* ceremony, and these may or may not include rites conducted by a Brahman priest or at a Hindu temple, depending on the locale and the family, but the *khimi chuwa* ceremony is the sine qua non of Thakali marriages: once this ceremony is completed, the marriage is considered official, and without it, it is not. Any additional marriage rites the family may select are not prescribed and may take any form the families of the bride and groom desire. These rites are optional and relate less to the relationships among Thakali than they do to the relationship of a particular Thakali family with its non-Thakali neighbors, friends, colleagues, and business partners.

It was common in the past for the Thakali to practice capture-marriage—a practice that is now rarely followed by any of the hill groups of Nepal—wherein a man, with the assistance of his friends and the friends of the woman (and often with her own knowledge and help)—would abduct a woman and keep her captive for ten days. During that time, an intermediary would negotiate with the woman's parents and try to get them to agree to the *khimi chuwa* ceremony. Usually after ten days, if the girl was not found, the ceremony was performed. Today, it is not uncommon for couples to elope, but the marriage is not considered official until the groom's family has supplicated the bride's family and the *khimi chuwa* is performed.

Once the arrangements have been made for the marriage and both sides are in agreement, representatives of the grooms' *phobe*—excluding the groom—come to the home of the bride's father, where the representatives of the bride's father's *phobe*—excluding the bride—await them. During this ceremony the bride's family (the wife givers) is considered to be higher in status than the groom's family (the wife takers), and the groom's representatives must stand during the ceremony—they are never offered seats—and must speak in very respectful tones to the family of the bride. The ceremony is usually presided over by a respected Thakali from a clan other than the bride's or groom's; this man will request that any outstanding demands or conditions or any reasons not to proceed with the marriage be announced at this time or that it be made clear that there are none. When no objections or difficulties are voiced, the groom's representatives offer distilled alcohol (N: *rākshi*) and then beer (N: *chang*) to male and female members of the bride's father's *phobe*. The bride's brother, wearing a silver Thakali neck ornament (T: *khāngalo*)[12] and a Nepali cap, and with a juniper twig in his mouth, offers the alcohol to the ancestors and informs them of the marital transactions.[13] When this has been transacted, the host announces that the bride has been transferred from one *phobe* to the other.

After the offerings of *rākshi* and *chang* are accepted, a representative of the groom's family must come in and show respect by touching his forehead to the feet of each member of the bride's representatives. The bride's lineage insists that this be done by someone of status—though it is never done by a person of the highest status—and as closely related to the groom as possible. The groom's party often tries to send a young boy to perform this part of the rite, but the bride's side may refuse to accept this. Twice I have watched the groom's designated representative sent back by the bride's lineage with the demand that he be replaced with an individual of higher status. In some instances this individual may simply press his palms together in front of his chest as a sign of respect instead of touching his forehead to the feet of each individual. In all the cases I have witnessed, the men of the bride's side have dispensed with actual contact between the groom's representative and their feet. The women were never so sympathetic and usually dragged the man's head down to their feet, laughing all the time.

After the marriage, it is customary for the bride and groom to return home to the bride's parents and then to visit all the households of the bride's father's subclan, but, until the *khimi chuwa* ceremony is performed, the bride cannot return home. The nonattendance of a close male lineage member at a *khimi chuwa* is a serious matter and usually occurs only when there is serious disagreement over the marriage arrangements: in most cases the refusal to attend by a principal member of the *phobe* will be enough cause to delay or cancel the ceremony.

An example may help to illustrate the significance of the *khimi tapne* rite: In 1980 a *joshi* (N: astrologer) had divined that the life force of the seven-year-old daughter of a Thakali woman who had had several miscarriages was responsible for the miscarriages, and he suggested that a solution was to arrange the daughter's marriage, thus transferring her to a different clan and redirecting her life force. The grandmother took the initiative against the desires of her daughter and her daughter's husband and arranged for the granddaughter's *khimi chuwa*, but when the time came most of the senior men of the *phobe* refused to attend, saying, "If Sita [the granddaughter] is unhappy later, how will we explain the fact that we drank *rākshi* at her *khimi chuwa*?" The grandmother persisted with the arrangements, the *khimi chuwa* was held, and the mother went on to have another child with no miscarriage.

Sita did not live with her husband, and her marriage was not consummated until she reached puberty. At that time she was permitted to choose to void the marriage or to go through with it. Because the *khimi chuwa* had been held, she was under considerable pressure to go through with the marriage, but, because most of the male members of the lineage had not attended, she had sufficient grounds to renege on the agreement.

In another instance, competition between two branches of a single lineage led to the breakup of a marriage arrangement and an ambiguous status for the jilted bride. A third-party emissary had been asked to arrange the marriage of a Bhattachan boy to a Sherchan girl. During the ensuing negotiations, the girl's father suggested that a second match be arranged between his son and the sister of the Bhattachan suitor. The emissary agreed. It was further agreed that the marriage ceremony of the Bhattachan boy and the Sherchan girl would occur first and that the ceremony for the Sherchan boy and the Bhattachan girl would not occur for a year. However, because the Sherchan man was older than his sister (and perhaps because he was unsure that the Bhattachan family would later go through with what they had agreed), the families agreed that the *khimi chuwa* for the Bhattachan girl would occur before that for the Sherchan girl. At the last

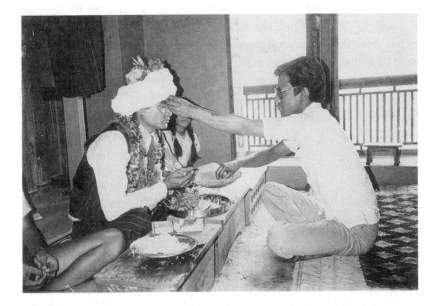

FIGURE 5.4 Thakali groom receiving blessing from a Chetri neighbor in Khani Khuwa

minute, one member of the Sherchan subclan refused to attend because of his rivalry with another branch of the subclan (and because he had expected to marry his own son to the Bhattachan girl). Despite this inauspicious incident, the ceremony went on as scheduled. Shortly after ceremony, however, the Sherchan groom-to-be, acting impulsively on rumors about the girl's affections, broke with protocol and confronted the Bhattachan bride-to-be. She confessed her disinclination to marry him. Scandalously, both weddings were called off. To justify the last-minute disengagement, the would-be groom's party insisted that the actual *khimi chuwa* had not been performed, arguing that the ceremony had, in fact, been a less-binding pre–*khimi tapne* ceremony called *dhān rākne*. Most of the other participants rejected this creative interpretation and insisted that the ceremony had indeed been a proper *khimi chuwa* and that the two individuals were betrothed. A great deal was at stake: if the *khimi chuwa* ceremony had not yet occurred, then the breaking of the agreement could be justified, and the unmarried status of the two individuals involved would remain unchanged. If the *khimi chuwa* had occurred, then the Bhattachan girl was effectively a Sherchan bride, albeit rejected, her "bone" was now of her groom's subclan, and she was no longer eligible to marry any other men of that subclan. In the event, the object of her affection, the son of the Sherchan who had refused to attend the ceremony, bowed to public opinion and considered her married (he married a Tulachan girl shortly thereafter).

Torongla

Devotion to lineage ancestors is also demonstrated during the Thakali festival of Torongla, so called because it falls in the Thakali month of Torongla (the Nepali month of Phagun, usually in March). For three nights, including the night before, the night of, and the night following the full moon, the Thakali feed their ancestors, who are thought to visit the household during this holiday. There are some variations — the families of *dhoms* begin this ritual one day early and so propitiate the ancestors for four nights, while in Myagdi and Baglung Districts the offerings to the ancestors are made on only one or two nights — but the pattern is basically the same. One member of each Thakali household rises before dawn and prepares the feast for the ancestors, which, in Khani Khuwa, is placed in the same storage-cum-ritual room used for the *kul devtā* ritual.[14] Many Thakalis all over Nepal stress the importance of this part of the ceremony; one explained to me in Khani Khuwa that "to be Thakali you *must* perform this ritual. You do not have to believe in it, but you have to perform it. The rest of the year you can follow Hinduism or Buddhism, but at Torongla you must feed the ancestors."

In migrant areas where this holiday coincides with the Hindu holiday of Holi, Thakalis merge their traditions with some of the secular activities surrounding that holiday. In the days before the festival begins, the whole house is whitewashed, replastered, and cleaned, as other *jāts* do before the Hindu holiday of Dasain. Thakalis explain that they, unlike other *jāts*, do this twice a year, once at Dasain and again at Torongla.

In addition to the household worship of ancestors and visits with close relatives, Torongla involves local Thakali communities through archery festivals, which are held in all areas of significant Thakali population density, including Kathmandu, Pokhara, Kasauli, and Bhairawa. In Thak Khola, these festivals are well attended. In Khani Khuwa, the archery games go on longer and involve more of the wider non-Thakali community than they do in Thak Khola. They often begin weeks in advance of the full moon, and members of all *jāts* are welcome to participate.[15] The games are usually played in teams, with a point counted for each arrow that hits the target and a bet placed on the outcome of each game. An additional bet is wagered against any player hitting the bull's-eye, and when a player succeeds, he collects an agreed-on amount from each player and uses it to buy alcohol and food for the other players. Food and alcohol are often provided on a concession basis, with the concession often given to a local family. In Khani Khuwa, refreshments are provided not by Thakalis but by Magar women, many of whom are married to Thakali men. Except in Khani Khuwa, Thakali women also gamble during this holiday, playing either cards or a traditional shell game.

In all Thakali migrant communities, Torongla is an important occasion for the celebration of the Thakali community. National efforts to restructure the Thakali community have had an impact on who is welcome to attend, however: non-Thaksatsae Thakali are often not welcome (see chapter 6). Other changes have also affected the activities and the way games are played. In Torongla, as in other festivals, tradition manifests itself in many new forms. In Kathmandu and Bhairawa, Western influences have slightly altered the games: in Bhairawa, they have replaced the traditional target with a new-style Western one, while in Kathmandu, where they retained the traditional target until the early 1990s, they have added a series of new events, including tugs-of-war pitting women against men and the Sherchans against everyone else.

Subclan Rites: *Khimi Ramden*

We crowd into a small back room of the Larjung Hotel. It is the sixth day of the 1993 Lha Phewa festival, and the dozen of us, eleven *dājyu-bhāi* (N: brothers, in this instance, male members) of the Sherchan Pompar *ghyu* and me (I am accepted as a fictive kin, whose status position is identical to that of my friend Jyoti) have gotten together to discuss how much money to contribute to the fund for our *celi* (T: sisters, in this instance women born into the *phobe*, most of whom have now married out), our coming visit to the Pompar ossuary, and our invitation to dine with the *celi*. Introductions are necessary as few of those present know all the others, and a great deal of

FIGURE 5.5 Archery during Torongla in Darbang

time is taken to establish kin connections and to discuss the health and general well-being of *phobe* members who were not able to attend the meetings.

Our members are generous, and we collect a large fund to which latecomers continue to contribute for the next few days. By the time we pass it on to the *celi*, we have raised more money than any other *phobe*, a fact in which the members take some pride. This money, a sign of respect to the *celi*, is used by them for their own feasting during the festival.

For the seventeen days of the festival, our *celi* and their husbands have taken over a house in Larjung where they reside and cook for themselves. Their husbands, our *juāi*, have used funds collected earlier for the repair of the Pompar *ghyu* ossuary, and they take us to see these repairs later in the afternoon. We move from the Larjung Hotel to their temporary residence (T: *cyāng*), where the *celi* have prepared a large feast.[16] This meeting is raucous and good-spirited, beginning with the greeting of old friends and relatives and moving on to the introduction of others. All these exchanges are spiced with good-humored teasing between the men and women of the

FIGURE 5.6 Archery during Torongla in Bhairawa

subclan. My ritual brother is relentlessly teased about his unmarried state, and every woman of the subclan makes a point of telling me it is now my responsibility to see that he gets married to a proper Thakali girl. They laugh when I reply that I have several women in mind and that since they had collectively failed to match him with a suitable Thakali girl, they should prepare themselves to accept my choice, even if she is American.

Later we climb up the hill over Larjung, pointing out along the way the area that used to belong to Pati Ram Sau.[17] The *juāi* show us their work on the Pompar ossuary. The Pompar men inspect it carefully, and then we settle there down to talk and drink while enjoying a panoramic view of the wide riverbed of the Kali Gandaki and its many meandering currents.

At the level of the named subclans (T: *phobe* or *ghyu*), there is a direct link between the ritual and physical landscapes. While lineage deities may be moved from house to house or region to region to continue the practice of *kul devtā puja*, the principal symbol of the subclan, the *khimi*, or ossuary, is never moved from Thak Khola.[18] The *phobe* are named extended

patrilineages or subclans usually associated with a specific locality or ancestor.[19] Existing *phobe* vary in size from three to fifty households. They are
effectual descent groups, and their members are supposed to have relatively
frequent face-to-face contact. A few subclans can trace all their members to
a common ancestor, but this is unusual; often, lineages within the same
subclan have to go back ten generations or more to find a common ancestor.[20]

Each subclan maintains a stone reliquary in Thaksatsae where a bone
fragment of each deceased member is placed. The reliquaries of most lineages are situated in fields belonging to the lineage in the hills above the
settlements of Kobang and Larjung. The subclan reliquary is of central importance, symbolizing, for both migrants and nonmigrants, the immortal
role of the ancestors and by extension one's own role and one's children's
place within the subclan. No matter how far a Thakali may be from Thaksatsae when he or she dies, a bone fragment should be taken from the cremation site and eventually brought to the ossuary of the subclan in Thaksatsae.

The right and obligation to deposit a bone fragment in the ossuary is
restricted to members of the subclan who are full-blooded Thakalis, that is,
acknowledged male or unmarried female offspring of a male Thakali subclan
member and a Thakali mother, and to Thakali women who have married
into the subclan. Having one's bone fragment deposited in the ossuary is the
manifestation of one's status as a Thakali and as an ancestor, and most subclans take strict steps to ensure that no inappropriate bones are deposited.
Consequently, the bone fragments of individuals who are not pure Thakali
are not deposited in the *khimi*.

The bone fragment of a married woman is deposited in the ossuary of
her husband's subclans, as she became of that subclan with her marriage.
The bone fragments of women who have married non-Thakalis are not welcome anywhere, as these women are considered to have passed out of Thakali society completely. (The bones of men who have married non-Thakalis
may be deposited in the ossuary, but those of their offspring by these marriages may not, as these individuals do not become ancestors.)[21]

One woman informant who had contemplated marriage with a non-
Thakali spoke to me at length of the fear she had felt when considering this
move, and she repeatedly stressed that her friend, who had married an American, had to have great courage to take such a step. My friend argued that
it would took tremendous strength to marry a non-Thakali, to sever your
connections to Thakali society and to the ancestors, and to accept that your
children would not be Thakali, that they could never perform the ancestor

worship rituals, and that you, their parent, would thus never become an ancestor.

The necessity of depositing a bone fragment is acknowledged by all Thakalis, migrants and nonmigrants alike, though it is not clear that the practice has always been strictly observed: by the late 1970s some of the ossuaries had fallen into disrepair, particularly those belonging to *phobe* whose members had migrated or were on the verge of dying out. Many migrated Thakalis, while they acknowledged the need to carry a bone of the deceased to Thak Khola, often argued over whether the responsibility fell to the heirs or to the *juāi*, the junior male in-laws of the deceased, and as a consequence bone fragments often languished for want of an individual prepared to carry them to the *khimi*.

Heirs may also be reluctant to take bone fragments back to Thaksatsae because they are uncertain of their reception by the members of their *phobe*. Subclan members residing in Thak Khola near the ossuaries do not always know migrants personally, and Thak Khole Thakali often assume that Khuwale Thakali are of mixed parentage, so migrants from that area are frequently embarrassed by the need to establish their right to deposit a bone fragment in the ossuary before they are permitted to do so. In the past two decades, many subclans have controlled access to the *khimis* by placing locks on their small doors. In 1984 some informants took me into the fields above Larjung and pointed out the new padlocks installed on the openings of their newly refurbished *khimis*. By 1993 almost all the *khimis* had padlocks.

There are no ossuaries outside Thaksatsae, but in the 1980s, because of the continuing antagonism between some Thak Khole Thakali and the Khuwale Thakali over the latter group's right to deposit bones in the *khimis*, there was a growing move to establish them in Khani Khuwa. As some Thakalis in Myagdi and Baglung Districts explain, the trip to Thaksatsae is time-consuming, the necessity to make it inevitably arises at inopportune times, on arrival they are inevitably assessed fines for sometimes failing to send a representative to attend obligatory meetings of the subclan, and it is often embarrassing when they cannot convincingly establish the genealogical rights of the deceased to have their bone fragments placed in the ossuary. Nevertheless, while they frequently express interest in establishing ossuaries in Khani Khuwa, all acknowledge that they would not do so without the consent of the Thakalis in Thak Khola.

In a few villages in Myagdi District, Thakalis have established shrines after the death of a relative that are used as a place for offerings to the deceased. They are simply called *chorten* (Tib.: reliquary) and are explicitly

distinguished from *khimi*s. Some informants vaguely hinted that bone fragments that were to go to the *khimi* in Thak Khola had been temporarily
stored in the *chorten* until someone had time to take them to Thak Khola,
but informants' answers were inconsistent on this point, and, understanda-
bly, no one was anxious to talk about what they did with the bone fragments
when they should have already been taken to Thaksatsae.

Most of the *khimi*s in Thaksatsae were renovated in the few years preceding the twelve-year Lha Phewa festival of 1993. Participants from outside
Thak Khola used the occasion to visit their *khimi* and check on the quality
of the work. Money for upkeep and renovations is raised among subclan
members, but the work is done or arranged by the *juāi*, the men who have
married women from the subclan.

The centrality of the *khimi* as a symbol of group membership emphasizes
the reliance on the concept of descent to draw social boundaries. These
rules, if enforced, would make Thakali descent more rigidly interpreted than
is characteristic of other groups in central Nepal. It must be noted, however,
that the strict interpretation of descent draws as many boundaries between
segments of the Thaksatsae Thakali community as it does between Thakali
and non-Thakali. For example, boundaries of descent create tensions between Khuwale and Thak Khole Thakalis and also between Thakalis in Thak
Khola who use descent to mark high status and others, like the *subba* family,
who sought and achieved high status through wealth but whose marriage
patterns in recent years have violated Thakali customs. Insistence on a strict
interpretation of descent can be and has been used as a strategy to diminish
the influence of some segments of Thakali society, but it is a clumsy and
imprecise strategy, with the unintended consequence of defining large portions of the community as "not-quite" or "impure" Thakali. Ironically, while
stigmatized for their imagined violations of rules of descent, some portions
of the Thakali community thus defined, like the Khuwale, otherwise adhere
more closely to recognizably Thakali forms of ritual practice.

While the interpretation of membership through descent occurs within
parameters that appear to be largely impermeable, such interpretation in
practice is fluid. The boundary is permeable in several senses: for example,
while offspring of one pure Thakali parent and one non-Thakali parent fall
into the ambiguous category of *celang melang*, their descendants can regain
full Thakali status after three generations of intermarriage with pure Thakalis. Also, through adoption or fictive kin (*mit*) relationships, non-Thakali
may be accepted in limited ways as Thakali during their lifetimes. In these

FIGURE 5.7 *Khimi* above the village of Kobang in Thaksatsae

cases, however, truly penetrating the boundary—being accepted as an an-cestor—likewise requires three generations of intermarriage.

While the rules seem clear, in fact, many of the Thakali have an ambig-uous status. One reason for this is the increasing frequency of marriages between Thakali and non-Thakali. Many of these mixed marriages have involved individuals from very prominent Thakali families. In fact, the great-est frequency of mixed marriages in the past two decades has probably been within the *subba* families. Many of these individuals have actively sought to acquaint their children with Thakali cultural practices and to involve them within Thakali society. A Kathmandu architect descended from a prominent *subba* family brought his daughters by a Brahman wife to Lha Phewa in 1993. They stood out not because they were from a mixed marriage but because they were among a small group outfitted in traditional Thakali dress. This kind of open activity has helped advanced discussion among the Thak-ali about the relative importance of descent versus culture in defining who they are as individuals and as a group. While membership in most, but not all, Thakali social organizations in the past two decades has been defined in terms of descent rather than culture,[22] many Thakali openly argue that if Thakali cultural practices are to survive they, as a community, may need more openly to include those of mixed descent who nevertheless adhere to key Thakali cultural practices.

Some informants—generally pure (N: *suddha*) Thakali—insist that the boundaries marked by rules of descent are impermeable, and they illustrated this by telling stories of individuals who were adopted as Thakali. There are numerous stories of non-Thakalis who have been granted some status as Thakalis during their lifetimes. However, given the emphasis that can be and is placed on purity of descent by many Thakali, it would be surprising to find non-Thakalis who had achieved equal social status with so-called pure Thakalis. In fact, informants generally responded to my queries about non-Thakalis who allegedly became Thakali by adamantly denying that these individual were accepted as Thakali and scornfully attributing the claim to some rival's imagination. For these informants, the measure of acceptance as Thakali had to span more than one generation: for an outsider to be truly accepted as Thakali, his or her children would have to be fully accepted within the community.

One scholar, however, has claimed that some non-Thakalis were given "full Thakali status" (Manzardo 1978:90 n. 12). By "full Thakali status" this scholar seems to mean acceptance within the Thaksatsae Thakali social sphere, participation in ancestor worship, and admission to the *thimten*, the sacred hearth in wealthy Thaksatsae homes in Thak Khola where the ancestor worship is performed. As I have described it here, "full Thakali status" would also include acceptance within the boundaries created by rules of descent, that is, permission to deposit the individual's bone fragment in the *khimi*, acceptance of his or her offspring as Thakali, and recognition of the individual, once deceased, as an ancestor.[23] While some non-Thakalis have been treated socially as Thakalis by members of a particular subclan—that is, they were referred to as Thakali and included in ritual and social interactions—few have been considered to be Thakali by members of other subclans, and even more rarely have their children found marriage partners among the Thaksatsae Thakali or their bone fragments been deposited in the *khimi*.[24] In effect, adoption entails full Thakali status only for the course of the adoptee's lifetime; it neither ensures that the individual will become an ancestor nor that his children will be accepted by members of other clans as Thakali and thus treated as eligible or desirable marriage partners.

Thakali boundaries are permeable in a more limited sense through ties of fictive kinship. While there is no formalized way in which a non-Thakali can be initiated into the group and given a full Thakali status that entails membership in a clan and in a *phobe* and full acceptance of his or her children as Thakali, even if that individual's spouse is Thakali, Thakalis willingly and frequently establish close relationships with non-Thakalis, formalizing *mit* (N: ritual friend) relationships or informally treating an outsider as a "brother."[25] *Mit* are welcomed by the extended family of their partners as if they have the same social standing as those partners.[26] These relationships frequently extend over several generations; thus children of individuals who considered themselves to be *mit* will continue to treat each other as family.

As some of my informants noted, the obvious paradox of a rigid calculation of descent is that there are increasingly fewer pure Thakalis. Most of the Thakali population, in fact, falls within the categories of *mang*, *pumi*, or *celang melang*, where their right to participate fully in some Thakali

FIGURE 5.8 Two Thakali women in traditional dress in the *thimten* of a subba family house in Tukche

rituals or to have their bone fragments placed in the *khimi* may be open to challenge. Consequently, the boundaries of descent, though rigidly drawn in theory, cannot be rigidly enforced without excluding most of the population.

Subclan Rites: *Jho Khane*

Each subclan usually has a *gamba*, an individual who keeps the documents listing each subclan member and manages the group's fund (*guthi*) and holds his post for one year. With an assistant (*gundal*) or two, the *gamba* does most of the preparation for the *jho khane* (N), or *jho cawa* (T), the yearly gathering of the named patrilineal subclans.[27] Most subclans hold feasts once a year, and each household is expected to send at least one member to attend; some subclans charge a fine to households that fail to send a representative.[28] These feasts are often held in Thaksatsae in the Nepali month of Asoj (September-October) around the time of the Hindu festival of Dasain, but there are numerous exceptions: some are held outside Thak Khola, and some in months other than Asoj. Some subclans hold them in the same location and at the same time year after year, while others rotate both the time and the place. Because most of these feasts are held in Thaksatsae, attendance by migrants has been irregular. As a consequence, the ties many migrants have to their subclans have loosened; in some cases, they no longer pay fines and no longer attend festivals, and their descendants are not recorded on the subclan registers. While few Thakalis can identify all the families in their subclans, in the 1980s many migrants did not know the names of their own subclan.[29] As the Thakali have spread across Nepal, it is uncommon to find subclans in which all the members have met each other face-to-face.

In cases of dissension within the subclan or in cases where the subclan has grown unusually large, groups have segmented along lineage lines, with one segment forming a new named subclan (see, for example, the cases discussed in the notes to table 2.1). Sometimes this simply means that the new group takes a new name, meets separately, and maintains its own *guthi* funds or fields. In other cases, particularly where the cause of division was dissension, one group will maintain the original *khimi*, and the splinter group will construct a new one.[30]

A group that has segmented but still shares a common ossuary often meets separately for the *jho khane* feast. For instance, the Sherchan

Dhom *phobe* is now split into three groups.[31] The first split occurred when migrants in Khani Khuwa became disgruntled with the attitude of the Dhom *phobe dhom*, who had became increasingly reluctant to travel to Khani Khuwa to perform rituals. Members in this area demanded their share of the subclan funds, established their own fund, and organized a separate yearly feast. This segment now includes more than thirty-five households and is supported by a fund worth more than one hundred thousand rupees that is circulated among the members at interest. The interest pays for a yearly feast held in the *bazār* of Burtibang in Baglung District. The second split in the subclan arose from personal argument between the descendants of two brothers who subsequently decided to separate their *khimi*: one branch, whose members were formerly residents of Tukche and closely connected—as *dhom* to the *subba* lineage—left Thaksatsae and now resides in Pokhara; the other includes households in the towns of Kasauli, Bhairawa, and Kobang. Members of these two branches came together at a funerary service in Bhairawa in April 1984 and made plans to collect money to refurbish a reunited *khimi*. Some members have also written to members of the Dhom *phobe* branch in Burtibang expressing interest in uniting all three branches, but others have reservations about this move.

Lha Phewa and Thakali Clans

Every twelve years members of all four clans gather to worship the clan deities (T: *lha phewa*, literally, "the appearance of the gods").[32] For this festival some of the named subclans have specific tasks, and each Thakali household, even those located outside Thaksatsae, is expected to send a male participant. For the duration of the festival each clan establishes a head-quarters in the village of Larjung where clan members coming from other areas may find lodging or food whenever they choose.[33]

As I have discussed in earlier chapters, Thakali clans are exogamous, patrilineal descent groups, membership in which is determined by birth and reinforced by ritual. Each clan has its own origin myth, deity, ancestor (*khe*), temple, common property or fund (*guthi*), and officers.[34] The unity of each clan and its interdependence with the other three are reinforced through periodic rituals that venerate the clan gods; the origin myths of the Thakalis make clear that while the veneration of the clan god is the responsibility of the members of each particular clan, veneration of all four gods is necessary for the well-being of the entire society. The images of the gods are four masks that are kept in their own temples in Thaksatsae, and propitiation of the gods can only be done in Thak Khola.

Each clan has two officials whose responsibilities are largely ceremonial and associated with the Lha Phewa ceremony. The propitiation of each clan god and the guardianship of the origin myth (*rhab*) of the clan ancestor (*khe*) are the responsibility of the hereditary clan *pāre*; each clan selects its *pāre* from a particular subclan. The clan *gamba* (Tib.: *rgan pa*, "old man, headman"), together with a committee, oversees all the practical arrangements for the Lha Phewa festival. The *gamba* is selected with the approval of the clan members and usually holds the post until he dies. The position is theoretically open to any adult male of the clan but frequently passes from father to son.[35]

Prior to 1993 the attendance of migrants at Lha Phewa had been irregular, but the festival still held significance for migrant Thakali, and interviews conducted in the 1980s indicated that most male Thakalis resident in Baglung and Myagdi Districts attended at least once in their lifetime. Those who are members of subclans with designated ritual functions attend more regularly. From Khani Khuwa, members of the Bhattachan Bara Ghorche *phobe* and both Dyatan *phobe*, for example, have sent representatives to the past ten Lha Phewa celebrations. Attendees at the 1993 performance all agreed that there were more migrant Thakalis in attendance than there had been at any previous festival in memory.

In the past, each clan had income-producing common property that was used to pay for the twelve-year festival. Today, many of the clan lands have been sold and replaced with a common fund that is administered by a member of the clan who lends the capital to clan members at a set rate of interest that may vary from 10 to 15 percent. The interest on the capital is used to finance the Lha Phewa festival.

Migration and Descent Group Rituals

Clan membership clearly continues to have importance in Khani Khuwa and other migrant areas. Most clan members use their clan name as a surname, and all clan members consider all other clan members to be relatives falling under the general category of *dājyu-bhāi* (N: literally "brothers," used to designate patrilineal relatives), however distant. Membership in a clan precludes sexual or marital relations with another clan member even when no common descent can be traced. Participation in clan rituals by members of migrant households requires that at least one member of a household make the trip to Thak Khola and the knowledge, stories, and contacts that result from these trips help to strengthen the sense of belonging of other household members.

Still, as should be apparent by now, the effect of migration on the organization of clans and *phobes* has been considerable, though there was apparently no major effect on the performance of clan festivals and *phobe* feasts and rituals until the migration of the 1960s. After 1960 there was considerable uncertainty about who would return for the celebration of the twelve-year festival in 1968, and many questioned the ability of the Thak Khola residents to continue to perform the festivals without the financial support of the wealthy families who had left. At first, there was diminished interest in performing the rites in Thak Khola, but now the migrants have begun to show interest in renewing many of the previous traditions and begun to formalize procedures to raise funds from all the Thakali communities to support what are perceived as traditional activities. Some subclans are relatively better organized than others and have maintained close ties among members despite migration; in addition to the Sherchan Dhom *phobe*, other well-organized subclans in Khani Khuwa include the Bhattachan Bhara Ghorche, the Dyatan and Chang Mhirki *phobes*, the Tulachan Jhong Man *phobe*, the Sherchan Lha Khang Dhungi and Norje *phobes*, and the Gauchan Ghocetan *phobe*.

The ritual landscape of the Thakali is tremendously varied but contains within it a set of rituals—Torongla, *kul devtā puja*, mortuary rites, and *khimi tapne*—that all Thakali acknowledge as important, despite the many variations in style with which these rites are performed. This set of rituals provides a shared battleground within which identity and authenticity are contested. The sharing of a ritual battleground helps to create and maintain extensive ties between migrant and nonmigrant Thakalis and among Thakalis within various migrant communities. The parameters of participation are contested and fluid, but for the most part this ritual field encompasses all the Thakali— including those who fall into ambiguous categories of *mang, pumi, celang melang,* or Khuwale—while generally excluding those of other groups from Thak Khola (like those from Panchgaon, for example).

6   Codifying Culture

The formation of a national Thakali organization in 1983 was the culmination of a series of attempts to formalize the Thakali community after migration had dispersed it among a wide range of locales in Nepal. This attempt to unify and codify cultural behavior that had become increasingly varied and open to ambiguous interpretations made public the contestations among the various Thakali factions more generally and specifically between those attempting to unite or reunite the *samaj* and the divergent interests of local communities.

Codification and Contestation

The tension between cooperation and competition was apparent in the processes of formally organizing local Thakali communities that began with the growth of the Thakali population in urban areas. The first formal Thakali local organization was the Thakali Samaj Sudhar Sangh founded in Pokhara in 1954.[1] This remained the only formal Thakali organization outside Thak Khola until a similar organization was organized in Bhairawa in 1973. In the 1970s formal organizations were later formed in Kathmandu and Kasauli.[2]

Before 1990 formal ethnic associations were not common in Nepal. The few that were organized—for example, the Tharu Kalyan Karini Sabha, which was first registered in 1950; the Nepal Tamang Ghedung, which was first formed in 1956; the Newar associations; the Nepal Bhasha Manka Kala, organized in June 1979; and the Nepal Magar Langali Sangh, formed in 1982—had to demonstrate the social nature of their activities and establish that they were not political or communal organizations. Thakali associations were also careful to stress their social and thus nonpolitical character.

Criteria for membership in the pre-1983 local Thakali organizations varied somewhat from locale to locale, but these criteria generally derived from assumptions of either shared descent or shared culture. In the Pokhara organization membership was restricted to "that individual or family who can assure the Managing Committee of being Thakali on the basis of language, culture, and morals."[3] The emphasis on culture at this point in time is interesting, but given the differences in opinion about Thakali "culture" and "morals," this criterion could hardly be called specific. In fact, the Pokhara organization considered all Thakali households in Pokhara to be members of the organization by virtue of their residence in the area. Even though the organization legislated a household tax or dues on its members, nonpayment did not result in nonmembership.

In most but not all instances membership in local Thakali organizations was effectively restricted not by references to "language, culture, and morals" but to members of one of the four Thakali clans from Thaksatsae. There were both formal and informal exceptions to this pattern, however: in Bhairawa, for example, families from Panchgaon were also accepted as formal members of the organization. While in most other areas Panchgaonle were not formal members, in almost all locales they were welcome to participate in community festivals such as Desh Puja, a community festival, and Torongla, the archery festival. This changed after 1983, when the national association specified that only members of the four clans could join the local Thakali *samaj* organizations. The number of local individuals thus formally excluded was very small, but the principle was seen as important and led to considerable controversy. Initially, many Thakali communities protested by refusing to sponsor local celebrations of Torongla. Over the past fifteen years this issue has reemerged from time to time as the Thakali have continued to debate the criteria for membership.

Over the years, these local organizations have performed a number of important functions for local Thakali communities. The most important may be the most intangible; they have provided a focus for the community, a cultural center for yearly festivals and other rituals, and in effect have helped to create a community from what would otherwise be simply a number of households scattered across an urban area. Some of the local communities have taken bold steps to reform traditional rituals. These reforms were apparently more concerned with convenience and with cutting the costs associated with particular rituals than with their religious content.[4]

Local community organizations have also overseen local rotating credit associations and have provided a forum for the resolution of disputes associated with these, a service for which organizations often extract a fee from each *dhikur* in their areas. They have also often provided social services both for needy members of the local Thakali community and for the urban community at large. This has most often taken the form of sponsoring poor Thakalis in local rotating credit associations or providing a needy family with the food concession at the yearly celebration of Desh Puja or Torongla. The Pokhara organization has also acted to "try to eradicate misunderstanding and internal conflict among Thakalis."[5] Conflicts between members of the Thakali community have been heard before the managing committee, composed of the officers of the organization.

The head of the local organization was initially called *mukiyā* in keeping with the tradition then prevalent in Thaksatsae wherein this term was used to refer to the headman of each village. Other migrant communities also have had *mukiyā*, either informally recognized or formally designated through social organizations. The original Pokhara organization designated three other officers, a secretary (N: *sachib*) and two *kumdals*, who visited each household in turn to discuss issues of importance to the community. Since 1983 local organizations have followed the example of the Thakali Sewa Samiti (National Thakali Service Organization) and replaced the position of *mukiyā* with that of *sabhapati* (N: chairman). Not much changed but the name: the responsibilities of the position remain essentially the same, and the *sabhapati* is still often referred to informally as *mukiyā*.

The authority and power of these local organizations remain contested, and their edicts can never be enforced nor behavior controlled. Manzardo and Sharma overstated the case when they argued that decisions of the Pokhara organization's "executive board" were "binding on all Thakalis" and that refusal to comply with "the board's orders" could result in a "complete social and economic boycott on the part of the other Thakalis" (1975:29). They also noted that the managing committee of the organization "is empowered to levy a stiff fine" on those who circumvent its authority (35). These contingency punishments imply more power than local organizations have in fact: in Kathmandu, Bhairawa, and Butwal, Thakali repeatedly stressed to me the powerlessness of the local organization in the face of recalcitrant members. Fines could be imposed but could not be collected if the member was unwilling, and social boycotts were easier to threaten than to execute. The tendency was to lead by example and to seek approval by acclamation: typically, leaders try to build a strong consensus before attempting any reform. Rules that appear to be imposed by a single interest group meet with stiff resistance and threaten the dissolution of the unity so vital to the continuation of these organizations.

Practices have often been less uniform than the rules imply. The existence of gaps between reform and practice is not new among the Thakali and can be traced back to the religious reforms pushed by the Tukche merchants in the 1920s. Prior to 1983, whatever influence these local urban organizations had was limited to urban areas and has little significance for migrant Thakalis residing in rural areas.

Beginning in the 1980s, a phenomenon in urban areas has been the formation of subgroups that represent more specific groups of individuals—youth, women, and so forth—whose interests are not well represented by the parent organization, which is dominated by the male heads of Thakali households. Other individuals within these households who are affected by the decisions of the organization are often dissatisfied that they play no role in the decision-making process. Subgroups run their own activities and raise funds independently of the main organization; for instance, the youth organization in Kathmandu raises money through donations accumulated by singing from house to house during the Hindu festival of Tihar. These funds are used to sponsor the social services run by the youth group for the Thakali community, support a library and study center for Thakali students, and supply food and clothing to needy families in Kathmandu. Although these groups are organized independently of the Thakali social organizations, they remain associated with them.

Forming a National *Samaj*

The attempt to reunite the widely dispersed Thakali community through the creation of a national ethnic association began in the late 1970s and was initiated by members of the *subba* lineage, most of whom by then resided in the main urban areas of Nepal. A variety of factors motivated this initiative. One early motivation for the movement lay with the desire of some members of the wealthy merchant families to regain some political control over the Thakali community, control they had relinquished when they had migrated from Tukche in the 1960s. While the *subba* lineage had dominated the Pokhara Thakali *samaj* association, and later the Kathmandu association, its members had been unable to regain the political influence or power they had had in Thak Khola during the Rana period and before their emigration. When the government shifted to the *panchayat* system in the 1960s, the *subbas* had already begun to pursue interests elsewhere, and they were without a local political constituency. By the 1980s the *subba* family had no remaining influence in Panchgaon and very little on the council of thirteen headman in Thaksatsae or in the local *panchayat*.

In the few years preceding the formation of the Thakali Sewa Samiti, the Thakali had become extremely conscious of themselves as a group. Beginning just before the 1981 performance of Lha Phewa, the twelve-year festival, individual Thakali began to publish articles, booklets, calendars, and other materials concerning Thakali traditions and history. This spate of publications continued for a few years after the 1981 Lha Phewa celebration: the Thakali journal *Khāngalo* began publication at this time.[6]

When a national organization was proposed again just after Lha Phewa in 1981, support for its formation came from many segments of Thakali society: Thakalis in urban areas welcomed the idea of improved contacts with Thakalis in Thaksatsae, the Thakali homeland, and to a lesser extent with Thakali communities in other regions; Thakalis in Thaksatsae wanted migrant Thakalis to bear a fair share of the costs of the complex of rituals and festivals held in Thak Khola; and all Thakalis stood to gain from the clarification and strengthening of their social identity in a society like Nepal, where ethnic or caste identity and differences can critically affect an individual's place in the social fabric.

Early attempts to form a national organization failed to achieve consensus on cultural, social, and organizational details. Disagreement over religious orientation and deep-rooted resentment against the descendants of the *subbas* and the wealthy merchant families of Tukche were two reasons for this failure. Often these two reasons were related as arguments over religious differences, which pitted middle-class Thakalis and their orientation toward the Thakali *dhom* against the *subba* descendants and their support for Hinduism, often reflected deeper political conflicts between the former *subbas* and their allies, on the one hand, and families who had made their fortunes more recently, on the other.

In November 1982 (Magh 15, 2039), a self-selected, ad hoc planning committee met and agreed on the procedures for the formation of a national organization to be called the Thakali Sewa Samiti (National Thakali Service Organization). Four sub-committees—the constitution subcommittee, the economic subcommittee, the social subcommittee, and the cultural sub-committee—drafted the relevant sections of a proposed set of rules. After these were published and widely circulated, a meeting was set for April 1983, in Pokhara, to approve the reports of the planning committee and the sub-committees. Participants were solicited and invited from among well-known Thakalis resident in diverse local communities across the country.

The fifteen members of the ad hoc committee did not represent a cross-section of the Thakali community: they came from the five areas considered important by the prominent Thakali families who organized the committee: four from Pokhara, four from Kathmandu, two from Bhairawa, one from Kasauli/Butwal, and four from Thaksatsae. There were no representatives from the more rural but heavily populated areas of Baglung, Myagdi, Gulmi, Parbat, Palpa, Syangja, or Chitwan Districts. Ten of the fifteen were Sher-chans, three Tulachans, one Gauchan, and one Bhattachan, and, of these, nine were either descendants of the former *subbas* or their affines. This disproportionate representation was at odds with the geographical distribu-tion of the Thakali population and the relative size of the four clans.

Institutionalizing Contestation

At noon on April 25, 1983 (Baisakh 12, 2040), more than fifty Thakali representatives from across the country gathered in the community center belonging to the Pokhara Thakali *samaj*. The actual number of participants varied from day to day as new representatives arrived and a few departed. The organizers of the meeting—the officers of the ad hoc committee—sat at a table along one wall facing the rest of the delegates, who sat on carpets on the floor. Delegates rose to speak when they were recognized by the chairman and frequently when they were not.

The *subba* lineage was well represented: the chairman, Anagman Sher-chan, was the oldest descendent of the *subbas*; the steering committee in-cluded two of his cousins; and among the delegates were two more cousins, a brother, a nephew, a niece, the widow of another cousin, and men who had married daughters of the *subba* lineage. Furthermore, the majority of participants were from the urban areas where interest in the creation of a national organization was strongest: the Thakali communities of Pokhara, Kathmandu, and Bhairawa, which collectively provided more than 60 percent of the delegates, were overrepresented, while areas like Myagdi District, which had no representatives, and Baglung District, which had two, were grossly underrepresented. Nevertheless, the representation of subbas and urbanites was proportionately less than it had been on the ad hoc planning committee. Part of the explanation for the overrepresentation from urban areas was simply that these areas were closer to the meeting site and transportation—accessibility in a few hours by road rather than in a few days by foot—was considerably easier; in fact, all the presiding officers of the planning committee and fully 75 percent of the participants in the general meeting came from areas accessible by road. Other participants came from Thaksatsae (six representatives), Butwal (six), Baglung District (two), Parbat District (one), Palpa District (one), Chitwan District (one), Syangja (two), Nepalgunj (one), and Dhanghadi (one). The representation at the meeting of each of the four clans, on the other hand, was close to their actual representation in the population. In general, women were underrepresented, but they were relatively well represented from urban areas: nearly 25 percent of the delegates were women, and all but one of these came from the urban areas of Pokhara, Kathmandu, and Bhairawa; the other came from the Terai town of Nepalgunj in far western Nepal.

The meeting was presided over by officers who represented established political power among the Thakali, but discussions often evolved from debates over issues to challenges to authority. There was no balloting: once the outcome was clear, decisions were made by acclamation, and elections results were recorded as unanimous. Debates were loosely regulated by reference to parliamentary procedures. There were impassioned exchanges, occasional bedlam, and frequent resort to humor, both to make points and to ease tensions when the debate became passionate. Heated presentations and shouting matches were not long sustained, but individuals dissatisfied with the direction a discussion was taking would raise an issue repeatedly. The meeting was scheduled to end on April 29 but had to be extended by another day in order to complete the negotiations.

The meeting provided an opportunity to play out in a public forum the underlying tensions of Thakali society, tensions that became increasingly apparent through the development of debates, the emergence of various factions, and the revelation of hidden agendas. Debates and disagreements returned to the same few substantive points: religion, cost cutting, and the allocation of representatives and fees. Debates over the first of these—religion—continually revolved around the questions "What are we?" "What is our history? "What are our traditions? "Are we Thakuri or Bhote?" If the meeting had a theme or a quest, these questions best characterize it. Much of the debate reflected sincere disagreement over substantive issues and honest confusion about ritual practices, but it readily dissolved into what sometimes might have seemed to be petty bickering over obscure points for the sake of argument. In any case, debates about religion, representation, and money were often thinly disguised challenges to the authority assumed by the ad hoc committee members in general and the descendants of the *subba* lineage specifically.

The first day of the meeting began calmly with requisite rituals honoring photographs of the king and queen of Nepal, the Thakali goddess Narijhowa (though for reasons that will become clear, many of the representatives insisted on referring to her as Mahalaxmi), and the four clan gods. This was followed by an award ceremony for special achievements by individual Thakalis. The rest of the day was devoted to a series of speeches outlining the purpose of the meeting and the history of the Thakali. Some of the speakers made references to descriptions of the Thakali by foreign scholars, and all stressed the need to determine "who we are" and "what our history is."

Little progress was made toward answering these questions until the second day. The morning session of April 26 began with an item-by-item review of the set of rules proposed by the November ad hoc planning committee and the various subcommittees. Among other subjects, these rules included detailed descriptions of who could be regarded as Thakali, the appropriate timing for rituals, who should and should not be invited to ritual occasions and when to invite them, the limits on costs for some common rituals, the allocation of representatives for the proposed *kendriya samiti*—the central administrative committee of the proposed organization—an itemization of the proposed organization's estimated costs, and an itemization of the fees to be allocated to regional Thakali organizations.

Factions

Factions among the delegation were clearly discernible by the second day. The dominant faction was composed of those who had organized the

meeting: it included most of the ad hoc planning committee, eight of the
nine descendants of the *subba* lineage, their affines, and several others, including the *mukiyā* of the Pokhara *samaj*. These individuals were descended
from families who had exercised considerable power in the Thakali community, and they included among them the most avid advocates of Hindu
dharma. This group controlled the meeting and remained on center stage;
its views were thoroughly presented, and its members were able to put forth
their ideas as if they represented the status quo. Since they had invited many
of the delegates to the convention and selected representatives from among
the urban populations most beholden to them, they could claim widespread
support. However, widespread resentment against what was perceived as
their high-handed style triggered considerable opposition.

One of the most vocal and vociferous of the interest groups that emerged
included a number of young, self-made, financially secure young men who
opposed the *subba* group on almost every issue. These Young Turks, almost
all residents of Pokhara, eloquently argued their perspective, and their artic-
ulateness persuaded a number of delegates to adopt their point of view. Their
constant interruptions created a great number of procedural obstacles for
the *subba* group, eventually forcing important compromises on the issues of
religion and representation.

A third distinct faction included nonmigrant Thakalis, that is, those who
still resided in Thaksatsae. These Thakalis had a number of specific concerns: they were worried that the reorganization of the Thakali community
would lead to a shift in focus from Thaksatsae to Kathmandu, and they were
concerned about the implications of this for the shrines and rituals located
in Thaksatsae and the costs associated with these.

Other factions formed among participants from rural areas, representatives of the youth group, and a group of Kathmandu-resident moderates.
These groups allied themselves with the *subba* group, the Young Turks, or
the nonmigrants on an issue-by-issue basis. None of these other groups consistently held a unique perspective, but any position taken by a member of
any one of them was usually supported by the other members of that faction.

Tradition

One concern shared by each of these factions was tradition, but their views
of Thakali tradition and customs varied considerably. The controversial

issue was raised early on the second day when one delegate challenged the proposed rules and inquired, "What is our dharma [religion, duty, religious duty]: are we Hindu, or are we Buddhist?" Discussion returned to this question throughout the rest of the weeklong meeting, even when the particular topic under discussion had little direct bearing on religion. Cries of "out of order" by some delegates encouraged the chairman of the ad hoc committee to stifle attempts to introduce issues not currently under discussion. Some argued that the Thakali should return to their traditional Buddhism; others that the Thakali should restore tradition, whatever it is; still others argued that they should embrace Hinduism because it was the religion of their Thakuri forefathers. The more progressive took the position that the Thakali should embrace Hinduism as a practical choice for the future, while a few argued that questions pertaining to religious practice should be left to individuals to decide for themselves.

For many delegates, the real issue was not tradition but political influence within Thakali society: tradition was merely one of the issues that served as a battleground for political legitimacy. The formal adoption of Hindu reforms, for instance, would confirm the lifestyles and reforms already followed in some urban areas, most particularly by the descendants of the rich Tukche merchant families, and help dust off and reinforce the old claim that the Thakali were descended from a Thakuri, and thus Hindu, prince. The *subba* group was quick to sense the strong sentiment among the delegates for tradition and couched its appeals for religious reform as a return to tradition, albeit an older tradition, or a more appropriate tradition, or the tradition of the Hansa Raja. The opponents of the *subba* group sought to reinstate or officially sanction the Thakali ḍhom as *the* traditional Thakali religious practitioner, perceiving that this would effectively isolate the *subba* group and mark them as outside the mainstream of Thakali society, as sellouts to the dominant Hindu culture, and as reformers willing to exchange customs for economic and political opportunities.

The positions taken with respect to religious orientation and tradition were not always politically motivated; among the participants were individuals who sincerely embraced Hindu dharma or Buddhist dharma, and others who sincerely advocated the exclusive use of the Thakali ḍhom. Sincerity, however, had little to do with knowledge. Those who asserted that the Thakalis were traditionally Buddhist generally had little experience with or knowledge of the Tibetan Buddhism once followed in Thak Khola, and their assertion that the Thakali were Buddhist merely reflected the stories their fathers and grandfathers had related to them about Thakali traditions.

The theme of tradition recurred through the third day's discussions, which were entirely devoted to the subject of religion, or dharma. By the afternoon of the third day, tempers were short, and, in an angry exchange about the appropriate role for Thakali *dhoms* and Brahman priests for various rituals, several of the Young Turks insisted they would leave a house if a Brahman priest were called to conduct a ritual, while members of the *subba* group retorted that they would leave if a Brahman priest were not called. After several shouted exchanges, the representative of the Thakali youth organization of Kathmandu respectfully directed a question about "the real or true dharma" of the Thakali to the elders who were present. He expressed the view that there was considerable confusion among the young about Thakali tradition and that most young people felt that "the traditions of the Thakali must be maintained if life is to have meaning." "But what is Thakali tradition," he asked, noting that there were apparently contradictory arguments concerning the history of the Thakali, including the story that they were descended from a Thakuri prince and the claim by members of other *jāts* that the Thakali were Bhote. He went on to argue that there was no reason for continued subterfuge and challenged the elders to state the truth, saying, "If we are Bhote, let us embrace that; if we are Thakuri, let us embrace that."

This appeal received a long reply from the leader of the Thakali organization of Pokhara, a man who had been trained as a Thakali *dhom* but now advocated that the Thakali community follow Hindu dharma. In a forceful and dramatic style, which often seemed to be directed to the dissidents and Young Turks, he began by recounting the story of the Hansa Raja, the son of the Thakuri raja of Jumla and the putative ancestor of the Thakali. The Thakalis became Buddhist, he argued, only because of the close proximity of Thaksatsae to Buddhist areas, and moreover, he continued, the Thakalis are not true Buddhist. For proof of this he referred to the non-Buddhist practices of the Thakalis *dhom* and the worship of Narijhowa. He went on to note that the Thakalis don't practice these religions in an orthodox way and that there is no clear tradition and no consensus on religious matters. For these reasons, he felt that Hindu dharma—which was, he claimed, the dharma of the Thakali ancestors—should be selected as the practical alternative. The last part of his presentation was interrupted by a delegate from Khani Khuwa, the *rastriya* (national) *panchayat* member from Baglung

District, who shouted to be heard over the speaker's voice: "We [Thakalis] are Buddhists, and even my father used to say that we are Buddhists."

This exchange was cut short by a sudden hailstorm, which made such an unbearable clatter against the corrugated metal roof that the meeting had to be delayed until the storm ended. When the hail ceased and the meeting resumed, Subba Anagman Sherchan, the chairman of the ad hoc planning committee, stood and said that the hailstorm was a sign that the ancestors did not want to hear this kind of argument among them. Despite this observation, the disagreements did not abate for long.

Subsequent subjects of discussion ranged from cutting the costs entailed in ritual performance through the revision of these rituals to clarification about the performance of specific rituals, but they always returned to the issue of dharma. Discussions about cutting costs arose so frequently that one participant finally complained, "Which is to be our criterion for reform: dharma or money?" Disagreements over where, when, and by whom a particular ritual should be performed were frequently recast as debates about the true dharma of the Thakali. Discussions about the details of ritual performances included who should be invited, the appropriate religious practitioner, when the event should take place, and how long it should last. Detailed discussions covered issues like the amount of money and goods to be given by both sides of a wedding party, the people who should and could be visited by the bride and groom after marriage, and the custom of stealing the shoes of the groom's brothers during a wedding.

Some of these issues reveal regional variations in the evolution of Thakali rituals. For example, in Thaksatsae and in Khani Khuwa, Thakalis continued to follow the custom of having specific categories of women weep in front of the *mhendo*, the pot or bamboo structure that holds the bone of the deceased during the funeral rites. This custom occurs at different points in the funerary rituals and in a slightly different style in the two areas. In urban Thakali communities, however, this custom is no longer practiced. Some delegates, particularly the urban advocates for Hinduism, felt that the community was better off without it; they argued that when women wept in front of the *mhendo* they were frequently satirical and often accused people of wrong-doing, thus initiating long, bitter quarrels that continued for years. Others, including many representatives from Thaksatsae and Khani Khuwa, noted that the Thakali shamans specifically called for weeping at certain points during the rites, and they asked whether banning this practice wouldn't make the death ceremonies incomplete. Still others supported the practice with emotional appeals, and a rural woman asked, "If you can't cry on the occasion of death, when can you cry?" Women representatives from Kathmandu noted that crying in front of the *mhenḍo* was a lost art, one no longer practiced by Thakali women residing in urban areas, and observed that were the tradition to be reinstated these women would have to be reinstructed.

The frequent requests by delegates for clarification about how a ritual should be performed reflected the widely held view that there was a single Thakali tradition that should be followed, that other Thakalis were following it, and that the questioner would, too, if only he or she knew how. Pressed to identify this tradition, many delegates called it Buddhism, but, as the leader of the Pokhara Thakali association had noted, the ritual practices of the Thakali had little in common with the more orthodox Tibetan Buddhism practiced by their northern neighbors in Thak Khola. Delegates, such as the Baglung District Rastriya *panchayat* member, whose families had never used a Buddhist priest but who had been raised on the notion that the Thakali were Buddhist, insisted that "we [Thakali] were originally Buddhist and should use a lama" and that "we [Thakali] have our own homeland and our own customs, why do you [the advocates of Hinduism] want these Hindu customs?" The advocates of Hindu dharma persisted with their contention that "the issue of our [Thakali] religion is unresolved," and they insisted that the best course of action was to decide on customs that were best for the future.

A clear difference emerged between those who advocated that the association adopt Hinduism and Hindu rituals as the appropriate form of Thakali ritual performance and those who were resisted the formal adoption of Hindu ritual practices. Many of the delegates were willing to accept that some Thakali, under some circumstances, followed Hindu ritual practices, but they were not willing to adopt these formally at the expense of traditional Thakali rituals. One participant offered the widespread opinion that he didn't think it was "wrong" to include the use of a Brahman priest "from time to time." He illustrated this with an example of how he had obtained a *mit*, a ritual friend, through the influence of a Brahman priest. That the relationship had been financially rewarding indicated to him that this kind of informal interaction should be acceptable.

Many delegates were distressed by the disharmony caused by the issue of dharma, and many appeals were made to the most vocal participants in this debate. These included statements such as: "If we continue with this

dissension, we will have nothing; we will have no *samaj*"; "We are supposed
to live in harmony"; "Why are we so much against dharma?" and "The statement that 'we [Thakalis] have no dharma' makes me sad." More moderate
delegates continually pressed for compromise and argued that the disagreement about religious orientation was misplaced: "This argument is unneces-
sary," argued one delegate who had been trained as a religious practitioner,
"Thakali ritual does not require any of the practitioners or details that divide
us today." And another asked, "Why do we contradict each other? Why don't
we leave these religious matters to the individual?" As it became increasingly
apparent that no consensus could be reached on most religious questions, this
position gained considerable support among the delegates and became the
basis for some of the compromises that allowed the meeting to succeed.

The conflicts over dharma that had evolved between the established
subba group and the Young Turks and others continued into the fourth day
until, in a clever move by those opposed to the *subba* group, my presence
as an anthropologist and my use of a tape recorder to record these debates
became the issue over which the Young Turks chose to challenge the ad
hoc committee. As the dharma debate became particularly heated, one of
the women from Kathmandu attempted to soothe tempers by gently asking
the other participants to watch their language, reminding them that "a distinguished scholar" was present and tape-recording the proceedings. Immediately, some delegates shifted the debate from the subject from dharma,
asking, "Who invited him?" "Who gave the ad hoc committee the authority
to invite a non-Thakali to attend the meeting?" they asked. "If we can't speak
our minds freely here, what use can be served by this meeting?" An argument
over my presence as an anthropologist occupied the next hour, until the
challengers finally welcomed me as long as I turned off the tape recorder.[7]

When approached privately, the Young Turks who had challenged the ad
hoc committee on this issue stressed that they had no quarrel with me personally, neither with my presence nor with my taping; instead, they insisted
that their intent had only been to challenge the procedures of the ad hoc
committee. By the end of the fourth day, I was warmly rewelcomed and
formally reinvited to continue my research.[8] The chairman of the ad hoc
committee approached me individually and apologized for the situation,
while the Young Turks expressed satisfaction over their ability to limit the
authority of the ad hoc committee. The whole exchange encouraged other
delegates to express opinions contrary to the *subba* group. The last two days
of the meeting proceeded more smoothly, with fewer outbursts and growing

consensus, and there were indications that the members of the ad hoc planning committee had been humbled.[9] The *subba* group became increasingly
willing to compromise, and consensus was soon reached on vaguely worded
statements outlining cultural and social customs.

Representation

Conflict over unequal representation also recurred throughout the six
days of the meeting, and this issue, too, emerged as an offshoot of the emergence of clear factions and the debates over tradition. As noted earlier, representation at the meeting was biased in favor of the *subba* faction and the
advocates of Hinduism. Other factions pushed for representation that more
accurately reflected the distribution of the Thakali population. Doing so
would also likely increase the number of supporters of the *ḍhom* tradition
and opponents of the formal adoption of Hindu practices.

One of the representatives from Baglung District, Tejab Gauchan—then
the Rastriya *panchayat* member from that district—vehemently challenged
the proposed allotment of representatives to the central committee, arguing
that the size of the Thakali population in Baglung District justified an increase in the number of representatives proposed in the drafted constitution.
Arguments about representation met with little success: other delegates dismissed the claim that large numbers of Thakalis still resided in Baglung and
Myagdi Districts, and they cited the nonattendance of individuals from those
districts as evidence.[10] The dismissal of the Baglung delegate's claim based
on the relatively small number of participants attending from Myagdi and
Baglung Districts failed to take into consideration the relative inaccessibility
of particular geographic areas, the ease or difficulty of transportation, and
the relative lack of communication between communities in Kathmandu
and Pokhara and some local Thakali communities, particularly those in distant areas of Baglung and Myagdi Districts. The fact is that few individuals
from Baglung and Myagdi were invited to the meeting, and neither was their
attendance desired by the chief organizers.

The allocation of delegates to the central committee revealed a distinct
bias in favor of urban areas and, most particularly, in favor of areas that were
home to the organizers of the meeting (see table 6.1). Kathmandu, Pokhara,
and Bhairawa were all well represented. The success of the Parbat, Palpa,
Syangja, Chitwan, Nepalgunj, and Dhanghadi Thakali communities in

gaining representation on the *kendriya samiti* despite their small Thakali communities was due in part to the attendance of influential representatives from these communities at this organization meeting in Pokhara. In contrast, Thakali communities from the two districts of Khani Khuwa were grossly underrepresented in proportion to their populations. Part of the reason for this was the lack of adequate representation of these districts at the meeting. Baglung District had two representatives, one of whom was very influential (but, unfortunately, the influential participant left before the final debate over the issue of representation). Thakali communities in Myagdi District sent no representatives, not because no one was invited but because the invitations were individual rather than solicitations of community representatives, because those invited were old or infirm, and because the communities were not yet sufficiently organized or motivated to select alternative representatives.

The decisions taken at the 1983 Pokhara meeting were not based on population distribution figures—no accurate count was available at that time—but relied on the impressions of the delegates concerning the population distribution of Thakali society. The agreed-on allotment of representatives to each region represents not a deliberate deviation from actual population density in each region but the delegates' estimate of the distribution of the population of the Thakali community. Among the participants were several individuals who had previously resided in either Baglung or Myagdi District—including a former Rastriya *panchayat* member from Baglung District, two retired British Army officers now residing in Kasauli, and another residing in Dangidi—but while many of them expressed views on the question of dharma that typify the Khuwale perspective, none of them championed the issue of representation. This imbalance has been redressed somewhat over the years to provide for more delegates from Khani Khuwa, but the representation is still far from proportional.

A New Social Order

On the final day, after a delay to film the event for Nepali TV and the requisite rituals of draping the photographs of the king, the Queen, and the goddess Narijhowa with garlands of fresh flowers, the resolution of outstanding questions about the amount of money to be collected from each household, the number of representatives to be selected from each region for the

TABLE 6.1 Representation to the Central Committee Relative
to Population Distribution

Locale	Number of households in 1983	Number of delegates in 1983	Households per delegate in 1983	Number of delegates in 1993
Thaksatsae	290	4	73	2
Pokhara	121	3	40	2
Kathmandu	119	4	30	3
Bhairawa	37	2	18	1
Butwal	110	2	55	1
Baglung Jilla	253	2	127	2
Myagdi Jilla	280	2	140	3
Palpa Jilla	21	1	21	with Butwal
Syangja Jilla	27	1	27	with Pokhara
Parbat Jilla	55	1	55	1
Chitwan Jilla	20	1	20	1
Nepalgunj	12	1	12	1
Dhanghadi	8	1	8	1
Gulmi	53	–	–	1
Totals	1406	25	626	19

central committee, and the nomination of individuals for the central committee proceeded quietly and amicably. There were no dissenting votes; all elections of representatives and officers were unanimous.[11]

The Thakali Sewa Samiti was established as an association for "all Thakali," and the question "Who is Thakali?" was clearly and narrowly defined by the statement that a Thakali is an individual who belongs to one of the four Thakali clans: Sherchan, Bhattachan, Gauchan, and Tulachan; all others identifying themselves as Thakalis were thus explicitly excluded from membership in the association.

The association was established with two representative bodies: a general assembly and a central committee. A greater share of the representation to the sixty-one–member general assembly and the twenty-five–member central committee was drawn from rural areas than was originally proposed by the ad hoc planning committee (see tables 6.1 and 6.2). The result of this re-apportionment was a relative reduction in the influence of both the *subba* group and Thakali living in urban areas.

The delegates also effectively formalized the loss of real authority by the traditional council composed of the thirteen headman of the Thaksatsae council. Until 1983 the relationship of the council of thirteen headmen and the local associations in migrant communities had been unclear. In the early part of the century migrant communities had often looked to the council of thirteen headmen for guidance on cultural issues but had avoided the po-litical influence of the council. In the 1960s many of the wealthy merchant families who had controlled the council in the previous decades migrated to urban areas, where they set up competing institutions like the Pokhara and Kathmandu *samaj* associations. Despite the diminution of influence

TABLE 6.2 Representation to the General Assembly, 1983

Locale	Proposed by planning committee	Approved by delegates
Thaksatsae	18	8
Pokhara	17	7
Kathmandu	17	7
Bhairawa	11	5
Butwal (Kasauli)	10	6
Baglung District	7	5
Myagdi District	8	5
Palpa District	2	1
Syangja District	3	2
Parbat District	4	2
Chitwan District	3	2
Nepalgunj	2	1
Dhanghadi	2	1
Pyutan	0	1
Totals	104	53*

*Eight additional members were chosen at large, for a total of 61.

that had followed the migration of the wealthy merchant families and the establishment of *panchayat* political structures, the Thaksatsae council had continued to have symbolic importance as the traditional political institution and as the Thakali authority within the homeland. Effectively, the Mul Bandej, the principal rules or constitution of the Thakali Sewa Samiti, formalized the limited role now played by the Thaksatsae council.

The National Thakali Service Organization was given authority over all Thakali communities, while the council of the thirteen headmen was recognized as the official local authority for Thaksatsae. In effect, the council of thirteen headmen was given equal status to and no more authority than the other local Thakali organizations. In areas that had had local community organizations, these were disbanded and reformed according to the rules of the national organization. In communities that had no formal, local Thakali *samaj* organization prior to April 1983, new organizations were formed. The council of thirteen headmen, however, was neither disbanded nor reformed according to new rules.

Representatives to the general assembly and the central committee were originally drawn from fourteen geographical areas and not merely from the five represented at the November 1982 ad hoc meeting. Moreover, representation from these areas was more proportional to actual local populations than had been originally proposed.

Codified Culture

In terms of culture, the actions taken by the delegates were limited. The first version of the Mul Bandej reflected the compromises reached by the delegation. It detailed the correct performance of a few cultural practices while vaguely describing many aspects of Thakali cultural practices. The text only partially resolved the most controversial issues and left room for a wide latitude of individual interpretation.

The Mul Bandej is not a ritual primer: there are no instructions concerning the performance of rituals, their timing, the appropriate ritual specialists to be employed, or the obligation to perform them. It is instead a list of reforms, but reforms not of a uniform and widely practiced tradition but rather of specific regional practices that are themselves peculiar aberrations or modifications of practices believed to have been followed at some time in the past in Thak Khola.[12] In short, it is a document that can only be understood when considered in the context of the wide variety of Thakali regional practices.

The original Mul Bandej was limited to a detailed set of guidelines concerning rituals that occur at specific times within the course of an individual's life cycle. Rituals covered by the manual ranged from ceremonies peculiar to a specific region (for example, stealing the shoes of the groom's party in order to stop the marriage procession and extort money in exchange for the return of the shoes) to those specific to particular religious dharma (shaving the head as a sign of mourning and other practices related to ritual purity, for example), as well as those practiced, in various forms, by all Thakali.

Under the heading "Cultural Preservation" the text discusses aspects of both life-cycle and calendrical rituals and singles out a few rites for preservation. In the ensuing years efforts have been made to continue the coming-of-age rite of *shyopen lawa*, the Thakali New Year celebration of Torongla, and Desh Puja, a festival created and celebrated only in Kathmandu and Pokhara. The text also included comments on such varied subjects as the use of the *khāngalo*, the silver necklace required for the performance of *khimi tapne*, the ceremony that sanctifies a Thakali marriage; the placement and worship of photographs of the four clan gods and the goddess Narijhowa; the twelve-year festival of the Thakali; and the preservation of temples and *gompas* in Thaksatsae.

The text does not advocate any religious tradition; nor does it specify the use of a specific ritual practitioner for any single rite. Instead, it states that a Brahman priest, Thakali shaman, or a Tibetan Buddhist priest may be used for mortuary rites but that one and only one of these practitioners should be employed. Support for the tradition represented by the Thakali shaman was demonstrated by the promise of financial support for the training of new shamans. The meeting also established a committee responsible for studying Thakali culture, customs, and history and pledged to raise money for the performance of *shyopen lawa* and Lha Phewa.

The text, written only in Nepali, also encourages the preservation of the Thakali language. One should note that the November 1982 meeting and the April 1983 meeting were both conducted in Nepali. For that matter, all meetings, including those of the council of thirteen headmen in Thaksatsae, are conducted in Nepali. This issue continued to draw the attention of urban Thakali communities throughout the 1990s, but, in fact, very few were willing to make the effort to educate their children in Thakali. Even those urban families who advocate education in that language have shown a distinct preference for educating their own children in English-medium schools.

Despite the gestures toward the preservation of Thakali culture, the text avoided any definitive statement about the nature and content of Thakali culture. The ability of the delegates to act on their emphasis on returning to tradition was stymied by disagreements, disputed evidence, and the vested interests of some urban factions. The result was a very partial redefinition or creation of tradition. The lack of consensus left room for considerable individual interpretation of customs, an unsatisfactory solution in the opinion of many delegates. The uncertainty related to Thakali tradition was reflected in the reliance on a definition of Thakali that emphasizes putative common descent rather than common culture. This tension between a criterion based on descent and one based on culture was to resurface numerous times in the following years.

Initial Responses to the Formation of the Thakali Sewa Samiti

Unquestionably, the formation of a national association both drew from and contributed to a growing group consciousness among the widespread Thakali migrant communities. After the formation of the national *samiti*, the Mul Bandej was printed and distributed to all Thakali communities, and a household survey designed by the central committee was conducted by the new local chapters of the national organization.[13]

In many areas steps were taken to formalize local community organizations. Thakalis generally expressed satisfaction with the formation of the national organization, though there were many criticisms of its goals and activities. There was, however, no consensus of criticism: it varied even within a particular region or community and was both substantive and petty. Not surprisingly, the most enduring criticisms have attacked the organization for its attempts to legislate ritual performance. Many Thakali argued that there should be no compulsion to perform rituals in a particular fashion and that they should perform rituals in accordance with their own desires and the means available within particular regions. Others worried that Thakali culture would be lost if the Thakali settled in different areas did not follow the same rules and traditions. In large part, criticisms of the Mul Bandej stem from the disproportionately urban bias in the representation to the organization meeting and from the awkward compromise reached among the factions at that meeting. The result was a document that failed to answer the questions the Thakali most wanted answered—Who are we? What are our traditions?—and instead offered detailed regulations about the minutiae of rituals as performed in the urban areas.

These regulations were immediately dismissed as region specific and encouraged more and more Thakali to assert that rituals should not be performed in some Kathmandu fashion but according to the desires and means available in particular areas or districts. As a Thakali shaman in Khani Khuwa sarcastically remarked, "The Thakalis residing in Kathmandu and Pokhara are very wise, and they make many rules and regulations, but they themselves do not follow the rules. It is the Thakalis living in Myagdi who follow the real traditions of the Thakali." Khuwale Thakali had little use for a document that occupied itself with a discussion of an upper limit on the value of wedding gifts and dowries that was far above their means. Over the years these criticisms have resulted in reforms of the Mul Bandej and a diminishing of the attempt to control ritual performance. Yet, simultaneously, the Thakali generally continue to express the concern that if Thakalis settled in different areas do not follow the same set of rules and traditions, Thakali solidarity will be undermined, and Thakali culture forgotten.

The Integration of the Khuwale

The reactions of Thakali living in Khani Khuwa to this increased consciousness and ethnic organizing revealed both their desire to be reincorporated into the national Thakali community and their continuing resentment over the way they were treated by the Thak Khole Thakalis. On occasion shunned by the Thak Khole, who, under some circumstances, considered the Khuwale to be more like Magars than Thakalis, the Khuwale noted that, ironically, it was they and not the urbanized Thakalis who followed the ancient traditions of the Thakali forefathers. Thakalis in Kathmandu might be rich, wise, educated, and great, they acknowledged, but it was these urban, educated Thakalis who regularly broke the very rules set by the Mul Bandej. If there were to be rules, they argued, there should be punishments for breaking them.

Though they were underrepresented at the organization meeting in 1983, Thakali from Khani Khuwa came to take an increasingly active role in the national Thakali community in the ensuing decade. New associations were formed in areas of Khani Khuwa with large Thakali populations. In the growing *bazār* town of Burtibang, for example, more than one hundred Thakali households joined to form a local association in July 1983, following the guidelines established by the Thakali Sewa Samiti. One representative from Burtibang had attended the April 1983 meeting, and through him the local association maintained close contact with the national association. This association became very active and quickly became a forum for the resolution of issues of all kinds affecting the Thakali community (including *dhikurs*, the pricing of goods in the market, the performance of rituals, funding for the training of Thakali shamans, collections of charity for seriously ill members of the community, interactions with non-Thakali *jāts*, and other social events such as deaths and elopements). The Burtibang group contributed over half the fees assessed to Baglung District by the national association and also agreed to change some local ritual practices to comply with the guidelines of the Mul Bandej. It had no difficulties raising funds, and fees assessed per household for marriages and births have been willingly paid by members. This *samaj* has continued to stay in close contact with other Thakali communities and has participated actively over the last decade in national events.

In other areas personal and political differences created local factions that made it difficult for a consensual association to emerge as smoothly as it did in Burtibang. Any attempt by one faction to organize the community was met with suspicion and undermined by the others. This was true, for example, in the Darbang area of Myagdi District. An association of seventy-five households eventually emerged in 1984, but it was unable to sustain attendance or interest in its activities. This association does not hold regular meetings, does not discuss as wide a range of issues as the Burtibang association, and, as a consequence, has had considerably less influence on the national association than other, more organized local associations.

These two examples, in Burtibang and Darbang, are instructive in their contrasts: the Burtibang community has continued to reach agreement by consensus and easily adopts new members into its midst, it is very influential locally, and it closely follows the guidelines set forth by the national association; the Darbang association has often disagreed with the national association, has little influence even in the local community, and has reflected the tensions between competition and cooperation characteristic of Thakali interactions in other fields, such as economics and politics.

In general, however, Khuwale Thakalis have demonstrated a greater willingness to become reengaged, either as individuals or as local communities, with the national Thakali *samaj*. Khuwale Thakalis attended the 1993 twelve-year festival in Thak Khola in record numbers and demonstrated a growing willingness to voice their resentment both privately and publicly.

Nationally Drawn Boundaries Locally Imposed

In the aftermath of the 1983 meeting, local Thakali communities were asked to reconsider not only the performance of public and private rituals but the boundaries of their communities. In areas where local *samaj* associations already formally existed, these associations were disbanded, and new associations formed. But this reformation did not occur without conflict that continued to reverberate throughout the Thakali community in the 1990s.

In Bhairawa a formal *samaj* had existed since 1973. When the association was disbanded in 1983 in order to reform it according to the new guidelines, Thakalis in the area were unable to reach agreement. At issue was the criterion for membership in the association. Prior to 1983 this *samaj* had included among its members Thakali migrants from Thaksatsae and Khani Khuwa as well as a number of Panchgaonle households. The membership criterion approved by the national organization, however, explicitly limited membership to members of the four Thakali clans of Thaksatsae. Adopting this criterion meant that Panchgaonle households that had been members of the local *samaj* for years would be excluded from the new association. Over the past fifteen years the Bhairawa community has remained divided on this issue, and what was once an active association has been barely able to function. As a consequence, public celebrations of Thakali festivals have occurred only sporadically.

In the Bhairawa area many members of the community openly criticized the Mul Bandej and continued to fault the Kathmandu community for failing to uphold Thakali traditions and yielding to the Hinduizing influence of the *subba* lineage. Many members of the community, though residing in a strictly Hindu area, argued that the Thakali are not Hindu and advocated a return to the employment of the Thakali shaman for mortuary rites and ancestor worship.

There are two important aspects to this revitalization movement. First, it arose among wealthy merchant families who had lived within a strong Hindu community for over twenty years. Unlike the *subba* lineage and its allies, however, who had embraced aspects of Hinduism, these families had retained strong ties to non-Hindu Thakali practices. Second, this community has supported a strict interpretation of both Thakali culture and Thakali descent. Thus their arguments set them apart from the reforming Thakali of Kathmandu on the subject of religious tradition and also from the Khuwale community (with whom they share views about appropriate religious practice) on the subject of impure descent (arguing that the Khuwale have been affected by inter-*jāt* marriages). Curiously, however, at the same time, they defend their affinity with locally resident Panchgaonle.

Disputes concerning the criterion for participation in *samaj*-sponsored events have continued to affect the public celebration of Thakali festivals elsewhere in Nepal. In Kathmandu the *samaj* has continually restricted participation in the festival of Torongla to the four Thakali clans from Thaksatsae; in Pokhara in 1984 tempers became so heated that a fistfight terminated the archery festival; in Burtibang, where the *samaj* usually follows the lead set by the national association but where large numbers of non-Thakalis, particularly Magars, have traditionally participated in the Torongla archery games, the local *samaj* decided that a ban on non-Thakali participation might be appropriate in Thaksatsae or Kathmandu but was inappropriate in their context; in Darbang there has been no discussion, and all remain welcome.

Throughout the past fifteen years, the national association has often appeared to lack direction and have no clear purpose, but local communities and individuals have remained involved for a variety of reasons. Many individuals have openly questioned the purpose and utility of the organization. Some individuals have wanted the *samaj* to champion specific causes. Many others, recognizing that the association has no power to force individuals to conform in ritual practice, felt the attempt to create conformity was misplaced. Many of these individuals would have preferred the association to focus on improving the economic and political prospects for the whole Thakali community. Some informants expressed the hope that in unity the Thakali community would be more competitive economically against larger ethnic communities such as the Newars and Marwaris. Nevertheless, however unintended, the organization has had a significant impact on the Thakali community. Most Thakali value the strengthening of social ties and identity that it has spurred. The association has served an important function as a forum where disparate elements of the wider Thakali community can come together to imagine, each in its own way, a unified community.

Ongoing Changes

The Thakali community and the Thakali Sewa Samiti have continued to evolve over the years since 1983. The later revisions of the Mul Bandej and the changing distribution of representatives to the general assembly reflect some of these changes. The revised charter for the Thakali Sewa Samiti, for example, places a high priority on the preservation of some key cultural practices. The purposes of the association include preserving and promoting the culture, rituals, and artistic values of the Thakali community; preserving language, dress, ornaments, songs, and dances; restoring and preserving gods, goddesses, temples, sculptures, and manuscripts; raising consciousness among the Thakali and encouraging cooperation; stressing economy in ritual performance without affecting authenticity; condemning superstitions and pompousness; making rotating credit practices more scientific and successful; improving the economic status of the Thakali community; and researching and publishing on Thakali history and culture.

As I predicted in 1987, the increasing group consciousness of the Thakali in Khani Khuwa has made them more active participants in the Thakali Sewa Samiti.[14] At first, this helped move the organization further from the influence of the urban faction and the *subba* lineage. Though the balance of influence shifted, however, controversy and conflict among factions has continued unabated. And while the process remains fluid and ongoing, the 1990s did witness continued tensions between these factions, with more emphasis on traditional and anti-Hindu practices.

Some of these tensions were played out at the first twelve-year festival held after the formation of the Thakali Sewa Samiti. This festival, in 1993, was managed and largely funded by the Thakali Sewa Samiti (the first time the event was not managed by the *tera mukiyā* of Thaksatsae), a circumstance that served to emphasize the tensions between migrants who dominated that body and those still resident in Thaksatsae.

The distribution of representatives to the central committee and the general assembly was revised several times and came to better reflect the actual distribution of the Thakali population (see tables 6.2 and 6.3). The percentages of delegates to the general assembly from Thaksatsae, for example, dropped slightly from 1983 to 1993 (from 17.3 to 12 percent of the total number of delegates), and the number of delegates to the central committee was reduced by half (from four to two). Smaller reductions were assigned to

Kathmandu and Pokhara. The largest gain was experienced by Myagdi District, which added one representative to the central committee (going from two to three) and more than doubled the number of delegates sent to the general assembly (from five to eleven, an increase from 7.7 to 13 percent of the total delegates).

Thakali membership in the Nepal Federation of Nationalities (Janajati Mahasangh) has also fueled conflict among the Thakali since 1990. The 1990 overthrow of the *panchayat* system and establishment of a constitutional monarchy created political space for anti-elite, anti-Hindu, sentiments to be expressed more freely in Nepal. Since 1990 ethnic associations and cultural revitalization movements have become more numerous and more public, leading to open conflict among hill Brahman and Chetri elites,

TABLE 6.3 Representation to the General Assembly, 1993

Thaksatsae	10
Pokhara/Syangja	10
Kathmandu	11
Bhairawa	9
Butwal/Palpa	9
Baglung/Galkot	4
Myagdi-Beni	3
Myagdi-Darbang	4
Dana/Tatopani	4
Parbat/Birethanti	3
Chitwan	4
Gulmi, Tamghas, Pyantan	2
Banke	2
Far West	2
Social workers	2
Intellectuals	2
Women	2
Youth	2
Total	85

orthodox Hindus, low-caste groups, and anti-Hindu hill groups. These conflicts became manifest immediately following the Jana Andolan (the people's movement) in April 1990 and intensified during the debates over the writing of a new constitution for Nepal. At issue was the degree to which the new constitution would enshrine two pillars of Nepali nationalism—the Nepali language and the Hindu religion—that privileged the culture of high-caste hill Hindus and marginalized the language and cultures of Tibeto-Burman hill groups. A new association representing the interests of the non-Hindu, non-Nepali-speaking populations—the Action Committee of Various Religions, Languages, and Nationalities (Bibidh Dharma, Bhasha, Jati tatha Janajati Sangharsha Samiti)—demonstrated in the streets of Kathmandu and petitioned the constitutional committee to ensure that the new constitution would acknowledge ethnic, religious, and linguistic diversity. In July 1990 twenty-two ethnic associations, including the Thakali Sewa Samiti, joined together to form the Janajati Mahasangh (Nepal Federation of Nationalities). This federation reflects contemporary attempts to introduce more flexibility in the boundaries of difference that had been drawn by the state. The Janajati Mahasangh seeks to redefine these lines to create one ethnic majority where there had previously been only numerous ethnic minorities.

In the decade since the passage of the new constitution, groups and individuals have defined themselves in opposition to Hinduism in increasing numbers. (The Janajati Mahasangh is described by its leaders as "fundamentally non-Hindu"). Beginning in 1992, many of the ethnic associations began to persuade their constituencies not to observe Nepal's major Hindu holiday, Dasain. Around the same time there was a proliferation of new historical accounts of ethnic origins that took the inverse of the previous Sanskritized histories (like that of the Thakalis' Hansa Raja). In the new histories, groups no longer trace their origins to a long-forgotten Hindu past but instead to some long-forgotten Buddhist, indigenous, or autochthonous past, explicitly citing their differences from Hindu populations. In 1991 census returns reported the first decline in the percentage of the population reporting Hinduism as its religion.

Many Thakali have protested the participation of the Thakali Sewa Samiti in the Nepal Federation of Nationalities, an umbrella movement composed of thirty-three Tibeto-Burman ethnic associations that takes an anti-Hindu position in opposition to the dominant Hindu elite of Nepal.[15] When the Thakali representative to the Janajati Mahasangh took his rotation as president in 1995, his friends and allies delayed the scheduled meeting of the Thakali Sewa Samiti central committee until after his term was over to avoid exposing him to open criticism during his term as president of the Mahasangh. Some factions of the Thakali community still see their interests as being best served by allying themselves with the Hindu elites of Nepal, while others support the efforts of the Mahasangh. In 1999 the central committee set up a subcommittee to reconsider the question of Thakali membership in the Janajati Mahasangh. Two years later, the issue remained unresolved.

The formation of the Thakali Sewa Samiti in 1983 was a significant catalyst for the reevaluation of Thakali society, and it both directly and indirectly helped to fuel the revitalization of some Thakali social practices. From its formation in 1983 until the fall of the *panchayat* system in 1990, the association provided an unusual forum within which the Thakali discussed and debated the social and political implications of ethnic solidarity and identity. Within this context, different positions were taken emphasizing either the importance of shared cultural practices or the primacy of putative descent. By 1990 more emphasis was placed on culture than descent.

After 1990, when political changes allowed these issues to be discussed more openly and when many other associations formed to focus on these issues, the Thakali Sewa Samiti continued to serve as a important forum within which social issues were debated and differences in the perspectives held by members of different Thakali communities aired. Throughout the period from 1983 to the present, debates within the association have tended to balance social and political concerns. Ironically perhaps, while before 1990 the Thakali Sewa Samiti's greatest significance lay in its status as a forum within which political debates could take place, after 1990 its greatest function may reside in its established encouragement of balanced perspectives on highly politicized ethnic debates.

7 Constructing Thakali

> We have only to speak of an object to think we are being
> objective. But because we chose it in the first place, the object reveals more
> about us than we do about it.
> —Gaston Bachelard

The differences in scholarly statements concerning the Thakali are provocative: aspects of Thakali religious practices and beliefs have been variously described as Buddhism, Hinduism, Bon-po, shamanism, scientific atheism, and sheer opportunism. Within the first decade of scholarly research, for example, from 1952 to 1962, different scholars observed among the Thakali the gaining in strength of Buddhism, an increased emphasis on their original "shamanistic cult," a movement toward Hinduism, and a secularization camouflaged as Hinduization. In the view of most analysts, each religious revival occurred at the expense of practices associated with the others. With access to almost identical ethnographic evidence, scholars agreed that Thakali culture was in the process of a major transformation, but their interpretations of that transformation and their estimates of its timing varied significantly. The most widely known and frequently cited version of Thakali cultural change opposes the Thakalis' alleged earlier alignment with Tibetan Buddhism to their ensuing emulation of high-caste Hindus.[1] Categorizations of cultural and religious transformation among the Thakali have taken three general forms: (1) the description of the Thakali as once-devout Buddhists who became Hindu; (2) the portrayal of the Thakali as Buddhist who only appeared to become Hindu, that is, they adopted many of the practices but not the values or beliefs of Hindu society, their conversion being characterized by one such scholar as a "camouflaged secularization"[2]; and (3) the assertion that the Thakali were never devout Buddhist and neither did they ever become

Hindu, though they pretended to be one or the other under different conditions.

The variety of characterizations of the Thakali raises questions about both the underlying assumptions and the sufficiency of the supporting historical and ethnographic evidence provided in the literature. The argument presented here builds on the work of earlier scholars of the Thakali but at the same time challenges not only the arbitrariness of the criteria by which scholars have analytically isolated, constructed, and named particular populations as Thakali but also the assumption of some scholars that there are discernible boundaries between one set of religious practices and another and their reliance on an explicit or implicit linear model of historical development.

Collectively, the arguments presented by previous scholars present a confused view of Thakali culture. The selection of evidence to fit preexisting interpretive structures and the reliance on imaginings of the past and assumptions of unilinear change make it difficult to sort fact from fiction, particularly with regard to the extent of Thakali devotion to or the chronology of their conversion to Buddhism and the impetus, nature, sincerity, and chronology of the alleged subsequent conversion to Hinduism. One would be justified in wondering whether these scholars are all discussing the same people. Often they are not.

Despite observations such as Sylvan Lévi's fundamental intertwining of religious strands, dichotomies such as Hinduism and Buddhism sneak into much of the scholarship on Nepal. Other distortions have arisen when ethnographers have attempted to reconstruct some idealized past of contemporary cultural formations and when scholars have presumed that what they observed at one moment in time reflected a process heading in one specific direction or another. In the past decade, building on additional information about the political and historical contexts in which ethnic identifications evolve and multiple studies conducted among people who identify themselves or are identified by others as members of the same so-called ethnic groups, there has been more widespread recognition of the ambiguity or fluidity of the boundaries of these groups and of the contemporary and historical heterogeneity found within these boundaries. Building on the work of others, it has become increasingly possible to conduct ethnographic studies that foreground the ways in which individuals and groups have acted to forge their own histories and identities within the context set up by the processes of Nepali state formation.

First Contacts, First Constructs

A brief review of scholarly encounters with the Thakali illustrates the various ways in which they privileged some evidence, applied interpretive structures, imagined the past, and projected the future. The first foreign scholar to record his visit to Thak Khola, Giuseppe Tucci, an Italian orientalist, spent a few days in Thak Khola in October 1952 during the course of a scientific journey to Nepal.[3] His description of the Thakalis as "trilingual, speaking Tibetan and Nepali as well as their own dialect," and his suggestion that they "represent the link between Nepal and Tibet" ([1953] 1982:45) conveys the feeling most visitors to the area have of reaching a geographic and cultural transition zone. His record of his encounter with a group of muleteers from "Tukuche" noted that "the people are Thakalis but they speak Tibetan, they wear heavy Tibetan coats and hats, they walk with the Tibetan slouch, and, above all, they smile like Tibetans" (48). One wonders who these people were. In photographs from the time, few of the Thakali from Thaksatsae fit this description, although it accurately describes many of the residents of Panchgaon or Baragaon who might have spoken Tibetan and identified themselves to an outsider like Tucci as Thakali.

Reaching Larjung in Thaksatsae, Tucci wrote:

We are truly at a frontier, ethnic, religious and linguistic. This is the place reached by the furthest impulse of Lamaism which has flowed back from the north and still holds out against the slow, implacable spread of Hinduism. As usual in areas where two cultures meet, the two religions overlap, and the people, fearful of the mysterious presence of occult forces, prefer for safety's sake to include the gods of both faiths in their prayers. However, Buddhism is definitely the predominant religion, indeed I would say it is gaining strength; the temples are new, and there is a small newly-built monastery in which they have ceremoniously deposited a complete copy of the holy scriptures (bKa'agyur) acquired in Tibet.

([1953] 1982:49)

Tucci described Thakali religious practices and beliefs as a syncretism of a number of traditions, and he saw no conflict among the cultural traditions contributing to this religious mixture; indeed, he noted that the overlap of faiths and the inclusive approach to deities was not uncommon in this region of South Asia and that in the minds of religious supplicants it was an effective means of worship. He insightfully added that:

> The transition from one religion to the next is not difficult anyway. The Brahmans are very strict about precepts with social value which give firm support to the solidarity of the community, protecting it from corruption or contamination, but as we have often noted they are very tolerant in religious matters. This liberal attitude of theirs is supported by the theory that manifestations of divinity are constantly being re- newed: the gods are symbols of a cosmic consciousness which has neither name nor form, but which is made comprehensible for us by means of these symbols.
>
> (49)

This echoed his more general comments about Nepal, in which he ob- served: "We have often seen that the religions do not compete with each other in this country [Nepal], but live in harmony in the same place" (66).

Tucci's observations underscore many significant points pertinent to this "frontier" meeting of Hinduism and Buddhism and the process of transfor- mation. His comments prompt four inferences, to which I will return shortly: (1) that in Tucci's judgment Thaksatsae was the farthest place reached by "Lamaism";[4] (2) that in 1952 he believed Buddhism was predominant and gaining strength; (3) that in his view the two religions, Hinduism and Bud- dhism, were not in conflict in these areas but "overlap" and live in "har- mony"; and (4) that he believed it was easy for the Thakali to continue old (that is, Buddhist and indigenous) practices while describing them to out- siders in new (Hindu) terms.

One year after Tucci, in 1953, Jiro Kawakita passed through Thak Khola, accompanying a Japanese scientific expedition to the area. Kawakita's per- spective on "Takali" religious beliefs was remarkably different from Tucci's.[5] Whereas Tucci found it plausible that the Thakali could be both "Lamaists" and Hindus, Kawakita took a quite different position, arguing that "in their religion they seem to adhere not much either to Hinduism or Lamaism" (1957:92).

Kawakita speculated about the origin of Thakali religion and claimed that the religion of the Thakali "came originally from *Hindu Tantra* and in the Thakali language is called *Jangri*" (1957:90).[6] He lamented that he was unable to learn much about the content of "jangrism" as a religion, but he imagined it to be a sort of shamanistic cult (91). Kawakita further suggested that religious practices based on the "*jangri*" were undergoing a revival.

While Kawakita, like Tucci, concluded that the Kali Gandaki valley is a transitional zone between the two cultural spheres of Hinduism and Buddhism (1957:223–27), his vision of reified "traditions" and fixed boundaries rather than an amorphous frontier area is evident in his attempt to map the furthest reaches of Lamaistic and Hindu influences in the Himalayas using such indices as the southern and northern limits of Lamaist and Hindu temples, monuments and shrines.

In 1956, three years after Kawakita's visit, David Snellgrove, during the course of an eight-month journey across the northern stretches of Nepal in search of Buddhist temples and documents, sojourned briefly in Thak Khola. What he found gave him no solace: "To what sorry pass has the 'Doctrine' come. In fact throughout the whole of the Kali Gandaki valley the women have constituted themselves as the chief guardians of what little Buddhist practice remains. They at least are not ashamed of confessing it" (1961:180). Snellgrove's report contrasts sharply with that of Tucci, who, only four years earlier, suggested that Buddhism was "gaining strength." This difference in opinions is partly attributable to Snellgrove's more orthodox definition of Tibetan Buddhism. His vision of a Buddhist past and his disapproval of the current lackadaisical Thakali attitude toward both Tibetan Buddhism and Hinduism are evident in his observations. The Thakali, he wrote:

> have also acquired "progressive" ideas, which have taken a virulent "anti-traditional" form. Thus they have no use for the Tibetan Buddhism which represents the whole culture of their forebears and even despise Tibetan itself as a language for dolts. . . . Many others who are free from "advanced" ideas of this kind share the same contempt for Buddhism as a result of their social contact with Kathmandu. They prefer to call themselves Hindu, but to them Hinduism means no more than the acceptance of caste laws and prejudices and it is significant that while the Buddhist temples fall into disrepair, not one Hindu temple has yet been built. . . . The older folk are bewildered, for no one in Tukchä [sic] has the necessary knowledge to argue the validity of the old religious tradition and they see the whole basis of life crumbling away.
>
> (177–78)

In the fall of 1958 Shigeru Iijima, accompanying the Japanese Scientific Expedition to Northwestern Nepal, led by Jiro Kawakita, stayed briefly in Thak Khola. He, too, described Thakali religion as "a syncretism of Lamaism, Hinduism, and a native belief called Dhom" (1963:48). Iijima conceptually divided Nepal into three major cultural areas: the Indic, the Tibetan, and the Himalayan. He then examined the extent to which the Thakali, whom he described as a "himalayan tribe" or "Mongoloid ethnic group" had adopted Indic culture. His Himalayan cultural area included the Thakali, Gurung, Magar, and other similar ethnic groups and was characterized by syncretic ritual practices including a complex religious amalgam of Lamaism, Hinduism, and native animism. This conceptual division has several disadvantages; for example, it lumps within its central category of "Himalayan" a diverse set of populations whose cultural traditions range widely and include a wide variety of indigenous practices that do not fit neatly into the other two categories

In contrast to earlier scholars, Iijima deemphasized the importance of the *ḍhom*, or *jhankri*. Whereas Kawakita, five years earlier, had reported that a revival of practices associated with the *ḍhom* was occurring at the expense of Hinduism and Tibetan Buddhism, Iijima suggested that the influence of the *ḍhom* had been reduced by a process of Hinduization (1963:51).[7] He did not address the *ḍhom* practices directly, however, choosing instead to limit his argument to Lamaism and Hinduism. He described the Thakali as a people who were slowly moving from Buddhism and their original religion of the *ḍhom* to acceptance within Hindu caste society.

In 1960 and 1961 Corneille Jest, a French anthropologist, accompanied Snellgrove on his way through Thak Khola to and from Dolpo. Jest would pass through again in 1963, 1965, and 1968. In his first article on the Thakali, he wrote: "ils constituent une ethnie très dynamique qui se trouve dans la zone de contact entre la culture hindoue et la culture bouddhique" (1964/65:26).[8] Within this contact zone, Jest, like others before him, was struck by the variety of religious influences: "Lorsqu'on parcourt la vallée de la Kali Gandaki, on est frappé par la pluralitie des formes religieuses. On passe progressivement d'une région hindouisée à une region où prédomine la religion bouddhique. En pays Thak, on trouve à la fois le bouddhisme lamaïque et des croyances magico-religieuses propres aux Thakali" (36).[9]

Jest discussed the two religious forms that he saw as significant for the Thakali—Buddhism and the "magico-religieuses" beliefs—and described the numerous Buddhist monuments and temples in the area, citing them as evidence for early Buddhist influence, but he concluded that the strongest attraction to Buddhism in Thak Khola in the early 1960s came not from the Thakali but from the Tibetan refugees residing in the valley. He devoted much more effort to describing "the ancient beliefs," the original religion of the Thakali that he describes as *"Bon-nag"* (1964/65:37).[10]

Jest also noted the Thakalis' attachment to Hinduism, their attempts to claim ancestry with the high-caste Thakuris,[11] and the story of the Hansa Raja, which conveys the relationship of the Thakali ancestors to the Thakuri of northwestern Nepal.[12] As noted in earlier chapters, this story exists in many forms, and the accuracy of some details is in question; most scholars assume the story was adapted and emphasized to support Thakali claims to high-caste Hindu status. Jest, on his part, has observed that "des Thakuri, inter-rogés, ont très violemment rejeté une possibilité de lien pouvant exister entre Thakuri et Thakali" (1964/65:33).[13]

Despite Jest's acknowledgment of Thakali cultural variety, he describes the Thakali as "un groupe d'une très grande cohésion attachés fortement à leurs traditions" (1964/65:42).[14] Given his description of the variety of cultural influences on the Thakali, it is not clear what these traditions are, but if the Thakali were as strongly attached to their traditions (whatever they might be) as Jest believed, perhaps they, or at least some of them, may not have been as open to rapid and dramatic cultural change as other observers of the Thakali have implied.

In 1962 Christoph von Fürer-Haimendorf and Dor Bahadur Bista resided in Thaksatsae for six months. By the time of this first extended stay by scholars in Thak Khola, Tukche was no longer the bustling *bazār* town that Tucci, Snellgrove, Iijima, and Kawakita had visited: trade with Tibet had been seriously reduced in the years following 1960, and many of the wealthier merchants had already begun to relocate.

Fürer-Haimendorf, like Snellgrove, believed that Thakali culture had earlier subscribed to the tenets of Tibetan Buddhism. He confidently speculated that "the Thakalis of the Kali Gandaki valley, undoubtedly once a preliterate tribal community not very different from Magars and Gurungs, adopted *the whole panoply* of Tibetan Buddhist culture complete with monasteries and nunneries" (1978:x; my emphasis) and that "though they retained some elements of an older tribal religion, Buddhism became the dominant ideological force. . . . There can be little doubt that fifty years ago the Thakalis must have presented a picture of Buddhist society subscribing to most of the values and beliefs of Tibetan Buddhism" (1967b:197).[15]

Having conjectured an orthodox Tibetan Buddhist past for the Thakali of Thaksatsae, Fürer-Haimendorf, like Iijima, went on to describe Thakali culture as one that had fallen away from these Buddhist practices and embraced Hindu forms of religious worship in their stead. He noted that in 1962, the year of his study, Buddhism was not the dominant ideology and in his opinion "the cultural atmosphere had completely changed" from the "Buddhist society" he believed to have existed in the early twentieth century to one increasingly influenced by Hindu customs (1967b:198): "There has been a steady trend towards the adoption of Hindu customs, and the gradual abandonment of habits and observances deemed incompatible with the claim to high caste status" (1966:148).

Fürer-Haimendorf noted the presence of practices using the ḍhom, describing these as the remnants of an older "tribal religion" and distinguishing them from both Buddhism and Hinduism. He suggested, however, as part of his argument that the Thakali were steadily embracing Hinduism and without making his own criteria explicit, that while Hinduism and the ḍhom practices are clearly distinguishable (presumably by the well-trained outside observer), nevertheless the Thakali sometimes confuse the two traditions.[16] He attributed the revival of ḍhom practices among the Thakali to their imagined similarity to Hindu rites, though he asserts that "the jhankri rites and exorcism of spirits could not by any stretch of imagination be classified as part of Hindu religion" (1966:146).[17] This restrictive definition of Hinduism also excludes a large portion of the religious practices common to Nepal's middle regions, regions that Fürer-Haimendorf earlier characterized as "deeply steeped in the belief in a hierarchic order based on hereditary and immutable status differences" (12). It seems likely that what presented a problem for Fürer-Haimendorf was not and is not, in fact, a problem for the Thakali. Unfortunately, Fürer-Haimendorf does not specify the criteria by which he would classify rites as part of the Hindu religion.

Unlike Tucci, who asserted that Buddhism and Hinduism could and did coexist in Nepal, Fürer-Haimendorf insisted that the two ideologies were opposed to one another and concluded that a "clash" between them was inevitable (1966:142). His analysis of the trends of Thakali cultural change recalls Iijima's conclusion that Thakali society was in the midst of a process of increasing Hinduization. To illustrate the transformation he saw taking place in Thakali society, he cited a list of cultural changes: in language use, dress, marriage practices, and diet. Fürer-Haimendorf predicted that the Thakali, having moved away from Buddhism, would become increasingly

Hinduized, especially in areas where they lived among Hindus (1967b:202). But while practices would become Hinduized, he saw values secularizing: in his judgment the Thakali acceptance of Hinduism was not a heartfelt conversion but a secularization disguised as Hinduization.

Bista's view of Thakali religious orientation is similar to Fürer-Haimendorf's in many respects. He described Thakali religion in 1962 as "a mixture of Buddhism, Jhankrism, Bonpo and Hinduism" (1967:85), noting that "they practiced, at the time of their rise to fame, a primitive tribal religion involving shamanism and animal sacrifice" (1971:54). Bista's and Fürer-Haimendorf's accounts diverge dramatically, however, in their estimate of the timetable for the Thakali conversion to Buddhism. Whereas Fürer-Haimendorf dated the Thakali conversion to Buddhism to the seventeenth century, Bista argued that both the Thakali conversion to Buddhism and their later turn to Hinduism occurred subsequent to the start of the salt monopoly in 1862. "Attracted by the complicated and colourful rituals of Tibetan Lamaism," the Thakalis turned to Buddhism "during the last quarter of the nineteenth century" (1971:54). Later, as "part of the process of sanskritization," Bista has speculated, the Thakali conversion toward Buddhism halted, and they turned instead toward Hinduism (59). In 1962, only ten years after Tucci witnessed a revival of Buddhism, Bista observed "widespread contempt" of both Buddhism and Bon-po. Bista, like Fürer-Haimendorf, also noted, in addition to the growing association with Hinduism, "a renewed interest in the revival of the primitive religion of Jhankrism" (1967:86).

Revisionist Constructions

In the 1970s two scholars whose work is markedly different contributed to revisionist views of sociocultural change among the Thakali. These views countered many of the earlier characterizations. Michael Vinding, a Danish anthropologist, and Andrew Manzardo, an American, have both, by suggesting that Buddhism was never as widespread or as "ideologically dominant" (Fürer-Haimendorf 1967b:197) as Fürer-Haimendorf or Snellgrove had assumed, challenged a major premise underlying Snellgrove's, Iijima's, and Fürer-Haimendorf's interpretations of Thakali culture (Manzardo 1978:177–80; Vinding 1982:293). They suggested that there is a strong basis for the assumption that the Hinduism of the Thakalis is shallow and that the citing of the Thakalis as "a textbook case of sanskritization" has been premature (Manzardo 1978:173).

Beginning in 1972 Michael Vinding lived intermittently in the village of Syang, where he has conducted research among the northernmost of the groups that claim Thakali status.[18] He was the first scholar to present a co-herent picture of the northern groups resident in the upper Kali Gandaki valley, and his research thus broke the pattern wherein scholars primarily focused on and reflected the view of the wealthy Thakali traders of Tukche.[19] Like scholars before him, he has described Thakali culture as "a mixture of indigenous and exogenous cultural elements" (1982:291); their religion, he has written, "is a combination of elements from an indigenous tradition known as *dhom*, Tibetan Buddhism, and Hinduism" (292). His observation that it is difficult to discuss Thakali religious beliefs and practices in general terms and his insistence that one must first distinguish among a number of subgroups on the basis of "ethnicity, locality, education, age, and sex" (293) are particularly important, since, as I shall show, the composition of the groups of Thakalis studied by previous scholars varied greatly. This is par-ticularly striking when one turns to Manzardo, who began research within a few years of Vinding but worked in radically different circumstances and among a significantly different group of people.

Vinding notes that there is more attachment to Buddhism among the northern groups residing in Thak Khola than among the southern groups, but even so he has concluded that the religious practices in the northern part of Thak Khola (Panchgaon) are by no means orthodox Tibetan Bud-dhist. He has suggested that when such groups consider themselves to be followers of Buddha, as some of the Thakali groups do, scholars should regard them as Buddhist despite the groups' unorthodox practice.

When Manzardo conducted his research, the situation in the upper Kali Gandaki valley was tense because of the Khampas of Tibet who had taken refuge in the valley from the Chinese, and the area was closed to outsiders. Consequently, Manzardo first began his work among the migrant Thakali community of the central Nepal market town of Pokhara, at a time when some of his Thakali informants were apparently less than forthcoming to outsiders. Whereas Fürer-Haimendorf had already hinted at Thakali duplic-ity by arguing that the Thakali emulation of Hinduism was a pretense hiding a secularization of their culture, Manzardo went further and asserted that the Thakali had manipulated both Buddhism and Hinduism to further their economic goals. He correctly noted that the evidence for widespread adherence to Buddhism was weak and that while the Buddhist structures in Thak Khola can be counted and dated, this methodology does not provide a clear idea of how widespread Buddhist practice was, when its influence began or increased, how orthodox the doctrine was that was followed, or how devoutly it was believed (1978:179).[20]

Manzardo originally argued that the Thakali deliberately manipulated their religious allegiance and symbols.[21] He asserted that "Hinduism and Buddhism are used politically by the Thakalis and have very little religious meaning to most of them" (1978:180; see also 1977a:78 n. 4).

Manzardo's applies to the Thakali Erving Goffman's concept of "impression management," a concept that, Manzardo has suggested, may not be applicable to all people "but certainly is to the Thakali."[22] Manzardo's argument has four parts. First, he has argued that the Thakali manage the impressions that others form of them. Second, he has insisted that this impression management entails the cooperation and acquiescence of the entire Thakali community (1975:32). This would be interesting, if true, but as Manzardo himself has recently acknowledged (Manzardo 1992), this part of his argument is overstated.

It should also be noted that, unlike Goffman, who is most concerned with discerning the techniques of impression management, Manzardo ties impression management to the motives and intentions of his subjects. He calls impression management "one recurrent feature of Thakali adaptation, the manipulation of several situations with the *avowed* aim of maximizing their position simultaneously within each of several status systems operating within Nepal" (1978:171; my emphasis).

The third part of Manzardo's argument stresses the importance of a shared "back-area" of religious rites that remains basically unchanged and hidden from the scrutiny of outsiders. He has argued that an indigenous tradition "based on beliefs which are idiosyncratic to the Thakali" (1978:232) has remained largely unaffected by the imitation of Buddhist or Hindu practices: "The Hinduism of the Thakalis, is shallow and the use of the Thakalis as a textbook case of 'sanskritization' has been a bit premature. Hinduization, like the Buddhist guise which came before it, seems to have been more window dressing than actual conversion to a new system" (173). This statement raises the analytical issue implicit in the ongoing discussion, namely, how can one distinguish among Hinduization, Sanskritization, actual conversion, and window dressing? What independent criteria can one apply to the data? What do these analysts mean to imply by their use of these terms?

My study partially supports Manzardo's claim that the Hinduism of the Thakali is shallow, but his assertion that "this furtiveness is a structural necessity" (235) is untenable. Moreover, his conclusion that the furtiveness "is due to the nature of the Thakalis' trade adaptation" limits the applicability of his theory to that portion of the Thakali population dependent on trade, a narrower applicability than he initially claims (235).

Fourth, Manzardo has argued that the trend of rapid communal social change undertaken to raise social status "appears repeatedly throughout Thakali history" (1975:32).[23] This notion of recurrent adaptation is perhaps the most compelling part of his argument. I support this view, in part, though the recurrent change I discuss is less instrumental than that imagined by Manzardo and is never the same for all parts of the group, as he envisioned.

Thakali Reconstructed

How could so many scholars reach such different conclusions in so short a space of time? Faced with varied characterizations, one must recognize that the widely accepted representations of the Thakali as a group that has achieved remarkable economic success, gained regional political dominance, and purposefully restructured its tribal hierarchy and altered its social and religious behavior is not equally true for all those who claim to be Thakali or have been treated by scholars as such. These characterizations are useful when one sorts out which are more accurate of residents in Panchgaon and which of Thakali from Thaksatsae; which are more accurate for traders, for agriculturalists or for pastoralists; and the degree to which some characterizations apply primarily to the Thakali traders of the Lha Khang Dungi subclan of the Sherchan clan who monopolized the salt trade for most of the period from 1862 to 1928.

An impediment to distinguishing ritual continuity from transformation may be the tendency to label a practice or a culture as belonging to a particular religious tradition based on the presence of certain cultural attributes. This tendency to classify a particular trait, practice, or belief as belonging to one or another cultural sphere, tradition, or religion is at best misleading. Some practices may be unambiguously traced, but the appearance even of these does not allow one to assume that their meaning is unchanged when it appears in a new context. The project of classifying religious practices and beliefs is, of course, always limited by the analyst's own system of classification.

For inhabitants of the Himalaya, the so-called syncretism of Buddhism and Hinduism does not present the same difficulty, or puzzle to be solved, as it does for the analyst. Thus "the moral turmoil" Fürer-Haimendorf (1966:142) imagined enveloping the Thakali may be a turmoil not in their minds but in his.

The plethora of contradictory characterizations of the Thakali raises questions about the extent to which the Thakali can be described as Buddhists, now or historically; the extent to which they can validly be described as Hindus; the sincerity and completeness of the alleged conversion from Buddhism to Hinduism; their motivation for any change; and the role of worldly and otherworldly aims in the alleged Thakali religious conversion.

The contradictions outlined above raise significant methodological questions about the admissibility and sufficiency of the evidence that has been used by scholars to determine and measure the historical development of religious orientation in general and any specific motivation for related Thakali cultural change. Not only is the cultural content or social process of the Thakali conversion to Hinduism generally unspecified, but the question of what we are to understand by Buddhism or Hinduism in this context remains unanswered. How appropriate to a study of Thakali cultural change is an analytic model based on the dichotomy of Hindu/Buddhist? The detected conflicts in values are not as problematic for the Thakali as they are for the analysts. The challenge, then, is to distinguish between religious belief and religious practice and to recognize that the incorporation of isolated practices does not necessarily imply a concomitant adoption of the meaning that that particular practice holds when it appears within another cultural system.

A study of Thakali cultural change, especially one that reconsiders the alleged decline of Buddhist ideology and the apparent adoption of Hindu practice, must examine the way in which the apparent heterogeneity of Thakali religious orientation can be related to specific subgroups, distinguished by such criteria as locale of residence, locale of birth, wealth, occupation, age, and sex.[24] This attention to both context and variety is fundamental to any attempt to discern the nature of religious practice among migrant communities, the potential motivations for religious change in these communities, and the way in which religious symbols are, and have been, manipulated over time in different ways by different subgroups. In the absence of such an approach, the conflicts mentioned in chapter 6 that arose at the 1983 organization meeting in Pokhara for the national Thakali *samaj* association and at the 1993 Lha Phewa celebration in Thak Khola have an inadequate context for interpretation.

The use of the term *Thakali* for various distinct populations in Thak Khola, a focus on subgroups of these populations by different scholars, and the attempt to offer diachronic explanations based on synchronic observations help to explain how so many apparently contradictory views have been put forth about the Thakali.[25]

A recurring theme in studies of Thakali is cultural change—particularly the dramatic rise of the Thakali to regional influence and the subsequent adoption of Hindu symbols—but quite frequently the appearance of drastic change in lifestyle, ritual practice, and social structure has distracted observers from cultural continuities. Unquestionably, some of the observed changes represent dramatic and sudden discontinuities with the recent past, but there has been a significant lack of consistency in the analysis of cultural change and continuity among the Thakali. One scholar has noted the exaggerated focus on Thakali sociocultural change and observed that "we Himalayanists have overemphasized and grossly simplified the Thakali case based on a limited understanding of both their recent and their distant past. Our vision of change and adaptation among them has been, in a word, myopic, without sufficient historical perspective" (Messerschmidt 1984:2).

Among the few points of consensus among observers of the Thakali is a general agreement that Thakali religious practices incorporate a mixture of Hinduism, Buddhism, and shamanistic rites. Scholars agree that Thaksatsae lies and has lain within the spheres of both Hindu and Buddhist influences. But there is little consensus concerning the history of Buddhist and Hindu influence in the area, the quality of the devotion to the various religious traditions, or the degree to which the practices are widespread. While there is little agreement about the beginning of Buddhist influence on the Thakali, it is accepted that there are numerous Buddhist temples and monuments and that there were new Buddhist temples in 1952.[26] While Buddhism was not practiced by the population generally in the early 1950s, older Thakalis, particularly women, appeared to be pious Buddhists (Snellgrove 1958; Tucci [1953] 1982; Iijima 1963).

It is difficult to determine the extent to which people who considered themselves to be Thakali also considered themselves to be Buddhist at any single point in time. The lack of convincing evidence allows considerable speculation that contributes to the confusing picture of the Thakali, and many issues regarding Buddhist influence in Thak Khola remain contested. Consequently, one scholar can hold that there "can be little doubt" that

Buddhism was previously the "dominant ideology" of the Thakali (Fürer-Haimendorf 1967b:197; see also Fürer-Haimendorf 1966, 1975), while another can suggest that they may never have been devout Buddhists (Manzardo 1978), and yet another that Buddhism may have been the dominant practice in parts of Thak Khola but it was never the dominant ideology (Vinding 1982:293, 315). Unquestionably the area fell within the sphere of Tibetan Buddhist influence, and some Buddhist practices may have been widespread, but this is too unspecific to be meaningful. It is also clear that the answers proposed have depended a great deal on each analyst's assumptions about what constitutes adherence to Buddhism. At the very least it seems reasonable to assume that practices on the frontier of Buddhist influence were less orthopraxic and the beliefs less orthodox than elsewhere.

Differing chronologies of Buddhist influence in Thak Khola have been proposed. Fürer-Haimendorf (1975) asserted that the Thakali had been Buddhist at least since the seventeenth century, Vinding (1988) dates the earliest influence to the eleventh or twelfth century, Bista (1971) says that the Thakalis turned to the north and adopted Buddhist rituals in the last quarter of the nineteenth century, and Manzardo says that Bista "must have gotten his chronology a bit confused" (1978:49 n. 2) and goes on to date the "imitation of the Tibetan culture" (emphasis added) from the fourteenth century.

Since these scholars are not always using the term Thakali in the same sense, it might make more sense to ask which people who claim to be Thakali were influenced by Buddhism and when, in what way, and to what extent this influence was manifested. Unfortunately, there is very little incontrovertible evidence that can support conclusions about Thakali culture prior to 1951. The few travelers' accounts provide no detailed information about the Thakali, and, for the period prior to the initiation of the salt monopoly system in 1862, there is no ethnographic information of any kind. Speculative histories of the area have relied on archaeological evidence, the oral traditions of the Thakali, and the few available documents and tama patra.[27] More recent textual research has begun to provide an understanding of the history of the region before the salt monopoly (Jackson 1976, 1978; Ramble and Vinding 1987). As Jackson notes, most of his information comes from texts found outside the area. As valuable as his information is for understanding the history of the area, one must be cautious in assuming that the history he has proposed for an area called Se-rib applies to the Thakali.

The evidence indicating Hindu influences in Thak Khola is extremely limited, but some accounts have drawn on it selectively while ignoring indications that contradict their contentions. For example, while it is clear that there are not, and apparently have never been, any Hindu temples in Thak Khola, it is nonetheless untenable to argue that the Thakali "used to be unfamiliar with the Hindu ideas of status distinctions prevalent in other parts of Nepal" (Fürer-Haimendorf 1966:140). One must recognize that Buddhism and Hinduism in the middle hills of Nepal have always been mixed with indigenous practices.[28] Fürer-Haimendorf's argument that Hindu influence in Thak Khola is relatively recent ignores two significant aspects of the upper Kali Gandaki valley that mitigated against cultural isolation. One is trade: while it is common to speak of the isolation of Himalayan populations, it is particularly inappropriate for people resident in an area that lies along one of the major trade routes through the Himalayas. Traders, including Thakalis, had used this route for centuries before the salt monopoly began in 1862. The other aspect Fürer-Haimendorf ignores is pilgrimage: the Hindu pilgrimage site of Muktinath lies just to the north of Thak Khola, and Hindu pilgrimages to Muktinath through the Kali Gandaki valley predate the Thakali presence in the area.

The dating of the Thakali shift toward Hinduism is particularly intriguing. Most events cited as Hindu reforms occurred in the 1920s, when Hitman Sherchan was *subba*; however, many of these so-called reforms were not so much reforms in favor of Hinduism as they were reforms of Buddhist rites. It might be more plausible to interpret the banning of the elaborate Buddhist rituals—including mortuary rites and feasts—as another example of the Thakali tendency to reform social practices by cutting their costs and not as an ideological reformation.[29] These bans seem less significant, if, as Bista suggests, the Buddhist rites undergoing reform had been adopted no more than forty years earlier.

One must also consider what Hinduism means to the Thakali. Snellgrove noted that "to them Hinduism means no more than the acceptance of caste laws and prejudices" (1961:177–78). Manzardo has called the Hinduism of the Thakalis "shallow" (1978:173). Fürer-Haimendorf has said that they are striving after status within the framework of Hindu ideas of pure and impure and higher and low status and that they are a caste because they think of themselves as a caste. This paraphrase of Dumont's comment on the absorption of "tribes" into the caste system is intriguing in this context. Do the Thakali think of themselves as a caste? While Fürer-Haimendorf has noted that the Thakali are lax in following caste rules and observed that there is "a wide gap between orthodox Hindu practices and the half-hearted observance of pollution rules by the Thakalis" (1966:150), both he and Iijima have reviewed many of the rituals and reforms that characterize recent Thakali religious practices, categorized most of them as Buddhist or Hindu, and provided a list of recently changed behaviors that, they have argued, provide evidence of Hinduization. This is a selective list that emphasizes change at the expense of continuity, thus including changes in dress and dietary habits and dismissing others, such as *chokor garnu* (literally, "to make pure"; a purification rite), because they have "no place in either of the two traditional religious systems" (1966:50).[30]

The practices most often dismissed in the tendency to identify Thakali religious practices as either Hindu or Buddhist are those that require the services of a Thakali *dhom*. All observers of the Thakali have noted the presence and persistence of "a survival of ancient beliefs . . . uninfluenced or influenced very slightly by Buddhism" (Jest 1981:55) or "a religion akin to the Black Bon and only slightly influenced by Buddhism" (Fürer-Haimendorf 1975:140–41), "a kind of shamanism related to the pre-Buddhist 'Black Bon' traditions of Tibet and the jhankri tradition of Nepal" (Vinding 1982:291), but few have recognized the significance of the continuity provided by these rituals.[31] The evidence from my research suggests that practices associated with the *dhom* remain a vital aspect of Thakali worship, a view supported by the appropriation of the *dhom* as the focus of a Thakali ethnic revitalization and as a symbol of the solidification of Thakali identity.

The conclusions of other analysts reveal particular biases in the interpretation of synchronic data. Snellgrove assumed that the "sorry" Buddhist practice he found in the "hands of old women" represented the remnants of a previous orthodox Buddhist society (1961:180). Iijima's declaration that the Hindu goddess Mahalaxmi was adopted by the Thakali "to fill the need" for a presiding deity betrayed both his narrow pool of informants and his own perceptions of religious necessity.[32]

In some cases, evidence cited to support the view that the Thakali were Buddhist is applicable to the Panchgaonle but not to Thakalis from Thaksatsae. In other cases, the changes cited as evidence for Hinduization were exaggerated, and the breadth of their acceptance overestimated. For instance, Iijima, Fürer-Haimendorf, Manzardo, and others have claimed that the Thakali adopted the Hindu ban on the consumption of beef and consequently banned the eating of yak meat. It has now been established that, whatever Thakalis may say they do, many Thakalis eat yak.[33]

A reliance on the analytic categories of Hinduism or Buddhism which that encourages the identification of this or that practice or attribute as

Buddhist or Hindu leads to an overstatement of the Thakalis' prior adherence to Buddhism and their contemporary leanings toward Hinduism and thus obscures the actual processes of change among the Thakali and hinders an inquiry into how widespread changes were. An analysis of this change must consider that practices adapted to a new cultural context often take on new meaning. Recalling Tucci's assessment of the interaction of the forces of Buddhism and Hinduism in Nepal, it is advisable to avoid treating Hinduism and Buddhism like reified entities or traditions:

> A deep study of the Thakali religious beliefs would demonstrate the imprecision of whatever denominational labels might be given to them. We would see that the former Lamaist still survives within every Hindu, but that the Lamaist in turn reserves a not unworthy place in the depths of his soul for Hinduism. In every soul we would see the two religions, not in conflict but coexisting by mutual consent and happily sustaining each other. And surely if we looked deeper still, we should find the secret fire of the original primitive beliefs is still burning.
>
> ([1953] 1982:50)

At issue is what it means to be Buddhist or Hindu in this context and the extent to which being Hindu (believing and doing Hindu things) and being Buddhist are exclusive or overlap. The more interesting questions to determine are when religious orientation is an issue and to whom and why, bearing in mind a number of historical influences and their effect on a number of distinct subgroups.

8   Beyond Sanskritization

Actual social change is never so great as is apparent change.
—John Dewey

My propositions serve as elucidations in the following way:
anyone who understands me eventually recognizes them as nonsensical, when he
has used them—as steps—to climb up beyond them. (He must, so to speak, throw
away the ladder after he has climbed up it.)

He must transcend these propositions, and then he will see the
world aright.
— Ludwig Wittgenstein

Narijhowa

Hugging the cliff above the village of Kanti, the Narsang Gompa com-
mands a majestic view of the upper Kali Gandaki valley. The history of this
temple is undetermined: the iconography of the images painted on the walls
and pillars is suggestive of Tibetan Buddhism, but there are no images associated with Tibetan Buddhism on the altar; instead, a locked vault occupies its center. In the vault is the rose-colored stone icon that represents the
goddess Narijhowa. It is perhaps ironic that the Thakali, so frequently accused of being overly materialistic and inadequately concerned with spiritual
matters, have locked their goddess in a safe, an act resulting from their
awareness of the statue's monetary value. The statue has resided in the vault
since it was recovered from a theft in 1982.[1]

Thakalis variously identify Narijhowa as the Hindu goddess of wealth,
Mahalaxmi, the Buddhist Tara, and Lha Jhyowa Rhangjyung.[2] Rites associated with the goddess Narijhowa involve a complex intermingling of indigenous, Hindu, and Buddhist elements, a hybridity that contributes to
multiple interpretations. These rites include *Ti*, performed on the request
of a worshiper who sponsors the rite and the feast that follows; *Narijhowa*

FIGURE 8.1 The inside of Narsang Gompa, including the safe that housed the statue
of the goddess Narijhowa after it was recovered from theft in 1982

choko, the purification of the goddess performed three times a year; and
shyopen lawa (T) or *kumar jatra* (N), a rite of passage for Thakali boys under
the age of fifteen. The religious officiant at Narsang Gompa is a member of
the Sherchan Dhom *phobe* and is trained in a Buddhist tradition: his functions and training are similar to what Vinding has described for the *dawa* (a
religious officiant in Panchgaon) of Syang village (a few hours walk to the
north).

Ti and *Narijhowa choko* involve individual Thakalis according to their
own inclinations. There is no obligation to worship Narijhowa, and some
Thakalis will never visit Narsang Gompa for this purpose. *Shyopen*, on the
other hand, involves the whole community.

According to myth, the performance of *shyopen* was one of the conditions
set by the goddess Narijhowa when she was captured by Thakali hunters
and agreed to reside permanently in the Narsang Gompa.[3] In the early part
of the twentieth century this rite was elaborately sponsored by wealthy

merchant families. After these families emigrated from Thak Khola in the 1960s, the continued performance of *shyopen* placed a considerable financial burden on the remaining Thakalis. The rite was discontinued for some years until several consecutive poor harvests persuaded farmers that the goddess was displeased. The ceremony was thus resumed, though initially at a more modest level (see Vinding 1978:183). After 1983 the Thakali Sewa Samiti supported the rite.

As a landmark in the ritual landscape of the Thakali, the worship of Narijhowa is instructive. First, it reveals the ambiguous interweaving of elements from various other South Asian traditions characteristic of the Thakali ritual landscape. Second, it is indicative of the difficulty of identifying the "real" or "true" Thakali traditions: though portrayed by the Thakali Sewa Samiti as a peculiarly Thakali goddess, Narijhowa is not actively worshiped by all Thakalis. Third, like some other practices, these rites are tied to a specific location. Fourth, the popularity of the goddess has both risen and fallen over time, and interpretations of the goddess (as, for instance, either a uniquely local deity or as a manifestation of the Hindu goddess Mahalaxmi) have varied.

The complex hybridity of this ritual complex has caused scholars to reach differing conclusions about its significance. Jiro Kawakita, for example, a Japanese anthropologist passing through Thak Khola in 1953, argued that *kumar jatra*, or *shyopen lawa*—the coming-of-age ritual under the auspices of Narijhowa held for young Thakali boys—was a good example of those festivals celebrated by the Thakalis that have what he called a strong "Indian flavour" (1955), while Christoph von Fürer-Haimendorf (1967b) cited the same ritual as an example of the Buddhist rituals of the Thakali.

Varied descriptions offered by the Thakali of the goddess, the rituals, and their origin contributed to the diversity of scholarly interpretations. Shigeru Iijima used a description collected from his informants in 1958 to illustrate his argument that the Thakali were undergoing a process of "Hinduization," or Sanskritization. The goddess, he noted is known as "Mahalakshmi" and was adopted by the Thakali to fill the "need for a presiding deity" (1963:49). As further evidence of Hinduization, he reported that the Thakali had come to regard their four clan gods as avatars of Hindu gods.

These characterizations of the Thakali as a group undergoing a process of Sanskritization were based on specific evidence, but those data were interpreted within paradigms that did not always recognize the ephemeral qualities of the examples. The Narijhowa ritual complex is a good example

of evidence that is malleable when put at the service of a preexisting interpretive structure. In the Thakali case, these structures are often built on
presupposed categories such as Hinduism and Buddhism and an imagined
straightforward unilinear process of transition between them.

Speaking of Thakali

While scholarly constructions of the Thakali have varied over the years
and, to some extent, reflected the academic trends of their time, there are
some common themes. Despite significant differences in the perceived
boundaries of the group that scholars delineated with the name Thakali,
scholars have usually described the Thakali as a group that has adjusted to
changing sociopolitical conditions and economic opportunities by turning
away from Tibetan Buddhist traditions and adopting or imitating the beliefs
and practices of high-caste Hindus.[4]

Thus the story of the Thakali appears, at first glance, to be a more or less
straightforward tale of successful elite emulation wherein a group adapted
to the changing economic and political opportunities brought on by the
formation of the Nepali state by consciously abandoning their old traditions
in favor of Hindu customs in order to justify their newly asserted claim to
high-caste Thakuri status. This is indeed the most commonly told tale about
the Thakali.[5] But this is a misleading reading and but a partial account of
the processes of cultural formation and transformation among the Thakali.
The overemphasis on one historical era (the time of the trading monopoly
from 1862 to 1928), on one activity (trade),[6] and one form of cultural change
(the process of Sanskritization) distorts the historical portrait of the Thakali.
The resulting picture of rapid, wholesale, unilinear cultural change is a
distorted one that fails to consider adequately either the rich complexity of
a variety of Thakali processes of adaptation and change or the persistence of
some significant cultural continuities. When one considers the broader historical, geographical, and cultural contexts, the processes of Thakali cultural
transformation are revealed to be both more and less dramatic than generally
portrayed.

The case of the Thakali illustrates the extent to which contemporary
identity distinctions in Nepal are a by-product of the attempts to forge the
artifice of a Hindu kingdom. The apparent shifting religious orientations
among the Thakali over the past one hundred years reflect a complex set of

political motives and identity choices affected by both the attempt to ma-
neuver for influence within the community and the pressures of the regional
status systems within which individual Thakalis have vested interests.

On Boundaries

Scholarship is bound up with the business of discovering, delineating,
and creating boundaries: of groups, cultures, fields of knowledge, and so on.
Boundaries and the categories they demarcate help make sense of complex
and overlapping cultural variations by drawing attention to specific discontinuities. Drawing boundaries along apparent discontinuities heightens our
sense of human diversity and allows us to make sense of it through contra-
distinctions. With respect to cultural variations, the marking of boundaries
draws attention away from others, and by emphasizing the demarcation of
boundaries, cultural variations are often made to appear more rigid or fixed
than they actually are.[7] With respect to social groups, concern with demarcating boundaries results in an overemphasis on the determination of analytical units. Similarly, presupposing overly rigid boundaries between such
conceptual domains as politics, religion, economics, and kinship obscures
and discourages some avenues of inquiry even as it encourages others.

What then is the nature and function of boundaries? As anthropologists
have become increasingly concerned with the processes involved in the
formation of ethnicity, we have come to acknowledge that categories and
typological boundaries obscure as much as they reveal. This analytical shift
in anthropological focus from reified units toward the processes of forming
and transforming categorical identities required that we rethink our expec-
tation of the inferences we draw from boundaries. The focus on process
rather than product redirects our attention to the formation and reformation
of boundaries and suggests that boundaries are permeable, fluid, and always
already in the process of becoming.[8]

The periphery of a category or an identity in the process of becoming is
perhaps better captured by the concept of *frontier* rather than *boundary*.[9]
Whereas boundaries serve to indicate the bounds or limits of anything,
whether material or immaterial, and represent an enclosing, a shutting in,
a fixed and specifiable limit, frontiers are zones of transition or "tracts of
indefinite nature" between groups, regions, and so forth.[10] Frontiers are like
an indeterminate zone where Wittgenstein's "family resemblances" overlap.

My concern in this study is not with discovering or demarcating boundaries but with understanding the nature and consequences of the search for them, the attempts to turn frontiers into boundaries.

There are elements of both discovery and creation in the delineation of domains. But insofar as each delineation of a boundary is a an act of creation, it is also, to heed Picasso, an act of destruction. Scholars scour for lines of fissure and then highlight them, drawing attention to and emphasizing fissures that often appear significant but may often prove to be nothing more than surface cracks in the facade, not lasting fissures in rock but transitory cracks in a thick mass of moving lava. The utility or necessity of heuristic delineations of domains should not lead us to conclude that they are rigid or final: closure, if it does exist, is ephemeral. We should follow Wittgenstein's wise admonition to discard or transcend our heuristic distinctions once we have used them and transgress boundaries as soon as we have demarcated them.

The fetishization of boundaries is glaringly apparent in both scholarly and lay discussions of social identity and groups.[11] Some scholars have insisted that significant distinctions emerge from the observer's objective criteria, while others rely on subjective indigenous categorical ascription. For example, Naroll argued that analytically useful units could be inferred from the observed distribution of a specific set of attributes including (1) biological self-perpetuation; (2) possession of fundamental cultural values; (3) a shared a field of communication and interaction; and (4) a membership that identifies itself and is identified by others as constituting a category distinct from other categories of the same order (1964). Bailey presents a similar list of attributes for "tribal" society, including (1) cultural autonomy; (2) territorial isolation; (3) absence of organic solidarity with other groups; (4) the absence of internal division of labor and social stratification; and (5) direct access to resources and means of production (1963:264).

Moerman and others effectively argued against objective criteria, building their arguments on Leach's observation that social units in northern Burma were produced by subjective processes of categorical ascription that had no necessary relationship to observers' perceptions of cultural discontinuities (Moerman 1967, 1968, 1974; Leach 1954).

Though Barth's emphasis on the persistence and maintenance of ethnic boundaries (1969) is often seen as a reification of ethnic groups, he makes the important point that ethnic groups must be analyzed and understood within appropriate social and cultural contexts; that is, groups can only be understood within the system of which they are a part.[12] Barth contends that by focusing on interaction, the emphasis of analysis "becomes the ethnic boundary that defines the group, not the cultural stuff that it encloses" (15). Barth's point does not so much quarrel with the substance of the attributes proposed for ethnic groups as argue for an emphasis on the interaction of groups. He correctly notes that while a classification of the attributions of ethnic groups purports to give an ideal model of a recurring empirical form, instead it implies a preconceived notion of the significant factors of their genesis, structure, and function.[13] The emphasis on interaction is important for understanding the Nepalese situation, where ethnic distinctions are the foundation on which the social system is based, but the separation of "cultural stuff" from "group boundary" goes too far in dismissing culture as an epiphenomenon or making it a dependent variable. The formation of group identity in the Himalayas is dependent on context, and cultural differences are a component in the process of forming and maintaining ethnic identities.

As noted above, it is tempting to find in the Thakali case support for an instrumentalist view of ethnicity that sees subjective claims to identity as deriving from the manipulation of culture in a variety of ways in order to mobilize collective sentiment and action in service of collective political and economic interests.[14] But while the instrumental manipulation of tradition is undeniably part of the Thakali story, it is important to resist the appealing simplicity of this view and to examine the Thakali case as part of a larger context within which social units are relational and shifting.

Berreman places the accent on the interplay between culture and behavior and, in his study of urban India, demonstrates that ethnic identity is only one among many statuses that a person may employ in society. He has argued that, in complex and fluid urban settings, ethnicity is but one of many social identities people use to cope with life, and his study demonstrates the importance of sorting out various claims to social status as they are expressed in particular ways in particular settings and then determining under what circumstances identity becomes a crucial issue (1972c). The value of examining process as opposed to defining and demarcating the boundaries of ethnic groups is the attention placed on the fluidity and flexibility of processes of identity formation over time. The boundaries prove not to be stable and continuous but permeated by "multiple and overlapping sets of ascriptive loyalties that make for multiple identities" (Cohen 1978:387). The process of defining ethnicity over time in central Nepal can be seen in terms of Cohen's description of a "series of nesting dichotomizations of inclusiveness and exclusiveness" within which the "process of assigning persons to groups is both subjective and objective, carried out by themselves and others" (387). Cohen's categorization of ethnicity as "an historically derived lumping of sets" can be extended to Nepal where each "lumping" outlines a potential boundary. Here as elsewhere "the division into exclusive groupings is always done in relation to significant others whose exclusion at any particular level of scale creates the we/they dichotomy" (387).

The approach that focuses on the existence of ethnic groups or collectivities within larger populations and defines them as those groups whose members share some patterns of normative behavior and an ideology of common identity—as culture-bearing isolates—miscalculates the fluidity of cultural identities. This approach is particularly inadequate and misleading for the understanding of what it means to be a member of such a group as the Thakali because of its implication that what some Thakalis do in one place or another or at one time or another is characteristic of the behavior of all Thakalis. The Thakali case makes it clear that the formation and transformation of ethnic groups must be examined within the context of the formation and transformation of social processes that contribute to intragroup variation as well as to us/other distinctions.

Emphasizing the processes and contexts of group formation rather than units also helps one elude the terminological ambiguity plaguing much of the scholarship on the Himalayas. Characterizations of the Thakali and other groups in Nepal by scholars have relied on terms such as *tribe, caste,* and *ethnic group* that have been inadequately defined and ambiguously applied. Considerable confusion results when groups such as the Thakali are variously described as an ethnic group, a tribe, or a caste group. While the use of the term *ethnic group* has generally replaced the term *tribe,* is becoming well established in the anthropological writings on Nepal, and is regularly applied to the Thakali and other similar groups, it is not used with a precise and explicit meaning. One of the more serious shortcomings of this vague use of terms is that it glosses over analytical problems by offering ambiguous descriptions in the place of analysis. The term *ethnic group* is often taken to imply a cultural coherence and historical endurance that a closer analysis would expose as inaccurate.

These terminological problems are not peculiar to the literature on the Thakali or on Nepal but relate to broader questions in South Asian studies concerning the relationship of caste, tribe, and social mobility and in the general anthropological literature concerning the emergence and evolution of group identity.[15] Though the growing use of the term *ethnic group* instead of *tribe* indicates a desire to reconsider the basic epistemological features of the units of analysis and to reconceive the context in which these units are located, most attempts to distinguish among the categories of tribe, caste, and ethnic group concede any possibility of sharply distinguishing among these categories.[16]

Much of the scholarship of South Asian continues to address the issues of intergroup relations by contrasting hierarchically ordered Hindu societies with the so-called tribal populations that are said to lack internal divisions of rank. Accordingly, the concepts of non-Hindu tribes and Hindu castes form an elementary opposition in the ethnology of South Asia. The proliferation of this analytical contrast has led to and formed the basis of overly simplistic teleological models of cultural transformation (I discuss these in the next section).[17]

Studies of South Asian groups and identities revolve around considerations of caste, focusing on a variety of aspects ranging from the hierarchy of local systems of units to underlying values of ritual purity and pollution. Research on the caste system in South Asia has revealed a wide variety in the local pattern of caste relations, but it is often argued that despite this variation there are certain basic principles, which include the hierarchical order of castes, the correlation between status in the hierarchy and ritual purity, and endogamy (modified by varying tolerance of hypergamous unions). The extensive body of theories relating to caste and caste systems includes numerous theoretical and methodological approaches to the subject. Studies of caste have been explanatory, descriptive, and intensive, concerned primarily with origins, structural-functional generalizations, and in-depth studies of microsystems, respectively. Theoretical perspectives range from socioeconomic, social-cum-political, and political-economic to structuralist and focus on either the attributes of the units of caste or the delineation of the interactional network of the system. Some have insisted on the specificity of the term *caste* to the South Asian context, while others have tried to maintain a comparative terminology.[18]

Some scholars of Himalayan cultures use the term *ethnic group* as an antonym of *caste* or *caste society*, approximately in the same sense as the terms *tribe* or *tribal* are employed with reference to India. Höfer (1979a) has pointed out the limited applicability of criteria such as Bailey's and Naroll's to those Nepalese populations that have customarily been designated as ethnic groups or tribes: centuries of exposure to cultural influences from Tibet, India, the Kathmandu valley, and the Malla kingdom of Western Nepal have undercut the cultural autonomy of most hill groups in Nepal; extensive migration makes the criterion of territorial isolation invalid in most cases; and many groups exhibit internal social stratification and rely on the services of specific occupational *jāts*.

In Nepali, the term *jāt* is used for all categories of groups: there is no distinction equivalent to the English categories *ethnic group, tribe*, or *caste*. Höfer notes that the distinction between caste and ethnic group in South Asia was introduced by Western research and administration (1979a:135); in Nepal, for example, this distinction occurs only in post-1951 legislation. However, while the use of the Nepali term *jāt* in place of *ethnic group, tribe*, or *caste* avoids the ambiguous implications inherent in the vague use of the English terms, it does not resolve the analytical problems. Colloquially and legally, the term *jāt* is used in numerous ways in Nepal. Höfer also observes that in the Muluki Ain of 1854, the first codification of the caste system in Nepal, the term is used to indicate four different concepts: (1) taxonomically distinct groups that have different status positions in the hierarchy but do not necessarily correspond to commensal units or endogamous units; (2) "caste-internal" status groups that are not commensal with other status groups of the same caste (*jāt* as used in [1]); (3) culturally and linguistically distinct groups that can embrace several castes (*jāts* in the sense of [1]); and (4) the legal status of a group in general (113).

These multiple uses of the term *jāt* in the Himalayas encourages the confusion of names, peoples, and cultures, insofar as the existence of a label is often taken to imply cultural or social boundaries. In Nepal, as elsewhere, attempts to clarify differences among populations result in the granting of too much coherence and systemic unity to cultures.[19] This focus on culture as a system of shared values, beliefs, symbols, and rituals overlooks the contradictions, conflicts, paradoxes, and disjunctions that compose its processual and dynamic core.

For example, ethnographers of Nepalese societies have tried to make some conceptual sense out of the tremendous cultural diversity of Nepal by carving out three categorical divisions, roughly relating these three divisions to three geographical areas.[20] Typically, the southernmost plains and low hills of Nepal are associated with Hindu caste groups. The highest plateaus and valleys along the northern border are associated with Tibetan or Tibetan-like groups, and the area lying in between—the middle hills ranging in

altitude from two thousand to over nine thousand feet—with a wide array
of groups speaking Tibeto-Burmese languages or dialects, as well as an as-
sortment of Nepali-speaking hill groups. Models of this type tend to attribute
dichotomous characteristics to the northern and southern divisions, allowing
them to contrast the Hindu south with the Buddhist north or the caste groups
of the south with the tribal groups of the north and central hills. The large
middle ground is then presented as an amalgam of northern and southern
characteristics (usually with a bit of indigenous animism thrown in) in the
process of embracing the Hindu customs and values of the south. While
these models have allowed quick comparisons, they encourage an ongoing
reliance on a number of simplistic and misleading dichotomies: for example,
Hindu/Buddhist, Hindu/non-Hindu, and caste/tribe. The oversimplification
inherent in these models has encouraged some ethnographers to make far
more complex attempts at categorization.[21]

The next step in this process of increasingly precise categorization and
reification was to isolate and describe each identified group as distinct and
separate.[22] The cumulative effect has been a fragmented view of Nepalese
society in which culture is treated as unquestioned and long-standing and
human groups are seen as coterminous with culture. While the attempt to
place some order on variation is analytically helpful initially, the oversimplification inherent in the attempt must eventually be transcended.

On Boundary Making

The Thakali attempt to define, codify, and describe their culture by tying
it to a perceived historical tradition parallels the endeavor of some scholars
of Nepal who have sketched out an ethnographic map of Nepal by defining
and circumscribing the cultural and historical boundaries of perceived ethnic and caste groups. Both the scholarly and the Thakali attempts to discover
(or create) the past and to fix cultural boundaries selectively use readings of
the others work to further their own projects. But there are differences in
interpretation, selective history, the political moment, and historical traditions that prove to be more elusive and ambiguous; indeed, they are not
discovered but are created. Scholars need to avoid making their conceptual
boundaries more rigid than those of the people they study.

The periphery of an identity in the process of becoming is more like a
vulnerable frontier than a fixed boundary. It is within the process of state

formation and the production of national cultures that the processes of ethnic boundary formation are pressured to turn ethnic frontiers into boundaries. Foster has observed that "the production of a national culture requires above all else the demarcation of boundaries" (1991:236). This process of demarcating the boundaries of a national culture sets off further processes of boundary delineations within the confines of nation-states. Fluid boundaries emerge at the frontier of cultural nationalism, a frontier between mainstream and peripheral categorical units of the emerging imagined community. Since identity is a multilevel question that requires attention to activities at the state, regional, and local levels simultaneously, the relationship of local social orders and wider agencies at the regional, state, and transnational level must be understood to avoid the inadequacy of synchronic models that presuppose the ongoing perpetuation or reproduction of existing sociocultural structures.

Thus an understanding of the process of group-identity maintenance and formation in Nepal and, in particular, an understanding of the development of differences among Thakali groups in central Nepal can only emerge from an examination of these groups in action, within their particular social contexts. That is, the emergence and adaptation of identity must be seen in the context of the group confrontation and interaction with the historical development and centralization of the Nepalese state and the dominant cultural system it represents.[23] The motivation for identity formation is both political and cultural; its expression depends on the circumstances in which communities find themselves, and, as happens among the Thakali, human collectivities may take many forms, not only in different social systems but within the same system. The emphasis, then, should be placed on process and not just on group maintenance, so that the interaction between behavioral and symbolic aspects assumes greater theoretical significance and both sociocultural continuity and change emerge as factors in the formation of ethnicity.

With more information on the political and historical contexts in which Himalayan ethnic identifications have evolved and with multiple studies among people who identify themselves or are identified by others as members of the same so-called ethnic groups, there has been increasing recognition of the ambiguity of the boundaries of these groups and the contemporary and historical heterogeneity found within these boundaries. Contrary to Holmberg's suggestion that, at least in some areas, ethnicity is no longer a significant process (1989:11 n. 2), ethnicity has emerged as an even more active factor.

Beyond Sanskritization

It is the received wisdom in studies of Nepal that the populations of the middle hills have been involved in processes of increasing Hinduization or Sanskritization. But what is one to understand by these terms? As the discussion above demonstrates, there is inherent in their use a loose assumption of unilinear processes of cultural change. Unfortunately, overuse and unexamined acceptance of the terms obscures complicated processes and motivations for change.

For some scholars *Sanskritization* refers to a process whereby historically autonomous tribal and Buddhist groups become acculturated to caste values (Fürer-Haimendorf) or Brahmanical caste ideology (Holmberg 1989:15). One of the most frequently cited examples of this process has been the experience of the Thakali. For instance, Fürer-Haimendorf has written that the Thakali, "though originally undoubtedly a tribal group, have become a caste because they think of themselves as a caste" (1966:160).[24] This view is similar to Barth's more general observation that the acceptance by "tribals . . . of the critical value scales defining their position in the hierarchy of ritual purity and pollution is the only change in values that is necessary for a people to become an Indian caste" (1969:28).[25] This point of view both fails to clarify who "they" are who "think" of themselves as a caste and omits the influence on a people of the way in which they are defined by others.

Fürer-Haimendorf also suggests that the change from tribe to caste reflects a change in the pattern of interactions of a group with other groups and with caste society. He leaves unanswered questions of how tribal people are absorbed into a caste society, what institutions are involved in the transition, which criteria we use to decide whether a particular people is to be considered a caste or a tribe, and whether there are differences in the social organization and values of tribes and castes. A large part of the analytical problem is the structural heterogeneity of the populations called "tribal" or "tribes" in South Asia. The term is widely used to distinguish nonstate groups. As noted above, there is a tendency within the scholarship of the Himalayas to use the terms *tribe* and *tribal group* casually, as terms of convenience, to distinguish hill populations from Hindu castes, and, as a consequence, a precise understanding of the theorists' intentions and the meaning of these terms remains elusive.[26]

The various means of group mobility in the hierarchical societies of South Asia have also been the subject of an extensive literature.[27] In South

Asia, as elsewhere, the tendency to imitate—in particular, to imitate so-called elites or superiors—is encountered more or less everywhere. In South Asia this tendency has been variously labeled "Sanskritization," "Brahman-ization," "Hinduization," or "Islamization," depending on the cultural traits being imitated. The terms have been frequently applied but with an ambi-guity that has left their use open to intense criticism. The terms *Sanskriti-zation* and *Hinduization* have often been applied to the Thakali in ways that impute a predictive as well as descriptive utility to the terms. Unfortunately, even the descriptive utility of these terms is extremely limited.

Kulke (1986) and Höfer (1979b) have identified Lyall (1882) as the first to formulate a theory of Sanskritization. Lyall identified two modes of "Brah-manic propagation." Lyall's first mode, "the gradual Brahmanization of ab-original, non-Aryan, or casteless tribes," occurs when Brahmans declare local gods to be incarnations of Hindu deities and offer "what are held to be the respectable high-bred manners and prejudices . . . and gods of a more refined and aristocratic stamp, as well as more powerful."[28] For Lyall, the most telling sign of a family's reception of "Brahmanism" was the invitation to a Brahman to officiate at the rites of passage (1882:103). Lyall also observed that Brah-mans will usually discover a decent Hindu pedigree for the family if they are of standing among their own people.[29] The second mode of "Brahmanic propagation," namely, the activities of devotees and spiritual leaders who found new sects, was not discussed extensively by Lyall.

Despite this early description of social change in South Asia, Lyall is not mentioned by later scholars working on social change in South Asia except for one brief citation by H. H. Risley, who took up the question of social change and identified four distinct processes involved in the transformation of tribes into castes: (1) the mobility of the "leading men of an aboriginal tribe" (this calls to mind Lyall's families who "are of standing among their own people"); (2) the mobility of members of a tribe who embrace the tenets of Hindu religious sects; (3) the acceptance of Brahmans and Brahmanical rites by a whole tribe; and (4) the gradual conversion of a whole tribe to Hinduism without the loss of its tribal designation or complete abandonment of its tribal deities (1892:xvi). Risley's first two categories are more or less identical with the two modes described by Lyall, and the last two processes are at least partially covered by Lyall's account of continued "social change."

The subject of the transition of tribes into castes was later taken up by both Sylvain Lévi (who discusses it in the context of Nepal) and Max Weber (who discusses it in the context of India).[30] But whereas neither Lyall nor

Risley placed their discoveries in the context of India's historical development, both Lévi and Weber did, noting that the integration of tribal groups
into caste organization had always been the work of Brahmans and, to a
lesser extent, of itinerant ascetics (Lévi 1905:30, 32; Weber 1958). Weber
drew a distinction between "intensive" and "extensive propaganda" that an-
ticipated the characterizations of "Sanskritization" and "Rajputization" described respectively by Srinivas and Sinha (Srinivas 1952; Sinha 1962).

It was M. N. Srinivas who popularized the term *Sanskritization*, defining
it as "the process by which a 'low' Hindu caste or tribal or other group
changes its customs, rituals and ideology, and way of life in the direction of
a high and frequently 'twiceborn' caste" (1967:6). This definition recalls
Weber's description of the intensive Hinduization of low castes and "pariah"
people. However, the merging of the process of a so-called tribe's acceptance
of the values of the caste system with the process by which a low caste
attempts to raise its status within the caste hierarchy of a given locale confuses two structurally different processes. Furthermore, it does not tell us
what is being imitated: dress, beliefs, behaviors, and so on. In practice, the
application of the term is often substituted for explanation.

The concept of Sanskritization has undergone several modifications since
it was first described by Srinivas. In his initial work on Coorg religion, Srinivas wrote:

> The caste system is far from a rigid system in which the position of
> each component caste is fixed for all time. Movement has always been
> possible, and especially so in the middle regions of the hierarchy. A
> low caste was able, in a generation or two, to rise to a higher position
> in the hierarchy by adopting vegetarianism and teetotalism, by San-
> skritizing its ritual and pantheon. In short, it took over, as far as pos-
> sible, the customs, rites, and beliefs of the Brahmins. . . . This process
> has been called "Sanskritization."
>
> (1952:30)

In this formulation, Sanskritization is equated with Brahmanization, or
the emulation of customs and beliefs practiced by Brahmans. This model
for Sanskritization, predicated on an imitation of high-caste Brahmans by
low castes, has been frequently criticized because of its identification with
the South India experience, where the ritual distance between Brahmans
and other castes is exaggerated and the Brahmans are economically as well

as ritually dominant. These factors do not occur everywhere on the subcontinent. Srinivas later revised his model of Sanskritization to broaden its application and emphasized the concept of a "dominant caste" that, he insisted, must supplement to some extent the concept of Sanskritization:

> In the study of Sanskritization it is important to know the kind of caste which dominates in a particular region. If they are Brahmins, or a caste like the Lingayats, then Sanskritization will probably be quicker and Brahmanical values will spread, whereas if the dominant caste is a local Kshatriya or Vaishya caste, Sanskritization will be slower, and the values will not be Brahmanical. The non-Brahmanical castes are generally less Sanskritized than the Brahmins, and where they dominate, non-Sanskritic customs may get circulated among the people. It is not inconceivable that occasionally they may even mean de-Sanskritization of the imitating castes.[31]

> (1956:496)

In this model, the cultural form of the social change is unclear, and Sanskritization appears as nothing more than elite emulation.[32] Srinivas later clarified his broadened definition of Sanskritization, specifying that there was more than one model of Sanskritization. He wrote: "I now realize that in my book on Coorg religion and my 'note on Sanskritization and Westernization,' I emphasized unduly the Brahmanical model of Sanskritization and ignored the other models—Kshatriya, Vaishya and Shudra" (1967:7).

The study of the Kshatriya model recalls Weber's mode of "extensive propaganda" and has been described further by S. Sinha, who argues that during the process of state formation in central India egalitarian clan-based tribal organization has adjusted to centralized and hierarchic political developments (1962:37). This process he calls "Rajputization" if families disassociate themselves from the tribe and claim high-caste origins by the means already described by Risley.

The broadening of the concept of Sanskritization (so that it applies to processes of change that range from the adoption of Brahmanical rites, practices, and beliefs to changes that can be characterized as de-Sanskritization) seriously undermines the analytic and even the descriptive utility of the concept: it is now used to cover all sorts of changes in South Asia that are characterized by the adaptation of the customs and values of higher-status groups. Srinivas's later formulation of the concept emphasizes the process of elite emulation over the particular cultural content transmitted by the process of change. Not surprisingly, then, in many instances where the term *Sanskritization* has been applied, neither the customs or values being imitated nor the agents of change belong to a group associated with a Sanskritic tradition. Srinivas's argument means that Sanskritization can have many local variations; the cultural values transmitted by these processes are mediated through locally dominant caste groups that may have "only a perfunctory knowledge of the Great Tradition" (Srinivas 1967:17). "Whether Sanskritized or not, the dominant peasant castes provide local models for emulation" (10).

Despite these refinements the concept is still frequently misused. Yet use of the term has become so widespread that is commonly used in lieu of explanation and even detailed description. Not surprisingly, given the popular characterizations of the Thakali as a tribe that has embraced Hindu customs in order to raise its status in the eyes of its neighbors, the Thakali have been cited by some scholars as representing a classic case of Sanskritization or Hinduization. Unfortunately, the broad application of the term *Sanskritization* and the oversimplified characterizations of the Thakali misrepresent the actual situation, leaving unresolved the issue of what processes of change the Thakali have experienced, and it remains unclear what dynamics of change are indicated when the term *Sanskritization* is applied to their situation. Insofar as some Thakali have emulated cultural aspects of high-caste Hindu culture, they can perhaps be said to have been Sanskritized, but where the Thakali have become established as the dominant local group, as they are in parts of Khani Khuwa and in Thak Khola, they must be considered not only as the emulators of some other elite group but also as the models for emulation. In other words, emulation by the Thakali and emulation of the Thakali can both be termed Sanskritization by Srinivas's criterion.

Nepal includes populations that have been strongly influenced by the Indian and Tibetan cultural spheres, as well as a large number of people only peripherally aligned with either. Sylvain Lévi (1905) observed that the two traditions of Hinduism and Buddhism were so closely interwoven in Nepal that it made little sense to classify Nepalese gods as either Buddhist or Hindu. Classifying religious beliefs and practices is always limited by the analyst's own criteria of classification, but it is important to remember that for most inhabitants of the Himalayas (as for scholars like Lévi), the syncretism of Buddhism and Hinduism provides no difficulty, no problem to be solved, no classification or clarification to make. The confluence of the two traditions in various forms in Nepal, coupled with the still-strong traditions of indigenous deities and ritual practices in the hills, creates a situation where there exists a complex and often confusing coexistence of socioreligious beliefs and practices. The Thakali are a representative case of this social and religious syncretism in the middle hills of Nepal. Although Buddhist influence in Thak Khola may go back more than four hundred years (Bista 1971; Fürer-Haimendorf 1966), an essential religious aspect of the Thakali includes indigenous ancestor cult practices (Fürer-Haimendorf 1966; Bista 1971; Manzardo 1978, 1985; Vinding 1982; Fisher 1987). At the same time, Hindu religious and social practices had to be accommodated if the Thakali were to interact successfully among the Hindu caste groups of central Nepal. Any attempt to sort out these various influences is misguided insofar as it is premised on the hope that understanding of a specific hybridity will stem from sorting out the sources of the various elements of which it is composed and not from grasping how these elements have been transformed in their current set of interrelationships.

Nepali populations are often described as caught between the two "Great Traditions" of Hinduism and Tibetan Buddhism, but the process of change from one to the other is not at all clear. By imagining the Thakali as caught between two ideal models we spend too much effort looking for evidence of changes from one tradition to another rather than carefully examining complex interactions. When Hinduism and Buddhism become reified abstractions they are often perceived as persisting unchanged and, in this ideal state, are perceived as two wholly separate and independent entities. Populations in Nepal, however, freely borrow from traditions that scholars have traditionally identified as Buddhist as well as those they have traditionally identified as Hindu.

In order to clarify aspects of Thakali cultural change, their interactions with other *jāts*, and the processes of social mobility in Nepal, we need to bear in mind a number of analytic distinctions with respect to sociocultural change in South Asia. Some of these distinctions have been noted by Kulke, who has suggested a reconsideration of the way we have applied terminology to processes of social mobility in South Asia (1986). The broad term *Hinduization*, he suggests, should be applied to the whole process of social change described by Lyall, while Weber's categories of intensive and extensive propaganda make a useful distinction between processes that begin on the periphery of areas of Hindu influence and those that start within Hindu areas (105). Sanskritization, Rajputization, and so on can then be reserved for special modes of either intensive or extensive Hinduization: where this use of Hinduization distinguishes a particular process of social change, the intensive/extensive distinction marks social context, and Rajputization and Sanskritization call attention to the cultural content that characterizes the cultural imitation in process. There must also be allowance for transitional stages of these processes, as the characterization of an initial stage does not ensure that a later stage will not evolve in an unanticipated direction. This approach allows us to distinguish between influences such as Westernization and revitalization, which may occur simultaneously with other aspects of cultural imitation.

This restrictive use of these two terms makes useful distinctions among criteria such as the nature of the change, the cultural direction of the change, the process, and the social context. One might also make two additional distinctions: (1) between groups that have deliberately adopted Brahmanic rites and those who include in their practices the observance of national holidays such as Holi and Dasain[33] that do not reflect wholesale adoption of, adherence to, or understanding of Hindu values; and (2) between groups that consciously imitate or adopt Brahmanic rites and those that are not aware of cultural change but have nevertheless incorporated aspects of the dominant cultural system.

With these distinctions in mind, the description of the Thakali case becomes more complex. The Thakali can be said to have gone beyond Sanskritization in the sense that their myriad processes of change fail to adhere to the unilinear model suggested by that. Over the past hundred years elements of the Thakali population have become Sanskritized, de-Sanskritized, and Westernized, as well as having revitalized aspects of their own indigenous practices. The insistence that we reject or move beyond the model of Sanskritization is not to suggest that no aspects of Sanskrit or Hindu culture have been adopted by the Thakali. What it does suggest is that we must not privilege these changes over others but must instead place them changes in a broader context that considers how different elements of Thakali society have integrated a variety of changes in different places and at different times.

9   Old Artificers in a New Smithy

I go to encounter the reality of experience and to forge in the
smithy of my soul the uncreated conscience of my race. Old Father, Old Artificer,
stand me now and forever in good stead.
—James Joyce

"Do you know what I suspect, Sancho?" said Don Quixote.
"This wonderful piece of this enchanted helmet must by some strange accident
have come into the hands of someone unable to recognize or realize its value. Not
knowing what he did, and seeing it to be of the purest gold, he must have melted
down one half for the sake of what it might be worth and used the other to make
this, which, as you say, is like a barber's basin. Be that as it may, to me who
recognize it, the transformation makes no difference."
—Miguel de Cervantes

"Have you heard," asked my friend Deepak excitedly, "what
was found in my uncle's house in Chairo after his death? They found the
crown and scepter of the Hansa Raja."

This news immediately caught wide attention. The story of the Hansa
Raja has had a controversial place in Thakali history. In its basic form the
story tells of a son of the high-caste Thakuri king of Sinja who wandered
around the Himalayas until he came to the town of Thini, where he married
the daughter of the Thini Raja and was given lands south of Thini, where
he settled down. This story has had particular significance for any Thakali
wishing to claim a connection between the Thakali and the high-caste
Hindu Thakuris. Despite the emphasis on this story, there has been very
little known of the historical Hansa Raja. Some accounts of the origin of the
Thakali identify the Hansa Raja as the ancestor of all the Thakali and identify
the four clans as the descendants of the four sons of the Hansa Raja and
Nhima Rani. Others speculate that the Hansa Raja was probably the ancestor
of only some of the Thakali.

Some identify Hansa Raja with the Pompar *ghyu*, the Sherchan subclan
to which my friend belongs.[1] The name Pompar, informants argue, appears

to be derived from the original word for "king." Members of the *ghyu* note that accounts of their ancestor Sonam-pompar parallel some stories of the Hansa Raja. Sonam-pompar is said to have come from the town of Sinja, in western Nepal, to Thak Khola, where he married Nhima Rani, the daughter of the ruler of Thini. The Thini Raja gave as dowry the land stretching from Dumpha to the Lhaki Forest. Sonam and his descendants settled in Chairo and paid tribute to the Thini ruler.

News of the discovery at Chairo prompted me to inquire about what exactly had been found, how they knew these items belonged to the Hansa Raja, and whether it was anachronistic that the Hansa Raja would have worn a crown as the symbol of his royalty. My friends had no answers and urged me to wait until we were able to observe the items ourselves.

The day after our arrival in Larjung for the twelve-year festival we went to the storage room for the Thakali council of thirteen headman where the items had been moved the previous month after the head of the lineage had instructed that they be turned over to the Thakali community. Filled with anticipation, I waited patiently as my Thakali companions crowded into the small room of the *kot ghar* and murmured sounds of awe and astonishment as they looked over and handled the items. When my turn came I saw nothing more than a carelessly heaped pile of rusted and pitted sword blades, an innocuous metal alloy helmet, and a two-and-a-half-foot-long club. Was this an old helmet or the crown of the Hansa Raja? A barber's shaving bowl or the helmet of Mambrino? My muted and cautiously skeptical observations elicited the response that half of the helmet must be missing; what I held, they assured me, was only the lining of the original crown.

My disappointment contrasted with their excitement. My companions believed they had found a tangible verification of the stories they tell and hear. I was not comfortable playing Sancho Panza, failing to see glory wherever it might be found or warning others against jousting with windmills, so I sought counsel elsewhere. Other Thakalis were less enthusiastic: some refused to go look; others referred to the find as a pile of rubbish. In the end, I again found conflict between the impassioned search for the past and a determined resistance to concluding that search, a fertile conflict that continues to give rise to multiple interpretations and narratives about history and culture.

This book has examined the changing conditions, opportunities, and constraints under which interrelated sets of Thakali and others have forged histories, visions, and procedures for organizing. It has explored the potential for conflicts that have arisen as people have constructed their identities and communities through innovation, resistance, and accommodation. In part, the Thakali case reveals contemporary identity distinctions in Nepal as a by-product of the historical attempts to forge the artifice of a Hindu kingdom. What appear at first to be shifting religious orientations among some hill groups over the past two hundred years reflect a complex set of political motives and identity choices influenced by both maneuvers for influence within these communities and the pressures of the regional and national status systems within which individuals had vested interests.

As an examination of the specific conditions under which people in central Nepal made their own history, this study has implications for our understandings of the interrelationships among nationalism, hegemony, culture, and processes of social and cultural change. The discussion of the Thakali presents one window on the complex ongoing process by which Nepalese society has been and continues to be molded as individuals and groups confront changing social realities and attempt both to adapt to them and to reform them.

The Thakali case is particularly instructive for these purposes. The deceptively straightforward tale of successful elite emulation, in which a group was said to adapt to the changing economic and political opportunities accompanying the formation of the Nepalese state by consciously abandoning their old traditions in favor of Hindu customs in order to justify their newly asserted claim to high-caste Thakuri status, plays to the Hindu elite vision of a nation slowly moving toward a Hindu homogenization. But the simplicity of this tale must give way to a range of conflicting characterizations of the Thakali that reveal the tale of elite emulation to be, at best, a partial account, a misleading artifice.

The foregoing inquiry into the contested and, in some ways, fluid boundaries of Thakali identity considered the complex and varying effects that the interpretations and reinterpretations of Thakali social identity and status by the Thakali and by scholars have had on different segments of Thakali society over the past hundred years.

The intriguingly contradictory assessments of the Thakali by the earliest scholars in central Nepal convey an inconsistent view of Thakali culture, particularly with regard to the extent of Thakali devotion to Buddhism and the chronology of their conversion to that faith and the impetus, nature, sincerity, and chronology of the alleged subsequent conversion to Hinduism. The overall image is one of cultural inconstancy. Other Nepalese have sometimes attributed this religious fickleness to the calculating, rationalizing character of the Thakali, portraying them as clever, greedy, and atheistic, professing any belief as long as it was to their advantage to do so.

How then did a heterogeneous and complex collection of people come to be perceived as the quintessential example of a unilineal process of cultural transformation and cited as a clear case of Sanskritization? The Thakali are not the only artificers who play a role in forging this simplified representation: anthropologists and the Hindu elite have also contributed to the contemporary forging of histories in Nepal. When foreign scholars first began to describe the Thakali in the 1950s, the Thakali followed a wide range of practices, which varied depending on locale, age, sex, occupation, and education: for instance, older Thakalis in Thak Khola, particularly women, actively practiced Buddhism; the merchants of Tukche professed to be Hindu; residents of agricultural villages maintained rituals associated with the Thakali shaman (*dhom*); and Thakalis in Khani Khuwa practiced a complex of religious rituals not dissimilar to that practiced in the agricultural villages of Thak Khola, with, of course, the omission of rites peculiar to local Thak Khola deities and the addition of rites associated with deities common to areas in Khani Khuwa.

Different scholars were attracted by different aspects of these changes and, attempting to account for how this cultural diversity came about and to indicate where it was heading, presented divergent chronologies and scenarios for the introduction of Buddhist and Hindu influences in Thak Khola. The argument presented here takes all these disparate streams as part of the same river: Buddhism has been influential in Thak Khola from at least the fourteenth century, but other influences, including Hinduism, have also been present, introduced through trading contacts, pilgrims, and, since the early nineteenth century, via the Thakalis who had begun to migrate to the mining areas.

Ethnic distinctions have been drawn in different ways at different times by different members or subgroups of the Thakali. This manipulation of cultural symbols has been conducted both consciously and unconsciously by different interest subgroups but never, as has sometimes been claimed, collectively by the Thakali as a whole.

In the late nineteenth century, after one branch of the Sherchan Lha Khang Dhungi *phobe* had gained control of the salt contract, some of the Tukche merchants, led by the family of Harkaman Subba, expended some of their wealth in sponsoring expensive Buddhist rituals, constructing private

Buddhist temples in their homes, and endowing public signs of their devotion (for example, the construction of new temples and shrines and the
performance of elaborate Tibetan Buddhist funerals date to this period). The
conscious adaptation to Hindu caste values began only in the early twentieth
century, initiated by the next generation of this small interest group of Tukche merchants in the 1920s. In other words, the conscious process of Hinduization began not with the expanded contact with Hindu society that
followed the unification of Nepal, or with the passage of the Muluki Ain in
1854, or with the initiation of the salt contract system in 1862 but toward
the end of the salt contract period, just as the Tukche merchants, led by
Hitman Subba, were expanding their trade networks to areas further south
and increasing their contacts with and contractual obligations to the Rana
government. A wealthy Thakali minority that stood to gain the most from
the creation of a distinct Thakali identity and, specifically, from the presentation of the Thakali as a high-status Hindu caste set out to define the four
clans from Thaksatsae as a distinct group, as Thakali, a group that could be
influenced by the wealthy traders and distanced from the more obvious
Tibetan Buddhist groups in the same region. The greatest influence of the
council of thirteen headmen dates to this time period (1925–35), as do the
religious reforms passed by the council.

The Thakali elite tilt, first toward aspects of Buddhism and then toward
Hinduism, was not equally embraced by other groups in Thak Khola or even
by other segments of Thakali society at large and Thaksatsae Thakali society
in particular; moreover, as noted, Thakalis outside Tukche largely ignored
or were unaffected by the religious reforms enacted by the council of thirteen
headmen. The migrants in Khani Khuwa, almost all of whom had migrated
there before the end of the salt contract system, continued to regard themselves as Buddhist, though most of them performed no Buddhist rites.

Two additional events—the extensive migration from Thak Khola after
1960 and the enactment of legislation in 1964 by King Mahendra, which,
though it did not abolish the caste system, removed government endorsement of it—have led to further differences in cultural practices among the
Thaksatsae Thakali *samaj*. The first event spread the Thakali population
even farther afield and at the same time removed the major Hinduizing
agents—the Tukche merchants—from Thak Khola, while the second reduced the impetus for the adaptation to Hinduism. Together, these factors
have contributed to the development of differences in cultural practices and
political and economic interests both among the various migrant Thakali

communities and between generations within the same community. For example, the youngest generation descended from the Tukche merchants has been educated in private schools, speaks Nepali and English as first and second languages (not necessarily in that order) rather than Thakali and Tibetan, professes scientific atheism as much as Hinduism or Buddhism, and is considerably less apt than its parents to accept unquestioningly the identification of the Thakali with Hinduism. Yet it is members of this younger generation who are spearheading the movement for a revitalization of Thakali tradition, albeit a tradition some of their parents insist never existed. Thakalis who have migrated from Thak Khola in the past two decades have adapted in varying fashions to their local social environments, sometimes doing without the service of a resident Thakali shaman for many years and sometimes employing the services of a Brahman priest for rituals that would have required a lama or shaman in Thak Khola, but most of these migrants have enthusiastically readopted the use of Thakali shamans when they become available in these areas, suggesting that the initial characterizations of these migrants as Sanskritizing were premature.[2]

As noted earlier, an analysis of Thakali cultural changes becomes clearer if one maintains a number of important distinctions; one of these is the difference between the conscious adoption of Hindu practices by the merchants of Tukche and the unconscious acculturation that altered Thakali society in many migrant communities. The deliberate adoption of Hindu practices by the Tukche elite appears to have been the first step in a process of "extensive Hinduization," similar to that described by Kulke (1986), wherein the local elite dissociated the four clans from Thaksatsae from other groups residing in Thak Khola and sought to identify the Thaksatsae clans with high-status Thakuris. Weber suggested that this kind of process results in a double legitimacy: it both endows the Hinduizing element with rank in Hindu society and secures their superiority over their neighbors and former peers ([1916] 1958:16). Among the Thakali, however, this process has evolved in surprising ways. At first the Hinduizing element, though it never fully achieved the Thakuri status it claimed, achieved a modicum of acceptance within Hindu caste society. But in the long run this process accorded higher status neither to the four Thaksatsae clans vis-à-vis other groups in the upper Kali Gandaki valley nor to the Tukche merchants vis-à-vis other elements of Thaksatsae Thakali society. In fact, as became clear in the account of the formalization of the national Thakali community, the identification of the descendants of the *subbas* and other elite merchant families with Hinduism has been used by other Thaksatsae Thakali factions to denigrate the relative status of this group within the Thaksatsae Thakali community. Rather than reaping the benefits of Weber's "double legitimacy," the Hinduizing element has found itself in a double bind that has further isolated from both the Thakuris and the Thakalis.

Sharma has argued that the Thakali claim to Thakuri status should not be interpreted as a serious attempt to have the Thakali accepted as belonging to the highest status category recognized by the Muluki Ain—that of *tagadhari*, the "wearers of the sacred cord"—but as an attempt to ensure Thakali acceptance within the second status—*namansinya matwali*, unenslavable alcohol drinkers—and above the third—*mansinya matwali*, enslavable alcohol drinkers (1977). In the Muluki Ain, these two latter categories are characterized by ambiguous internal ranking, an ambiguity reflected by the casual attitude in the middle hills toward commensality, inter-*jāt* marriage, and other aspects of ritual purity (see also Höfer 1979a:64).

The application of the term *Hinduization*, however, to the slow acculturation of the Thakali in migrant communities in Khani Khuwa overstates the Hindu nature of this cultural change. This process occurred in a relatively less rigid social environment than that within which the Tukche elite resided after moving to Kathmandu. While the Thakali in this region profess to have lost or forgotten much of their culture and direct questions about Thakali customs to Thakali residing in Thak Khola, they continue to perform a wider set of Thakali rituals than do migrant Thakali communities elsewhere. Thakali customs clearly underwent some modification in Khani Khuwa, but these changes only superficially reflect Hindu influence. Class is more operative than caste in these communities, and relative status is more often affected by wealth and power than by caste status.

Both the slow acculturation of Thakalis in Khani Khuwa and the deliberate identification with Hinduism by elites in Tukche were accompanied by interesting secondary processes of elite emulation and social change. These include the aforementioned attempt by other groups in Thak Khola to associate or reassociate themselves with the Thakali of Thaksatsae by laying claim to be of Thakali status. In Khani Khuwa, as well, other groups have come to emulate the Thakali, who, as rural elites and middlemen, have come to occupy an intermediate position between the local communities and the nation, from which, through webs of social relations, they articulate different social groups. In this capacity the Thakali, who have become increasingly Westernized through contacts with development agencies, modern education, overseas trading experiences, and service in the British army, are the agents or catalysts for change, serving as a model for emulation by other *jāts* in the region.

Two other significant processes of social change in the Thaksatsae Thakali community have become apparent in the last two decades. One is the revitalization of Thakali culture, a reemphasis on the uniqueness of Thakali identity and Thakali rites. The development and spread of this revitalization refute linear visions of change like that of Fürer-Haimendorf, who predicted that "all those Thakalis who now live dispersed among the castes of the multiethnic Nepalese society will gradually be assimilated to the ideology of the dominant Hindu castes" (1967b:202; see also 1966:151). Revitalization was clearly illustrated by the sentiments most frequently expressed at the April 1983 organizational meeting for the national Thakali *samaj* association, by the actions of local Thakali communities following that meeting, and the efforts of the Thakali at the twelve-year festival in 1993.

This process of revitalization has had several paradoxical effects. First, though it has worked against the interests of the previously dominant Hinduized Thakali elite, many of them have come to embrace aspects of it. Second, the Thakali revitalization has not brought the Thaksatsae Thakali culturally closer to the claimants of Thakali status in the upper Kali Gandaki valley, for while the Thakali of Thaksatsae are reemphasizing rituals involving animal sacrifices for the ancestors, the Marphalis and other Panchgaonle Thakali are reemphasizing a more orthodox Buddhism (Parker 1985:205–7; Vinding 1982:295 n. 20).

The implication for scholars is that we must be cautious not to assume that the occurrence of changes often superficially labeled as Sanskritization necessarily indicates a cumulative or directional influence. In other words, the process of Sanskritization is neither one-way nor irreversible.

The second ongoing process of change is the formalization of the Thakali *samaj* and the widespread efforts to coordinate their actions as a single unified community. The emergence of Thakali as a status and the consolidation of the Thaksatsae Thakali as a distinct cultural group began in consort with the extending arm of the Gurkha raja and has evolved along with the development of the state. Interestingly, one could draw a parallel between the initial step in the process of Hinduization and castification of the Thaksatsae Thakali and the emergence of these Thakali as a tribe (in Fried's [1975:114] or Moerman's [1974:54] sense of "a secondary socio-political phenomenon" [54] that emerges through interaction with the state) or as an ethnic group (described earlier as a collectivity with a subjective identity that cooperates to further common interests). This process was marked by the increasing importance of the council of thirteen Thakali headmen in Thaksatsae, the cultural reforms of the early twentieth century, and the increasing group consciousness of the Thaksatsae clans as a distinct group of Thakali.

The 1983 emergence of the Thakali association brought the four clans together in contemporary Nepal as an active political interest group, a process similar to what Dumont termed the "substantialization" of caste (1970:222). For Dumont, substantialization occurs when caste systems transform into collections of "closed groupings corresponding to modern ideas of social stratification" by shedding their religious basis (413 n. 112e). Leach and Gough have also concluded that when castes act as corporations or as political factions they are acting "in defiance of caste principles" and "cease to be a caste" (Leach 1960:6–7).[3] The current study indicates that the two processes of revitalization and substantialization are not necessarily mutually exclusive but may reinforce each other: revitalization may be the means by which the substantialization of a group is effected.

This analysis of the emergence of a particular form of Thakali identity has important implications for future research in Nepal, not least the conclusion that the widespread practice of classifying the peoples of Nepal as this or that tribe, caste, or ethnic group is inappropriate and limited. Labels such as Tamang, Magar, Thakali, Newar, Gurung, and so forth do not mark unchanging isolates with historical depth and cultural continuity. Many of these labels denote status in the caste hierarchy of Nepal, but the correspondence between these labels and particular bounded behavioral groups or distinct traditions is limited. The labels may be used by a wide variety of individuals in particular contexts, especially when dealing with representatives of the state or outsiders, to claim a status that may influence political and economic opportunities. But among the peoples indicated by any one of these labels, the social categories are both more finely subdivided and more flexible.

The emergence of Thakali identity, for example, is intertwined in the relations of the Thakali with other groups in Nepal that took form within the historical processes associated with the development and centralization of that nation. In the Thakali case, a group of merchant families moved within the hierarchical values of the caste system of Nepal, first accepting the concept of caste status and then maneuvering for a higher one. As Thakali evolved as a recognized status and as the Thakali of Thaksatsae evolved as a group, emphasis was placed on external rather than internal differentiation, that is, on boundaries distinguishing the Thakali of Thaksatsae from others rather than on divisions among the Thaksatsae Thakali.

Ethnic groups are not static, either culturally or socially: they are a dynamic product of interest-group articulation and cultural identity. Within Nepal, there are many examples of groups that have attempted to raise their relative status in terms of the caste system and in doing so have changed practices and identified themselves as higher-status groups (see Bista 1971; Holmberg 1980; Höfer 1978). Some Nepalese groups expanded and others closed their ranks in response to the growing influence of the Nepalese state.

The question that emerges is thus not only what ethnicity is but when and where does ethnicity become an issue. An analysis of where and when ethnicity is activated can reveal the manifold forms ethnic groups may take within different regional systems of integration. Particular cultural traits are relevant to particular adaptations and interaction systems, and, as among the Thakali, migration and social changes lead to increasing variations in the cultural traits shared by all segments of a society. For ethnic groups, different symbols become manifest at different levels of the social system. Some broadly acknowledged symbols—for instance, among the Thaksatsae Thakali, those that evoke the ancestors, for example, *khimi, khe, khāngalo,* Lha Phewa, Narijhowa, and the four clan gods—identify a group in all situations, while others—such as the Thakali identification with trade, language, dress, and the like—may be manifest within particular regions or subgroups of the society.

Thakalis in different migrant communities (for example, Khani Khuwa Thakalis) place greater emphasis on the performance of particular Thakali rites than on the purity of descent, while others (including Thakalis from Thak Khola) draw the ethnic boundaries along lines of descent. As noted earlier, Thakali endogamy and descent are casually treated in Khani Khuwa, where the Thakali attitude toward descent is more characteristic of that of Nepali caste society in general than of the attitude of Thakalis in Thak Khola, where the emphasis on the purity of descent is more rigidly upheld. One effect of the creation of the national *samaj* association was to draw attention to the criteria for membership in the Thakali *samaj*. Paradoxically, despite the essential role played by the descendants of the *subbas* in the reunification of the Thakali *samaj*, their present acceptance of Hindu culture and current tendency to marry non-Thakalis leave them in a position to be excluded in the future on the basis of both culture and descent. During the past few years they have responded to this danger by publicly embracing visible aspects of Thakali culture, ostentatiously reacquainting their children with the public performances of Thakali rituals that have been the focus of the revitalization movement.

The Thakali case demonstrates that ethnicity is not an inherent quality that is simply passed on from generation to generation; it is a dynamic process and emerges fully only through interaction and conflict. The current search for ethnic coherence draws its authority from a claimed connection to the past, to tradition. But the meaning created or extracted from that past, which is an important criterion of coherence, is created as an ethic designed for the present. Durkheim argued that society "feels itself drawn in divergent directions. But these conflicts which break forth are not between the ideal and reality, but between two different ideals, that of yesterday and that of today, that which has the authority of tradition and that which has the hope for the future" (1964:470). Thus, as I noted in the first chapter, the recent attempts by the Thakali to define their identity and clarify their cultural practices suggest that to return to tradition they must first create it—or re-create it—but this process of re-creation establishes it in a way in which it has never existed before.

Recognizing the contested nature of Thakali history and identity, I was heartened when the analogy I used at the Lha Phewa workshop between Thakali culture and the meandering of the Kali Gandaki River struck a chord with many who heard it. In subsequent visits to Nepal and Thak Khola, I have frequently found myself introduced as the professor who likened Thakali culture to the Kali Gandaki River. On one evening several years after Lha Phewa, while sitting with friends in a small Tatopani inn above the hot springs, my host recounted almost verbatim to his guests my entire comments from the 1993 workshop. Ironically, my comments have now become an object of my own study as, on occasion, new acquaintances, not knowing precisely who I am, but upon learning that I am interested in the Thakali, begin to explain, "You see, Thakali culture is like the Kali Gandaki River . . . "

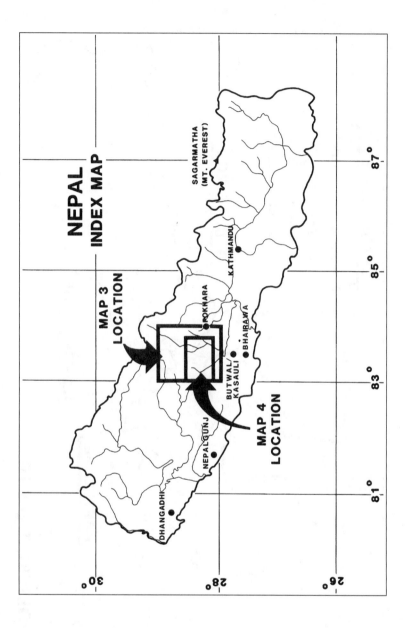

NEPAL
INDEX MAP

MAP 3
LOCATION

MAP 4
LOCATION

SAGARMATHA
(MT. EVEREST)

KATHMANDU

POKHARA

BHAIRAWA

BUTWAL/
KASAULI

NEPALGUNJ

DHANGADHI

30°

28°

26°

81°

83°

85°

87°

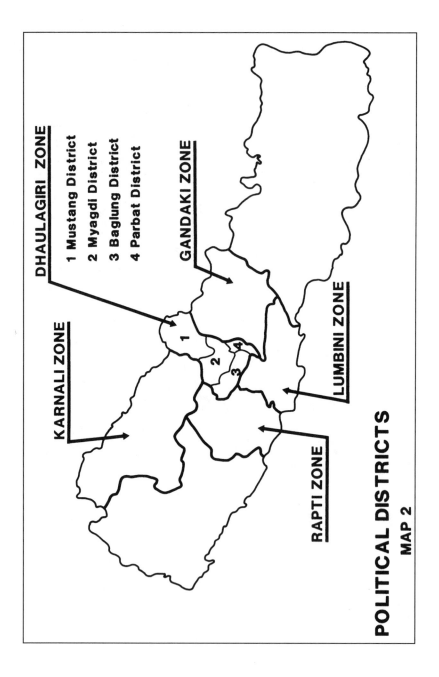

KARNALI ZONE

DHAULAGIRI ZONE

1 Mustang District
2 Myagdi District
3 Baglung District
4 Parbat District

GANDAKI ZONE

LUMBINI ZONE

RAPTI ZONE

POLITICAL DISTRICTS

MAP 2

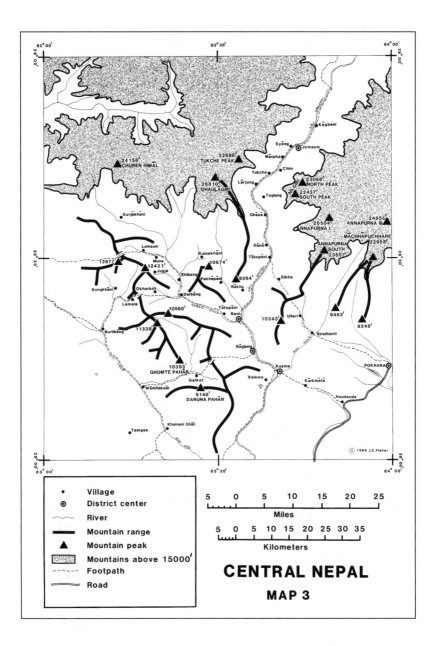

Village •

District center ◉

River

Mountain range

Mountain peak ▲

Mountains above 15000′

Footpath

Road

5 0 5 10 15 20 25
Miles

5 0 5 10 15 20 25 30 35
Kilometers

CENTRAL NEPAL

MAP 3

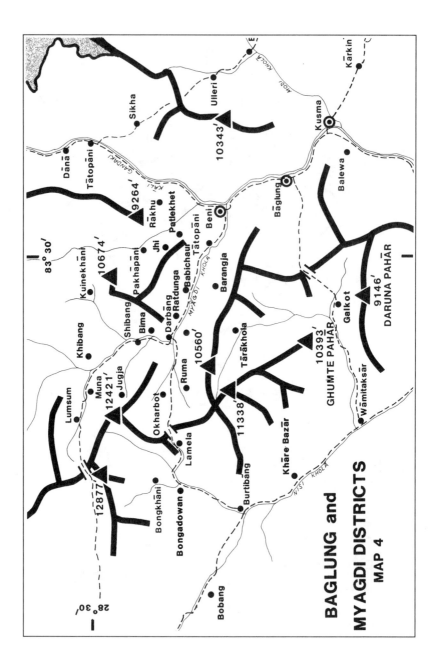

BAGLUNG and
MYAGDI DISTRICTS
MAP 4

Notes

In appended translations, "T" stands for "Thakali," "N" for "Nepali," "Tib." stands for "Tibetan."

Preface

1. In April 1983, when the same woman spoke in Thakali at the Pokhara meeting to form a national Thakali association, many attendees praised her, and no one objected.

2. The irony of my status as a fictive in-law was reflected by the name by which I was known throughout Khani Khuwa: *juāi saheb* (N: *juāi*, son-in-law or brother-in-law; *saheb*, a title of respect similar to the English *sir*; see Turner 1931:221, 603). The combination allowed my companions to address my dual status as foreign scholar and fictive son-in-law with a mixture of humor and respect, as well as with both intimacy and distance. The mixture varied depending on the circumstances and the disposition of my various fictive in-laws.

1. Introduction

1. Following the conventions of the people I studied, I use the appellation *Thakali* to refer to the four clans—Sherchan, Gauchan, Bhattachan, and Tulachan— of Thaksatsae. When necessary to distinguish them from other individuals or groups also identifying themselves or identified by others as Thakali, I use the designation *Thaksatsae Thakali* or *the Thakali of Thaksatsae*.

    The artificial term *Tamang Thakali* introduced by the Danish scholar Michael Vinding has been used by him and other scholars to distinguish this group from other groups who identify themselves as Thakali (but who are not recognized as such by the members of these four clans). See, for example, Vinding 1998, Heide 1988, and Fisher 1987. The Thakali of Thaksatsae themselves never use this term, and many have expressed a dislike for it. In deference to them, I employ the more preferred artificial term *Thaksatsae Thakali* when necessary to avoid confusion. The various applications of the term *Thakali* and the meaning behind these conflicting claims are discussed in chapter 2.

2.   *Thak* refers to a specific area in the upper Kali Gandaki river valley. *Khola* (N) is a river or valley. The Thakali are, literally, the people from Thak or Thaksatsae (N: *sātsae*, "seven hundred": the term *Thaksatsae* is often taken to refer to the original seven hundred households of Thak). The proper application of the term *Thak Khola*, however, like the designation *Thakali*, is disputed.

3.   The four clan *rhabs* tell of the travels of the clan ancestors and gods from various places in the west and north to Thak.

4.   Throughout, and consistent with colloquial use by the Thakali, I refer to the four clans by their contemporary names: Gauchan, Sherchan, Tulachan, and Bhattachan. In the *rhabs*, and at an earlier historical period, the four clans were referred to by other names: Cyogi, Ḍhimchen, Sālgi, and Bhurgi, respectively.

5.   *Khāni Khuwā* is a term used by the Thakali to refer to an area of the Baglung, Myagdi, and Gulmi districts where there were once many active mines.

6.   I first went to Thak Khola in 1981. I conducted research for my Ph.D. dissertation from September 1982 to October 1984, working primarily, but not exclusively, with Thakali communities and networks outside of Thak Khola (see Fisher 1987). I have returned periodically to Thakali communities both in and outside Thak Khola since then, including extended visits in 1987, 1991, 1992, 1993, and 1997.

7.   See chapter 8 and Fisher (1987).

8.   Though they represent only a tiny percentage of the total population of Nepal, the Thakali have caught the attention of many scholars. Prior to 1950, there were few written accounts of the Thakali or Thak Khola. Since that time, foreign, Nepalese, and Thakali scholars and laypeople have written a great deal about the people and the valley. For an annotated bibliography see Vinding and Bhattachan (1985). In addition to individual scholars, the multidisciplinary Nepal German Project on High Mountain Archaeology has worked in Mustang District (including Thak Khola) in the 1990s.

The Thakali are also mentioned in most travel and trekking books about Nepal. These books echo the most commonly held stereotypes about the Thakali: *Insight Guides*, for example, discusses them under the heading "The Clever Thakalis" and proclaims them the most successful entrepreneurs in the Nepal. *The Rough Guide* describes them as "ingenious traders" with "entrepreneurial flair."

9. The narratives told by scholars about the Thakali and the evidence they use to support these narratives are discussed in more detail in chapters 3 and 7.

10. For example, Bista has written: "The case of the Thakali of the upper Kali Gandaki is unique in the political history of the various tribal groups of Nepal. In a dramatic fashion the Thakalis succeeded in winning political power and authority, gaining ascendancy within their own group and restructuring their tribal hierarchy in relation to other groups of the region" (1971:52). Similarly, Manzardo has written: "In the degree to which they have been able to adapt to change and improve their standard of living the Thakalis are a unique group in the middle hills of west central Nepal" (1978:iv). Messerschmidt and Gurung refer to the "history of economic success" enjoyed by the "dynamic" Thakalis and have designated the Thakalis as the "likely winners of a prize for tribal entrepreneurship" (1974:197). See also Fürer-Haimendorf (1966).

11. Fürer-Haimendorf, for example, has described the Thakali as "fundamentally a trading community" (1981b:175; also see 1985:141). Manzardo's analysis also focused on "Thakalis who are involved chiefly in commercial enterprise" (1978:iv), though he has acknowledged that "many, if not most of the Thakali, are not traders" (1977a:63).

12. Manzardo and Sharma, for example, have written that changes "brought a rapid end to their way of life" (1977b:434) and that the "basic theme of communal change in order to enhance status appears repeatedly throughout Thakali history" (1978:32). See also Snellgrove (1961:177); Fürer-Haimendorf (1967b:197–98); Bista (1967, 1971); Manzardo (1978); and Messerschmidt (1984).

13. Many travelers and scholars have commented on this migration, including Jest, who writes: "Certaines familles sont émigré et se sont installées au sud de Dana, dan la vallée de la Kali Gandaki, ou dans la vallée de la Mayangdi et de la Bhuji Khola, plus a l'ouest" (1964/65:32). Gauchan and Vinding observe that "a significant number of Thakaali have—mainly in the past three decades— settled more or less permanently outside Thaasang where they are engaged in various kinds of business" (1977:99–100). See also Fürer-Haimendorf (1975:142; 1981a:177); Messerschmidt (1973:29 n. 20); and Manzardo (1978:22, 50–51 n. 6). But except for occasional mentions, no study has yet addressed the status, number, or social situation of the Thakali who have migrated out of Thak Khola.

Gauchan and Vinding have noted that "too many problems concerning migration among the Thakaali-speaking groups are still unsolved, so a complete study of this interesting subject is badly needed" (1977:100 n. 9). Manzardo has observed that the history of trade through the Thak Khola valley is well described but has added that "too little attention has been paid to aspects of trade in the middle hills" (1978:190). For a study of Thakali migration, see Fisher (1987).

14. Michael Vinding and Donald Messerschmidt attended this gathering. At the time I was conducting research in western Nepal and was unable to accept the invitation. Michael Vinding later repeated his conclusions in an interview with Krishna Bhattachan: "People can change their language and culture, but not their race. When a Thakali looks in the mirror he sees a mongoloid face, not the caucasoid face of a Thakuri. This proves that the bulk of the Thakali's ancestors were of mongoloid stock" (Bhattachan 1985). See also Vinding (1998:393). As many of my informants often impressed on me, this view was decidedly unpopular.

15. See Bourdieu 1977; Sahlins 1981; Ortner 1984.

16. See also Roseberry, who describes culture as "a rather inchoate set of lived experiences, feelings, and relationships within a political and economic order of domination. Because it is not a closed system, it is in a constant process of construction and reconstruction" (1989:75).

17. This emerged partly as a by-product of an anthropology striving to understand human diversity by assembling information on one culture at a time before making comparisons (see Moore 1989:28).

18. Bentley, from a more extreme position, says, "Conceptions of ethnic identity, while symbolically constructed fictions of shared descent, are not entirely arbitrary" (1987:36).

19. The raja of Gurkha, whose eighteenth-century conquests formed the basis for the modern state of Nepal. For an account of the unification of Nepal, see Stiller (1973).

20. July 1990 Columbia University workshop on writing a national constitution.

21. I mean not only to acknowledge that what follows is interpretation and not mere observation (see, for instance, Geertz, who writes, "What we call our data are really our own constructions of other people's constructions of what they and their compatriots are up to" [1973:9]) but to stress the heterogeneity of Thakali constructions of what they are up to and their attempts to understand what it means to be Thakali.

2. Drawing Lines

1. The Chimang *bemchāg* discusses the alteration of the boundary by the Parbat Raja. See Ramble and Vinding (1987) and Vinding (1998:61).

2. *Khola* (N), means "small river, valley, or hollow." Kawakita has asserted that the Thakali people can be referred to as Thak (1957:86). More commonly the

area is called Thak and the people Thakali. Snellgrove identified T'hak as the Tibetan name of the region and Thākkhola the Nepali name (1961).

3. For example, see Kawakita (1957:86) and Turner (1931:293). Turner offers two transliterations of the term: Thakāli and Thākāli. The latter term, however, is used in other instances to refer to a chief or chieftain (1931:295).

4. Glo Mantān, an area in northern Mustang District near the Tibet-Nepal border, is the traditional seat of the raja of Mustang. The Tibetan name was transformed into the Nepali name Mustang, which is now applied not only to the town of Lo and to the raja's former domain but also to an administrative district that includes all the area stretching along the upper Kali Gandaki valley from the border to Dana (see maps 2 and 3). I use Lo to refer to the traditional seat of the raja and Mustang to refer to the district.

5. More recently, Vinding has employed the term *Thak Khola* to refer to the area between Ghāsa and Jomsom (1998:9, 447).

6. Jackson notes that Thak seems to have come from the local Tibetan dialects, but he has not found it in the oldest Tibetan language sources. Tucci cites the biography of the lama San's rgyas bzan' po (Jackson transliterates this as Sangs-rgyas-bzang-po), which reports the visit of the lama to T'ag p'yogs, which apparently refers to the area now called Thaksatsae (Tucci 1956:13). Jackson claims that this reference cannot date before the late 1600s or the early 1700s (1978:196 n. 2).

    A number of tales purport to explain how the area got its name. Kawakita recounts an unlikely tale of a man of the Thapa *jāt* who died near Tukche, thus giving his name to the river that came to be called Thapa Khola and then Thakhola (1957:87). Some residents of the valley relate the name to the strong winds that blow from north to south through the valley; in this version, men walking the valley are said to have turned to their companions and complained "Kasto thakai khola!" (What a tiring valley!). Another account links the name of the river to a minister of the government named Thapa who was washed away in a flood, thus lending his surname to the river. According to this account, Thapa Khola later became Thak Khola and the people residing by the river Thakalis (this account is also related in I. Tulāchan 1992:3).

7. Baragaon (N: *bāragāū*, "the twelve villages") is used to indicate the area composed of a number of heterogeneous populations lying along the Kali Gandaki and Muktinath Khola between Jomsom and Lo. The inhabitants of this area are colloquially called Baragaonle.

    For divisions of Thak Khola, see, for example, Fürer-Haimendorf (1975:134) and Jackson (1978:196). Some scholars, including Vinding, refer to Thāksātsae as "the southern part of Thāk Kholā" (1998:447).

8. The British were interested in opening up trade with Tibet, and they were well aware of the importance of the Tibetan salt trade in the area. See, for instance, Field (1959).

9. In the 1860s, Captain Montgomerie of the Survey of India proposed the idea of using natives from the Himalayan region to explore the areas beyond the sphere of British control. These explorers, commonly referred to as *pundits*, were trained in the clandestine use of surveying instruments and dispatched on journeys into Tibet under Montgomerie's direction (see Montgomerie 1868, 1875). Rudyard Kipling's novel *Kim* is also based on the adventures of these explorers.

10. Snellgrove reports that the local name in Jomsom for a man from "T'ha-k" was "T'ha-k-pa" (1961:174 n). This term is not now used in the area below Tukche in Thak Khola but may, like Thakali, be a term used in interactions with outsiders, in this case, with Tibetan speakers.

11. The population of the Thakali of Thaksatsae in 1997 was approximately eleven thousand. Another three to four thousand belong to the other two clan-based groups.

12. Scholars have referred to the area as "Thak Sat Sae" ("the seven hundred Thaks" [Bista 1967]), "Thak Sat Sae" ("the seven hundred Thakali households" [Manzardo and Sharma 1975]), "'Thāsang" or "Thāksātsaye" ("the seven hundred Thāk [Thakli houses]" [Gauchan and Vinding 1977:99 n. 8]), "Thaksatsai" (Vinding 1984), and *"thāksātsae"* (Vinding 1998:447).

13. This name is variously transcribed as Tamang, Tamhang, Tamāng, and Tahmang. Despite the familiarity of the name with the term *Tamang* now used to refer a group to the east, the connection between the Thakali and the Tamang remains unclear. Tamang, the designation for the eastern group, is sometimes written Thamang (MacDonald 1966:28). Prior to 1932 the Tamang were known as *"murmi," "lama,"* or *"bhote"* (Höfer 1979a:147–48). It has been suggested that there are relationships among all these groups and those of the Thami of east Nepal (Allen 1978:11; MacDonald 1966:42 n. 9; Oppitz 1968:98). These relationships are still to be established.

14. In earlier papers and publications I followed the convention established by Vinding.

15. The term *Thaksatsae Thakali* suggests a linkage with a specific place, Thaksatsae, and yet many of the migrant Thakali have never been there. Nevertheless, all the Thaksatsae Thakali know of Thaksatsae (though they will often refer to it as Thak or Thak Khola), and it continues to hold significance as the final resting place where the bone fragments of every deceased Thakali are returned, placed in the appropriate lineage ossuaries.

16. For an account of the history of this period, see chapter 3 as well as Fürer-Haimendorf (1975) and Messerschmidt and Gurung (1974).

17. The transliterations used here are the versions most widely used by the Thak-satsae Thakali. These names are variously transliterated by different scholars. Some variants include: *bhāta-can* (T: *phur-gi*), *ser-can* (T: *thin-can*), *tula-can* (*sal-gi*), and *gau-can* (*cho-gi*) (Jest 1964/65); Bhattachan (Burki), Sherchan (Dimzen), Tulachan (Salki), and Gouchan (Choki) (Fürer-Haimendorf 1981a); and *gaucan, tulacan, shercan,* and *bhattacan* (Vinding 1998).

   Gauchan and Vinding have claimed that Chyoki was originally called Cho-ghyu, and they translate the Thakali word *ghyu* as "clan." Cho-ghyu, they report, later became Chyogi and then Chyoki. Similarly, by their reasoning, Sālki was originally Sāl-ghyu, then Sālgi and now Sālki. Bhurki was originally Bhur-ghyu and then Bhurgi. Ḍhimchen *ghyu*, according to their informants, has always been Ḍhimchen. According to informants' reports, the Ḍhimchen ancestor refused to changed his clan name when the four Thakali ancestors settled in Thak Khola (1977:97–98 n. 3). See also Vinding (1981).

   Today the Nepali names are always used by Thakalis outside the Thak Khola and are generally used within Thak Khola. Fürer-Haimendorf dated the use of the Nepali names to the 1930s and ties their use to the movement to justify a claim to higher caste status (1981a:3). In the migrant communities of Myagdi and Baglung districts, the Nepali names appear on documents that date to the early years of the twentieth century. No informants recall the use of any other names for the four clans. Between 1982 and 1997 there was a marked increase in the use of the Thakali clan names by migrants and Thaksatsae residents alike. This change coincides with the cultural revitalization efforts of the Thak-ali Sewa Samiti (see chapter 6).

18. Manzardo noted that as of 1978 no scholar had yet compiled a complete listing of the *phobes*. Since then, Michael Vinding and I have separately compiled listings of these subgroups. See Fisher 1987 for a comparison of the information compiled by the author, Vinding, Jest, Fürer-Haimendorf, and Manzardo. The Thakali also compiled their own list in 1984.

19. The term *ghyu* is similar to the Tibetan *rgyud*, which Jäschke glosses as "lineage" ([1881] 1958:124). The Thakali employ the terms *phobe, ghyupa,* and *ghyuwa* in similar ways to refer to different levels of patrilineal groupings. The Nepali term *thar* (caste, clan, subcaste, lineage) is likewise used in a variety of ways. The terms are not always used interchangeably by the Thaksatsae Thakali, as Manzardo (1978) has suggested, but different terms may be used for descent groups of the same organizational complexity, and in certain cases the term *ghyu* or *ghyupa* may be used to refer to clans as well as some subclans.

20. Other scholars have employed different terms: Manzardo has used the word *gyu* to refer to the four clans and the term *phophe* for the patrilineages (Manzardo 1978:65); Fürer-Haimendorf has called them *gyuba* (1981a:7); Vinding has called the subclans *phobe, phowai,* or *ghyuwa* (1981:209).

21. This was not always the case. Documents from the the the late nineteenth century generally list Thakali for a surname. Even today there are notable exceptions to the use of the clan name as a surname. For a discussion of the relative benefits of using the term *Thakali* or the clan name as a surname, see Manzardo (1978:84 n. 2).

22. For accounts of Panchgaon, see Parker (1985), Valeix (1974), and especially Vinding (1981, 1998) and Gauchan and Vinding (1977).

23. The village is call Mhowa in the local dialect of Thakali, and the inhabitants are referred to as Mhowatan. Vinding has transliterated this name as Mhatan (Gauchan and Vinding 1977), Mahawatan (Vinding 1978), Mhowatan (Vinding 1981), and Mawatan (Vinding 1998). Fürer-Haimendorf (1978) and Manzardo (1978) both refer to the village as Marpha (N) and the group as Marphali. For an introduction to Marpha, see Valeix (1974); Gauchan and Vinding (1977); Vinding (1981); and Parker (1985).

24. The Nepali names for the Marphali clans are now in common usage. According to Vinding, these names were introduced in the 1950s (1981:211; 1998:178). According to Thaksatsae Thakali informants, the Marphali clans copied the *chan* endings from the Thaksatsae Thakali. Fürer-Haimendorf (1967b) dated the use of Nepali clan names in Thaksatsae to the 1930s. In Khani Khuwa, however, these names appear on documents from the early twentieth century.

25. Vinding has observed that the Marphali avoid the name Puntan, which they were often called by other residents of Thak Khola, and deny that it means "people of leprosy," as has been claimed by other scholars (Iijima 1963:49; Kawakita 1957).

26. Manzardo (1978) has referred to this group as Panchgaonli. Bista and Fürer-Haimendorf considered the Marphali and the Thini, Sya-ngtani, and Cimtani as one group, which they referred to as Panchgaonli. Vinding (1978, 1979, 1979/80b, 1979/80b) and Jackson (1976, 1978) have referred to this group as Yulngasumpa or Yhulkasummi Thakali, or Yhulkasompaimhi. The inhabitants of these villages do not refer to themselves by this name, instead using Thini, Syangtani, and Cimtani.

27. More infrequently, they are called Syangtani, Thinel, or Cimtani by speakers more familiar with the groups in the valley.

28. See Gauchan and Vinding (1977:181), Vinding (1981:213), or Vinding (1998:181–2) for a list of these descent groups.

29. See Vinding (1981) for a description of these.

30. Among the Chimtani, Syangtani, Thinel, and Marphali, these groups still play an active political role in a system that exists alongside the Nepali political system.

31. Vinding has called this group Rhongtā Khāmpa and said that some of them are descendants of the Tibetan-speaking people of Nubri (Gauchan and

Vinding 1977:181). Fürer-Haimendorf has argued that in the early part of the nineteenth century Tukche was controlled by Tibetans, who spent six months of the year in Thak Khola and six months on the Tibetan plateau (1975:142).

32. Bista reported that the hundred households of Tukche previously supported more than a thousand servants (1971:57). Today, many of the descendants of these servants are found in Tukche, where they look after the homes and fields of emigrated merchants.

33. The assertions of scholars are addressed in more detail in chapters 7 and 8.

34. *Jāt* (N) means "sort, kind; tribe, nation; caste" (Turner 1931:213).

35. Sharma (1977) has described the tactics used by the Tukche merchants to further their claim to Thakuri status.

This process of social mobility is similar to that described by Kulke (1986) as "extensive Hinduization," and in the imitation by the Thakali ("tribal" in Sinha's terms) elite of a Thakuri (rather than Brahman) cultural model it resembles Sinha's "Rajputization" (1962). It differs, however, in that the Tukche elite did not attempt to raise their own status above that of all other Thaksatsae Thakalis but instead strove to improve the status of the entire endogamous group: the four clans of Thaksatsae. For a further discussion of this, see chapter 7.

36. Kawakita (1957) and Iijima (1960) date the formation of the council to the 1930s. There were previously headmen, *mukiyā*, in the villages of Thak Khola, but it is not clear that they were formally organized in a single council. Manzardo and Sharma refer to this council as the "traditional" political system of the Thakali (1975; see also Manzardo 1978). Vinding (1998) also believes the council is of long standing.

37. Fürer-Haimendorf (1966, 1967a) and Iijima (1960) list many of the changes undertaken at this time.

38. Many of the reforms were justified by referring to the excessive expense of the practices then current. Cost cutting is a recurrent theme in Thakali history. It is a central focus of Manzardo and Sharma's 1975 account of the early days of the Pokhara social organization, and it was an important issue at the 1983 meeting I attended in Pokhara where the Thakali formed the national social organization, as well as at subsequent meetings of the Thakali Sewa Samiti. Fifty years after they were enacted, it was difficult to determine whether the 1930 reforms arose as cost cutting disguised as religious reform or as religious reform disguised as cost cutting.

39. Members of these latter groups did not have a profitable role in the salt trade after 1862 and were often forced to serve as bond servants (N: *badha, badhiteni*) and wage laborers to the Thakali merchants. Thakali from Thaksatsae did not become bond servants to these merchants.

40. Sharma (1977) has described the tactics used by the Tukche merchants to further their claim to Thakuri status.

41. See also observations by Manzardo and Sharma (1975) and Bista (1967).

42. The four major subdivisions of Thakali society have generally been called clans by scholars. The more organized subgroups of these four divisions, the *phobe*, conform more closely to the anthropological concept of clan. A *phobe* consists of numerous lineages. The four major divisions, the so-called clans, might better be termed *phratries*. For the sake of simplicity, however, I use the conventional clan for the four divisions and call the subdivisions *phobe* or subclans.

    Fürer-Haimendorf, like most other scholars, stressed the fundamental equality of the Thakali and insisted that the four clans are of equal rank. Bista has argued that the original clan structure was hierarchical. He added that the order of rank was altered, at least in ritual contexts, when the *subba* lineage gained wealth and political authority (1971:56).

43. In 1997 this prohibition was challenged by a marriage between the offspring of two prominent Dyatan *phobe* families in Kathmandu. Many members of the Thakali community expressed dismay and disapproval, but the marriage took place nevertheless.

44. *Khaccar* (N), used for "mule," "mongrel," "bastard": offspring of parents of different *jāts*.

45. Sharma notes a similar situation within the Chetri caste of Nepal: the Chetri recognize *jharra* and non-*jharra* status. The latter is the result of mixed marriages and can be ameliorated through appropriate marriages. After three generations, full status can be restored (1977:288).

46. Gauchan and Vinding give the form *pumishyā* for females (1977:131 n. 35).

47. Gauchan and Vinding have reported this but lacked the statistics to verify the claim. It is a difficult claim to verify because information about suspected witches is not usually discussed in public, and once gained it is not politic to verify the information with those who are said to be witches. My own data on kinship and marriage indicate a tendency for those of *pumi* status to intermarry, but within recent generations the status seems to be of less concern. This is consistent with the easing of other marriage restrictions and with the statements of informants, some of whom lament the imminent disappearance of pure Thakali as the offspring of more and more pure families marry Thakali of impure status.

48. Fürer-Haimendorf contended that because of the "somewhat arrogant attitude" of the people in the first group, people in the second are denied active participation in the Thakali coming-of-age rite *shyopen lawa* (1981a:2). However, his informants did not suggest that marriage was discouraged between these groups.

49. I discuss these associations in chapter 6.

50. This percentage was first derived from a survey I did in 1984. There has been no significant change since then, though the Thakali outside Thaksatsae have continued to move from place to place.

51. Scholars have also had this problem. Manzardo wrote that "at first glance I thought I had run either into a group of local Magars who were claiming Thakali caste-standing for purposes of status-building, or an isolated group of Thakalis separated from the network itself" (1978:191).

52. Hirachan is usually the only Marphali clan mentioned.

53. One reason for this may be that Hinduism is by and large less concerned with orthodoxy than orthopraxy, but, in central Nepal, the concern with appropriate practice is limited to a very narrow set of practices, adherence to which does not indicate the full-fledged Hinduization described by Fürer-Haimendorf and others.

54. The *thimten* is a separate room in homes of wealthy Thakali families in Thak Khola that contains a separate hearth, not used for household purposes, and is the preferred site for *lha chuji* or *kul puja* ceremonies. Access to the *thimten* is said to have been restricted to pure Thakalis, at least during the course of the ceremonies. Thakali homes outside Thak Khola are not built in the same design. Many large Thakali homes in Myagdi include a large central room with a centralized hearth that is not used for cooking and serves as the site for the *lha chuji* ceremonies. The restriction of access does not apply in Myagdi: ceremonies are attended by those who are not pure Thakali and even by those who are not Thakali at all, including Magar spouses and anthropologists.

55. In relative terms, intercaste marriage occurs most frequently among members of the *subba* lineage. It is a curiosity that within this lineage an abnormally large number of women have married non-Thakalis. This is often attributed to the fact that the children of this lineage are better educated than most of the eligible marriage partners. The result is that many of the women from this lineage have married well-educated and gainfully employed non-Thakalis and foreigners.

56. The differences between the behavior of Thakali women resident in Thak Khola and the behavior of Thakali women resident in Myagdi and Baglung districts are quite striking. Women born and raised in the migrant areas are very conservative in behavior, rarely drink, are less flirtatious, and distinguish themselves from Magar girls, who interact with men in Rodi and at festivals. Thakali men and boys, on the other hand, frequently trek from village to village for festivals and spend their nights singing and flirting with Magar women. It is inevitable that these experiences result in occasional offspring and marriages.

3. *Forging Histories*

1.   Gauchan and Vinding (1977) present what they term a "retelling" (and what
     Manzardo [1978] calls "translations of a very loose sort") of the *rhabs*. Also see
     Vinding (1992). For an indication of the difficulties of accurate translation, see
     Gauchan and Vinding (1977:104). Fragments are also found in Jest (1974).
2.   *Gamba* (T): "clan leader," "headman." Manzardo has claimed that "the Thak-
     alis rewrote their origin mythology, arranging for certain older versions to be
     conveniently lost in a fire" (1978:49). This is not entirely correct; only one
     version was lost in a fire, and there is no evidence to suggest that the loss was
     arranged (though it was certainly convenient for those individuals who wished
     to present a different account of the Thakali past). More to the point, given
     the difficulty Manzardo reported in collecting information from the Thakali,
     it seems unlikely that anyone would have confessed to such a deliberate act.
     The cause for Manzardo's suspicion may be that the *pāre* responsible for the
     safekeeping of the *rhab* was a member of the same *phobe* as some of the most
     ardent proponents of the myth tracing the ancestry of the Thakali to the Thak-
     uri prince the Hansa Raja. The one *rhab* that has been rewritten recently is
     quite different from the other three in that it combines the story of the Hansa
     Raja and the tale of the four ancestors and their four gods coming from Sinja
     to Thaksatsae. The Gauchan *gamba*, with the assistance of the Sherchan elders,
     rewrote it as he thought "it ought to be" (see Gauchan and Vinding 1977:136
     n. 13). Basanta Bhattachan (1992) has raised questions about this interpretation.
3.   The following summaries of the *rhabs* are based on Gauchan and Vinding
     (1977), Vinding (1992), and accounts of informants.
4.   Gauchan and Vinding noted this same claim (1977:110 n. 2). They also cite
     Messerschmidt's observation (1976:17) that the progenitors of the Lamichane
     Gurung were called Chan.
5.   A version of this story cited by Manzardo involves four sons of the Jumla Raja
     who migrated to different places in Nepal (1978:42 n. 13). One of these sons
     was the Hansa Raja, and another became the Gurkha Raja, an ancestor of the
     present king of Nepal.
6.   Fürer-Haimendorf has dismissed the myth of the Hansa Raja and termed the
     use of it by some Thakalis to justify their claim to Thakuri status "tortuous."
     There is insufficient evidence either to demonstrate the veracity of the oral
     versions told by some of the Thakali or to establish that the narrative was altered
     after the beginning of the salt monopoly. See Fürer-Haimendorf (1975:140)
     and Vinding (1978:191–92). The Hansa Raja is mentioned in one other written
     local text, the Chimang *bemchāg* (see Ramble and Vinding 1987).
7.   For historical and archaeological work on the upper Kali Gandaki valley, in-
     cluding Lo, Baragaon, and Panchgaon, see Jackson (1976, 1978, 1980, 1984),

Mishra (1994), Pohl and Tripathee (1995), Ramble (1997), Ramble and Seeber (1995), Schuh (1990, 1994, 1995), and Seeber (1994, 1996). Local sources include oral traditions and village chronicles (*bemchāg*) from Panchgaon. On the Chimang *bemchāg*, see Ramble and Vinding (1987) and Rai (1994:111–14, appendix B). On the Marpha *bemchāg*, see Shuh (1990, 1995).

8. Vinding has speculated that Serib may be Panchgaon (1988) or both Panchgaon and Baragaon (1998). For an account of the kingdom of Serib, see Jackson (1976, 1978) and Vinding (1988).

9. On Yarlung, see Haarh (1969), Richardson (1962), Snellgrove and Richardson ([1968] 1980), Stein (1972).

10. On the history of Ladakh, see Francke ([1926] 1972), Petech (1939), and Snellgrove and Skorupski (1977, 1980). On Jumla, see Sharma (1972), Stiller (1973), and Tucci (1956).

11. The southernmost of these forts, Garab Dzong, on a plateau about one kilometer southwest of the village of Thini, reportedly had four monasteries in its charge. Some scholars have speculated that Garab Dzong was an important center of Serib. Recent efforts at dating the site indicate that settlement began there in the 1530s, and there is evidence of additional construction through the late 1700s (Schmidt 1992–93:23). The fort in Kagbeni in Baragaon has been dated to 1568 (Gutschow 1994:27).

12. Bon was the religion of Tibet before the introduction of Buddhism. Inhabitants of the Himalaya continue to practice it in both its reformed and unreformed versions.

13. According to the bibliography of a thirteen-century Bon priest, he had 198 disciples from Lo and 246 from Serib (Jackson 1978:207).

14. See also MacDonald 1989:170. Jackson identified Mu-Khun as present-day Muktinath. Ramble and Vinding (1987:21) concur in this identification.

15. Mon is used by Tibetans to refer to southern, non-Bhote neighbors. Jackson (1978) speculates that its use with Se may indicate a specific Mon, perhaps the Mon of Se-rib. Vinding thinks that this reference probably refers to the Thakali of Thaksatsae (1988:172 n. 28).

16. For accounts of these struggles, see Jackson (1978) and Vinding (1988).

17. The temple at Kobang also appears to have been a trading post, even in the fifteenth and sixteenth centuries, where goods from the lowlands were exchanged for those from the highlands. See, for example, Jackson (1978:218) and Schuh (1995:44).

18. See, for example, Ramble and Vinding (1987).

19. This is indicated in several *tama patra* (N: copperplate edicts) still in existence.

20. Shrestha (1976:77 f). See also Jackson (1978:222, 223 n. 104); Vinding (1988).

21. Because of the difficulty of the terrain, an army would have had to hike approximately five hundred miles to reach Jumla, which is about 125 linear miles

away (see Hamilton [1819] 1971:286; Kirkpatrick 1811:291; and Stiller 1973:185).

22. While the title *subba* indicates a status conferred by the central government, the exact nature of this status varied. Hamilton reported that after the conquest of the dominions of the Chaubisi "rajahs," a "subah" was usually put in place of each deposed raja, and affairs were conducted by these officers as they had been under the raja ([1819] 1971:104). He described a "subah" as an "officer of revenue, justice and police" (105). Landan variously translates this title as "District Lieutenant" ([1928] 1976, 2:10) and as "Captain" (2:94). Kawakita notes that in general the position of a *subba* in the central government was relatively low. But whereas in provincial towns a *subba* was subordinate to the governor, in remote outlying districts the position carried considerable influence (1957). Snellgrove glosses "suba" as "district magistrate" (1961:177). See also Vinding (1988) and Iijima (1960).

23. *Ijaradar* (N: contractor; holder of an *ijara*, or contract for the collection of revenue or the management of mines).

24. Regmi (1972:138). Thak, as used here, appears to refer specifically to the area of Thaksatsae. In the documents cited by Regmi, areas to the north of Thaksatsae are usually referred to as Panchgaon or by their village name, for example, Thini.

25. Regmi (1972:140). *Mukhiy* (N: headman of a village; chief, leader).

26. Regmi (1972:140); Vinding (1988:10).

27. The tax went from 6,900 rupees in 1802 to 13,000 rupees in 1811. In 1809 Subba Bhawani Datta Thapa was authorized to collect 15,000 rupees, but this was reduced to 13,000 rupees after a few months (see "Royal Order to the Budhas of Thak," Regmi Research Collections (henceforward RRC) 40:35–56; and "Royal Order to Premakhad Budha," Poush Sudi 5, 1866 [January 1810], both cited in Regmi 1972). By 1862, when the Thaksatsae villages appealed for a reduction in the land revenue tax, it was only 12,500 rupees per annum (see *The Appeal to Inhabitants of Thak to Return Home*, Aswin Sudi 6, 1855 [September 1798]; *Abolition of Ijara System in Thak-Theni*, Shrawan Badi 1, 1859 [July 1802]; *Ijara Grant to Dware Bhawanand for Revenue Collection in Thak*, Aswin Sudi 1, 1864 [September 1807]; and *Orders Regarding Revenue Collection in Thak*, Baisakh Sudi 10, 1868 [May 1811], all cited in Regmi 1972:140).

Manzardo has cited another interesting document, dated Sambat 1875 (Manzardo lists this as 1802 A.D., but it is, in fact, 1818 A.D.), that supports the view that the Thakali were involved with tax collection well before they gained control of the salt contract in 1869 (1978:49 n. 3).

28. Hamilton ([1819] 1971:272–74). Stiller (1973) dismisses as relatively insignificant the amount of wealth available from mines but also notes that while the

mines of Parbat were never rich enough to attract outside invaders, nevertheless they made Parbat a more financially stable state than her neighbors.

Fürer-Haimendorf (1975:139) speculated that Thak Khola passed under the control of the rajas of Galkot, but it appears much more likely that the area was administered from Parbat (Malebum), which was then in alliance with Galkot.

29. Agrarian taxes contributed 75 percent of the total revenue in 1851. Most of this was collected in the Terai, however; the hill regions contributed very little agrarian tax revenue in the middle of the nineteenth century.

30. See Regmi 1979:37–45. The Gurkha army doubled between 1816 and 1837 and became better equipped over that period of time (see vol. 1f22, Hodgson Papers, India Office Library, London). This would have increased the demand for metals.

31. See, for instance, "Ijara Grant to Subba Ram Prasad Thakali for Mines in Western Nepal," Baisakh Sudi 15, 1942 (May 1885), RRC 52:507–8, cited in Regmi 1988:136, 143.

32. Data I collected includes information on fifty-seven extended Thakali lineages in Khani Khuwa. These lineage histories include information on literally thousands of Thakali.

33. Manzardo (1978) suggested that the Thakali may have initiated the mining operations in Galkot in 1915, but this seems unlikely.

34. Thakalis along the main trails from Baglung, Beni, Jomsom, and Pokhara are more recent migrants, and the Pokhara community probably dates back no earlier than 1950.

35. A competitive system had been introduced into the revenue collection system in the Terai in the 1820s.

36. See, for instance, "Order to the Baglung Khai Hatti Taksar Goswara," Badi 10, 1957 (1900 A.D.), RRC 70:220–41, cited in Regmi 1988:141.

37. "Order to Subba Ram Prasad Thakali," Chaitra Sudi 1, 1942 (March 1886), RRC 54:45–51, cited in Regmi 1988:143. A *dharni* is a unit of weight amounting to around five pounds.

38. "Order to Nab Subba Naib Ra Gurugharana Panditju," Jestha Sudi 4, 1930 (May 1873), RRC 82, 608–9, cited in Regmi 1988:144.

39. Regmi 1988:136.

40. "Order to Subba Ram Prasad Thakali for Mines in Western Nepal," Baisakh Sudi 15, 1942 (May 1885), cited in Regmi 1988:143–44.

41. If Thakakuti refers to the area and not simply to the town of Tukche, his statement that it "may contain one thousand houses" (Hamilton [1819] 1971:273) could be accurate.

42. According to Fürer-Haimendorf (1975:142), Tukche, at the beginning of the nineteenth century, was controlled by Tibetans.

43. The story of the salt contract and subsequent political and economic events in Thak Khola has been related in other sources and will be reviewed only briefly here. For more thorough accounts of the period of the salt monopoly in Thak Khola and the *subba* system, see Fürer-Haimendorf (1975:142–46); Bista (1971); and Vinding (1988:12–17). Fürer-Haimendorf cites copies of government orders still existent in Thak Khola as the basis of his account. Additional information concerning the Gurung usurpation of the contract can be found in Messerschmidt and Gurung (1974). See also Manzardo's speculative reconstruction of events during this era (1978).

44. In September 1855 (Aswin Sudi 12, 1912), Subba Dhansaram and Subba Balbir successfully petitioned the king to have Thakalis recruited as soldiers, as was the custom during the time of the Malla kings, rather than as porters. These two individuals were authorized by the government to recruit a regiment of Thakali soldiers (Regmi 1977c:251–53). Note that these two individuals were already referred to as *subba*.

45. Balbir was a Sherchan of the Lha Khang Dhungi subclan. In the nineteenth century, Thakali was generally used as a surname. In the twentieth century, the clan name was generally used.

46. Iijima has suggested that Balbir got his title of Subba as a reward for his services in the Nepal-Tibet War (1855–56) (1977b:75). Vinding has rejected this and suggested instead that Balbir got the title in his capacity as customs collector in Dana (1988). The fact is that Balbir was already referred to as *subba* before his involvement in the 1855 war in Tibet (Regmi 1977c:251–53), so the title did not initially derive from either his service during the war or from the salt monopoly contract that he held in 1869. Vinding has speculated that Balbir may have held a customs contract before 1855; this is plausible, but as yet no evidence either supports or refutes this.

47. Regmi 1977a:689–96. The records relating to this event do not detail the basis of the suit.

48. This account is from Fürer-Haimendorf (1975:142, 188). I agree with Vinding (1988:188 n. 98) that the relationship between payment of taxes and the initiation of the salt monopoly is unclear in this account. The tax of 12,500 rupees Fürer-Haimendorf calls a "consolidated tax" appears to be the homestead tax, and Fürer-Haimendorf does not indicate whether it was reduced or abolished after the introduction of the salt monopoly.

49. Orders issued in 1876 (1933 N.S.) in the name of Subba Balbir Thakali and his son, Kavi Ram Thakali, authorized them to procure on a monopoly basis salt purchased from Tibet by the people of Baragaon, Panchgaon, Thak, and Ghelung (Regmi 1977b:195). Kavi Ram won the contract with a bid of 82,000 rupees. The monopoly arrangement continued unchanged until 1885 (1942 N.S.).

50. Regmi, "Ijara Grant to Subba Ram Prasad Thakali and Others for Salt Mo-
    nopoly in Dana," Ashadh Badi 1, 1943 (June 1886), *Regmi Research Chronicles*
    53:146–48, cited in Regmi 1988:244.
51. The main office remained in Dana, but the branch office at Tukche became
    the center of the trade during this time.
52. Ram Prasad is often referred to as Ram Prasad Thakali in documents of the
    time but as Ram Prasad Gauchan by contemporary informants. My informants
    still tell many stories about Pati Ram Sau and Captain Ram Prasad. Pati Ram
    reportedly claimed to be so rich that he could stop the flow of the Kali Gandaki
    by damming it with his money. The actual cause of his eventual impoverish-
    ment remains obscure, but there are two widely repeated folk accounts. The
    first alleges that Pati Ram foolishly boasted about his wealth to the Rana prime
    minister, who found ways to make it his own. The second draws its clue from
    an oft-repeated ditty—"Pati Ram ko dhan, Ram Prasad ko jilli milli" (Pati Ram's
    wealth, Ram Prasad's frivolities)—that succinctly illustrates the allegation that
    Pati Ram's wealth was depleted by Ram Prasad's excesses. Ram Prasad is alleged
    to have been an obese man who would travel by horseback from the site of his
    mines in Myagdi to Thak Khola. During the journey a servant would jog along-
    side his horse carrying a water pipe with a copper bowl so large that, once filled,
    it could be smoked throughout the daylong ride.
53. By 1902 the bid for the contract had reached 119,001 rupees, representing an
    increase of 267.4 percent since the beginning of the monopoly. See Regmi
    (1977b:161–63); and "Ijara Grant to Subba Harka Man and Ganesh Bahadur
    Thakali for the Salt Monopoly in Dana," RRC 87:649–84, cited in Regmi
    (1988:244 n. 17).
54. My information about Thakali migration derives from household and settle-
    ment surveys and family histories collected in 1982–84 among migrant com-
    munities throughout Baglung and Myagdi Districts, in Bhairawa, Kasauli, Po-
    khara, and Kathmandu. This information includes data on nearly one thousand
    households. This information was updated and supplementary information col-
    lected in 1987, 1992, and 1997.
55. For example, one of the first permanent Thakali homes in the *bazār* of Baglung
    in Baglung District, which is still occupied by the founding family, was estab-
    lished in 1911. See also comments by Bista (1967); Kawakita (1974:259–60);
    and Jest (1964/65).
56. Ortner tells a story of a visit to the Solu-Khumbu region by a government agent
    to enforce the ban on killing cows and eating beef. The Sherpas readily con-
    fessed to the practice, which was punishable by death or enslavement. The
    agent let them off with a fine, showing more concern for practicality than
    ideology by observing that "if this crime is to be punished by death or enslave-
    ment, many people will be put to death or enslaved" (Ortner 1989).

57. My earlier research established that many of the Thakali families who now live in the area just south of Thak Khola along the Kali Gandaki River and on the trail to Pokhara moved there after 1920 (Fisher 1987). See also comments by Jest (1964/65); Kawakita (1974:259–60); and Bista (1967).

58. Many Thakali credit Hitman *subba* with convincing the Thakalis to move to lowland Nepal.

59. In the 1980s Anagman was the well-respected senior member of the *subba* lineage. As an old friend of his tells it, he went to Kathmandu to study and decided he wanted to enter into government service. His father approached the Ranas on his behalf, and they agreed to give Anagman a position. The position given to him, revenue officer in the Terai, was not at all what he wanted, but by this point there was no way to refuse the assignment. Hitman was worried about him because he was so young and sent a senior accountant for the family along with him. In the event, Anagman stayed in the Terai for twenty-three years before he was able to return to Kathmandu. After he settled in Kathmandu, he arranged for the education of the younger generation.

60. Both Hitman and Mohan Man held a contract on grain trading during the two decades after the end of the salt monopoly. By 1930 the customshouse had moved to Jomsom, and in 1954 it was moved to the Tibetan border. Hitman left Tukche in 1944 to tend to contracts in Nepalgunj, Bhutwal, and Bhairawa. Around the same time, Mohan Man went to Janakpur. Hitman's activities were particularly diverse: in 1945 he held a contract for trade in cloth, from 1946 to 1949 he had a monopoly on trade in cigarettes, and during the same period he had lumber contracts in Mechi District. He and his brother also owned two stores and a large rice mill in the Terai town of Bhairawa.

61. Nationally, forests passed mines as a source of revenue in the 1860s. Thakalis moved into the exploitation of forest resources only after their move in the 1930s to the Terai, where easier transportation made commercial forestry a viable activity.

62. Bista (1971) attributed this geographic distribution of the Thakali to two causes: he suggests that high taxes emanating from the salt trade contract drove out the poor and that economic opportunities lured the rich. The causes of migration are broader than this, however, as is the time period over which migration occurred. There was considerable migration before the salt contract system, and a large number of migrants are middle-income households.

63. He is unclear about the exact dates for this movement. In one place he dates this period of migration as 1956–60 (Manzardo and Sharma 1975:28), and in another he reported "real expansion was not to take place until the 1960's" (Manzardo 1978:100).

4. Separation and Integration

1. Nepal currently supports more than 10 people per one cultivated hectare. In the Terai this ration can be as low as 3 per hectare, while in the middle hills it is often as high as 15 people per hectare.

2. Both Bista and Manzardo have suggested that this is also the case for the Thakali (Bista 1967:80; Manzardo 1978). This is not correct.

3. A number of studies have attempted to devise migration typologies for Nepal. A 1971 CEDA study uses four categories of migration: (1) seasonal migration; (2) traditional settlers; (3) former settlers; and (4) permanent settlers. The difference between traditional settlers and permanent settlers is based on an arbitrary time period. Another CEDA study (1973) distinguishes three categories of population movement: (1) seasonal; (2) recurrent; and (3) permanent. Both these studies are concerned with movement into the Terai and do not consider intrahill movement. Dahal, Rai, and Manzardo (1977) key their typology to the major economic resource in the village of emigration: land. This study distinguishes between reversible migrants—those who continue to maintain access to land in their villages of origin—and nonreversible migrants—where ties of land and social interaction with the village of origin are severed. Reversible migrants include traders, transhumant groups, labor migrants, and "extended farmers" (defined in Dahal, Rai, and Manzardo [1977] as those who "have sufficient cash to purchase land outside their home area for the purpose of investment through the production of cash crops" [38]). As will be seen, none of these typologies is completely satisfactory to explain or analyze Thakali migration.

4. Most studies in Nepal, including the CEDA studies of 1971 and 1973, are concerned with migration into the Terai and do not consider the intrahill migration that is typical of the Thakali.

    The applicability of categories to particular migrants, as in the case of the Thakali, is not always easy to determine: permanent migrants, for example, are often distinguished from other categories on the basis of an arbitrarily defined time period. The Dahal, Rai, Manzardo typology considers more variables than most, but its utility is limited by its underlying assumptions. This typology is keyed on land as the "single axis on which categories of migration can be oriented" (1977:25–26). This step was taken not on the basis of the data but because the authors "feel migration is due to economic factors, particularly those perceived by villagers themselves" (25). Economics undoubtedly plays a major role in most migration in Nepal, but the extent to which economic factors, particularly land, are the primary cause of migration needs to be established. An additional problem with this typology is the classification of those who have severed their ties to land in the village of origin as nonreversible migrants and the assumption that "with the loss of land comes the concomitant loss of social relations with the village of origin" (40). In the Thakali case, the loss of land does not necessarily lead to a loss of social relations nor is the resulting migration irreversible.

5. Manzardo, who did a lot of his research in Pokhara, dates the first Thakali migration to Pokhara to the period subsequent to the end of the salt contract system (1978:100). The number of Thakali households in Pokhara remained low until the 1950s. By 1954 there were approximately twenty Thakali households in Pokhara (Manzardo and Sharma 1975:28). Kawakita has noted that as early as 1953 the Thakali were a prominent feature in the Pokhara market (1957).

6. Manzardo and Sharma 1975:40 n. 8; Manzardo 1978:273. The number of Thakali households in urban settings changes constantly as some families move on and others move in. Fürer-Haimendorf (1981a) counted eighty-five Thakali households in Pokhara in 1976.

7. Kawakita noted that Tukche presented a "lively appearance" and estimated the town's population at one thousand (1957:55–56). Iijima (1960), Snellgrove (1961), and Tucci ([1953] 1982) also describe it as a bustling town.

8. Tucci calls it a "family" but refers to them by the clan name Sherchan ([1953] 1982).

9. Fürer-Haimendorf's survey was conducted from February to April 1976, when most seasonal migrants would be in the south. His figures consequently only account for permanent residents. If seasonal migrants were included, the percentage of Thakali residents would be higher.

10. Manzardo offers only this statistic with no population or household figures to support it (1978:47).

11. The Nepali word used in these instances, *samaj* (N) is glossed as "association, league, society, meeting" (Turner 1931:587). The Nepali word *samaj* is used for all three levels of integration discussed here: the *gāũ*, or village community, the local Thakali *samaj*, and the Thakali *samaj*, which includes all members of the four clans.

The term *community* has both colloquial and technical usage: the English word *community* derives from the Latin *communis*, meaning "fellowship, community of relations or feelings," but in medieval Latin it was used concretely in the sense of "a body of fellows or fellow townsmen" (*Oxford English Dictionary* 1971:702). Within the anthropological literature it is a topic of extreme importance and has received a great deal of attention (see, for example, Redfield 1961; Marriott 1955; Klass 1978).

The discussion in the present study uses the terms *community* and *samaj* much as the Thakali do referring to the multiple levels of social organization recognized by the Thakali themselves.

12. Vinding (1981:206) found close to one thousand households in the upper Kali Gandaki valley, of which 70 percent were Thakali (see chapter 2 for an explanation of Vinding's use of the designation). Thaksatsae villages are more homogeneous than many of the villages in the upper Kali Gandaki valley, and the households that do belong to non-Thakali service *jāts* are usually situated on the outskirts of the villages.

13. Until the formal organization of a national Thakali *samaj* in 1983, local Thakali communities were formally organized in only three areas: Pokhara, where the *samaj* was first organized in 1954; Bhairawa (1973); and Kathmandu (1978). The Thakali communities of Butwal/Kasauli and Galkot were not formally organized before 1983, but in some respects they functioned as a cohesive body.

14. Iijima, for example, has commented on the qualities of "community solidarity" (1963:46), Manzardo has stressed cooperation and "cohesion" (1978:93), and Fürer-Haimendorf has referred to the Thakalis as a "homogeneous and indivisible society" (1966:147).

15. This is true even in Khani Khuwa. For example, eleven of the fourteen shops and the most frequented hotel in Darbang *bazār*, most of the shops and hotels in Burtibang *bazār*, and the prominent hotels in Beni and Baglung are all owned and run by Thakalis. Many of the Thakali who have migrated from this area operate hotels in Tansen, Kasauli, and Kathmandu.

16. See tables 5.3 through 5.5 in Fisher 1987:175–78.

17. Molnar (1981:69) reported that lenders often took 10 percent from the principal at the time of the loan and then charged an annual interest rate of 10 percent on the total loan. Vinding (1984:13) reported that interest rates for loans from individuals in Thak Khola varied between 15 and 36 percent, despite the government law.

18. In Darbang, for example, Ram Prasad was previously the poorest of the nine brothers, but after three of his five sons joined the British army, the household, which formerly lived in a one-room, thatch-roofed wooden house, was able to construct the largest stone home in the *bazār*. Locally, he is no longer known by the nickname "Shorty" but instead is called "Three Aces," a reference to his three veteran sons.

19. This is true not just for Thakalis but for all ex-Gurkha soldiers (Höfer 1978; Hitchcock 1966; Caplan 1970).

20. A good account of *dhikur* can be found in Messerschmidt (1978). Valuable additional references are found in Vinding (1984), Fürer-Haimendorf (1975), Bista (1967), Manzardo (1978), Manzardo and Sharma (1975), and Messerschmidt (1972).

The term is variously transliterated. Here I have used the form *dhikur*, as it is found in the documents I translated.

21. This kind of economic cooperation is not exclusive to the Thakali; socioeconomic cooperation is common among the Tibeto-Burman peoples of the Himalayan region. A number of studies include information on mutual-help systems
in this area: among these are Gorer's 1967 account of Lepcha *inzong*, Pignède
(1966) on the Gurung agricultural cooperative called *nogar*, Nepali (1965) on
guthi, Okada (1957) on *mit*, and Miller (1956) on the Tibetan systems of *ganye*
and *kidu*. Nor are rotating credit associations peculiar to Nepal: institutions
similar to *dhikur* have been noted in Indonesia, China, Japan, Vietnam, and
Africa.

22. See Geertz (1962:243); Ardener (1964:201); Messerschmidt (1978:142).

23. Geertz noted that this cooperation is founded on the participants' sense of
mutual value and not on a general ethic of the unity of mankind (1962:244).

24. Some informants claimed that up to three *dhikurs* might be organized to assist
a needy individual; if after these opportunities the individual had still not succeeded in business, no one else would take a chance with him.

25. Numerous stories are offered to account for the evolution of the *dhikur* from
systems based on the cyclical loan of grains. Messerschmidt (1978) and Vinding
(1984) each offer an account of the origin of *dhikurs*. Messerschmidt relates
the term to a Thakali compound word *Dhu-kor*, which he glosses as "grain
rotating turn by turn." An additional version relates the name to the Thakali
phrase *Dho kuisi*, which can be glossed as "grain collection." According to this
account, the villages of Thak Khola used to pool a set amount of grain that was
taken in turn by each family. The grain was used either to produce alcohol for
sale, to sell outright, or to trade for salt or livestock. Vinding says that grain
dhikurs had no interest payments; most of my informants say that these grain
dhikurs had interest that accumulated with each rotation and was paid by everyone whether they had taken a rotation yet or not.

26. Hitchcock has reported *dhikurs* among the "Chandel Magars" of the Bhuji
Khola region in western Myagdi and Baglung Districts (personal communication cited in Messerschmidt 1978:154), and Messerschmidt has found them
among Gurungs in some areas and in one Tamang village (1978). They are
found among all Thakali populations wherever they reside (see observations by
Fürer-Haimendorf 1975; Manzardo and Sharma 1975; Manzardo 1978; and
Vinding 1984). It seems apparent that the current spread of the custom is
related to Thakali migration throughout the middle hills of Nepal. While, as
Messerschmidt (1978) points out, it may be true that the Thakali merely elab-
orated on a custom borrowed from Tibetans, it is clear that the Thakali have
developed the custom into a sophisticated economic instrument.

27. Manzardo claims that Thakali *dhikurs* rarely include members of other *jāts*,
thus giving Thakali businessmen a distinct trading advantage (1978:97). He
thus contends that the pattern of Thakali *dhikurs* supports his argument that

Thakali economic success relies on groupwide cooperation. Information from migrant communities contradicts this argument. The pattern of Thakali participation in *dhikurs* in Khani Khuwa differs from that described for other areas, and the role attributed to *dhikurs* in promoting Thakali ethnic solidarity, in strengthening either ethnic or local community harmony, and in serving as a financial institution makes an examination of its permutations in Khani Khuwa particularly relevant to this study of Thakali identity and social interaction. Over the past few decades there have been some apparent changes in the form and functioning of *dhikurs* among the Thakali; this is particularly true for migrant communities.

28. This is consistent with Messerschmidt's evidence (1978) that sustained local residence is no longer a criterion for membership in a *dhikur*.

29. Manzardo contends that Thakali *dhikurs* are ethnically exclusive, and therefore Thakali businessmen gain access to the capital and supportive advice associated with *dhikur*—he asserts that this is especially true for the poor and inexperienced—and are sheltered more fully than members of other groups, giving them a better chance for commercial success.

30. Messerschmidt also notes exceptions that throw doubt on Manzardo's contention: he notes that some Thakali *dhikurs* include members from Panchgaon and Baragaon, as well as Tibetans resident in Thak Khola (1978:144).

31. *Dhikurs* are "played" (N: *dhikur khelne*) and have "players."

32. Vinding (1984) has noted that most *dhikurs* in Thak Khola succeed, and Manzardo (1978) has noted that all the members of a dhikur have a vested interest in the economic success of those who initially take the fund.

33. This resentment is not peculiar to the Khani Khuwa area: two decades ago Kawakita quoted a woman in the village of Ulleri who noted that Thakali had not been allowed to settle in the village because of the widely held belief that allowing even one Thakali household a foothold in the village would result in the villagers' eventual indebtedness to the Thakalis who would inevitably follow on the heels of the first and come to possess much of the village land.

5. Ritual Landscapes

1. N: a tailor, a man of a low-status caste group.

2. For example, ritual boundaries of purity and pollution are not rigidly observed in all Thakali communities. In the instance noted at the beginning of the chapter, for example, a low-caste *damai* was allowed to wander freely in and out of the room where the ritual was performed, and the anthropologist had access to all ritual objects and sites. This would not have been allowed in Thak Khola.

3. Hindu priests are very rarely ever called to Thaksatsae.

4. The kinship terms commonly in use by the Thakali include terms of both Thakali and Nepali origin.

5. Fürer-Haimendorf and Jest have reported extravagant celebrations of these rites by the prominent trading families of Tukche (Fürer-Haimendorf 1981b; Jest 1969).

6. Tucci has noted that juniper (N: *dhupi*) is also held sacred by the "Bonpos," and he writes that "the smoke of the juniper drives off evil spirits and for this reason the Buddhists make use of it in certain rites and for exorcisms. In popular liturgy it is known by the name of sang" (1956:14). Holmberg has observed the same use of juniper among the Tamang of eastern Nepal (1980:209).

7. See, for instance, Manzardo 1978:56 n. 14, 67.

8. For a discussion of these ritually impure categories, see chapter 2. For a discussion of restricted access to the *thimten*, see Manzardo (1978:58)

9. In Khani Khuwa, the ritual is usually called *kul devtā puja* and not *lha chuji* or *lha chuwa*.

10. I also received a copy of this videotape.

11. Vinding (1984) has described a ceremony in the village of Syang in Panchgaon that bears many similarities to ceremonies performed by the Thakali of Thaksatsae.

12. Many Thakali informants assert that the silver necklace used by the Thakali for this ritual originated from Rajasthan.

13. On only one occasion that I witnessed was a *khāngalo* not available. Not every family owns one, and so one is often borrowed for the occasion, but in this particular instance the groom's party had neglected to bring a *khāngalo* from their own village, and the nearest one was several hours' walk away. It was replaced by a women's necklace made of turquoise and coral, formerly popular in Thak Khola. This substitution was a subject of great mirth, and the groom's representatives were teased mercilessly.

14. Some informants report that one must feed the ancestors, the former servants of the ancestors, and the birds.

15. Though I have never witnessed the participation of a Brahman or an individual from a low caste.

16. Though Larjung village was the home of some prominent ancestors of the subclan (it was the site of Pati Ram Sau's principal home, and some believe it was the home of the Hansa Raja (see Basanta Bhattachan 1992), no member of the Pompar subclan currently owns a house in Larjung.

17. See the discussion in chapter 3.

18. In recent years some of them have been moved from one field to another, but none of them have been moved from Thaksatsae.

19. For a complete list of subclans, see table 2.1.

20. Fürer-Haimendorf reported that he found no lineage whose members could trace descent to a common ancestor (1981a:7).
21. Some informants claimed that the bones of the children of mixed marriages are placed outside the *khimi* but never inside.
22. See the discussion in chapter 6 about the membership in the early Pokhara *samaj* and the Thakali Sewa Samiti.
23. Manzardo does not address these specific issues in his discussion of "full Thakali status."
24. Manzardo has also referred to the existence of separate *khimi* for those adopted into the group (1978:90 n. 12). This is inconsistent with my informants' vague replies when pressed to reveal what happened to the bone fragments of adoptees and the *celang melang*. It may be that they are placed outside the *khimi*, or that they are quietly discarded elsewhere, or that they simply disappear. I found no evidence of separate *khimi*, and my informants insisted that the bones fragments of individuals from these categories would not be placed in the subclan's *khimi*.
25. *Mit* is the masculine form, *mitini* the feminine; it means "fictive kin" or "ritual brotherhood." See Okada (1957).
26. My own connection with the Sherchan Pompar *ghyu* is through a *mit* relationship. My relationship with the Tulachan Jhongman subclan is as an in-law through the *mitini* relationship my wife has with a Tulachan woman.
27. Vinding has stated that the post of *gamba* is nominated by members of the subclan and that it is open to any man living in Thak Khola (1981:210). Fürer-Haimendorf has stated that the *gamba* is the oldest member of the senior generation (1981b:9). I know of exceptions to both these statements. There are numerous instances where the post of the *gamba* or *gundal* is held by an individual residing outside Thak Khola, and sometimes a distinction will be made between the senior member of the subclan and the individual who is keeping the documents and managing the groups fund.
28. For a description of the organization of this feast, see Fürer-Haimendorf (1981a:9).
29. It is not clear that all the names were ever known by every Thakali, but it seems apparent that migration has contributed to this incomplete knowledge (see also Fürer-Haimendorf [1981a]). Since 1983 there has been an effort to reeducate the Thakali about the subclans and to reestablish connections. Most of those in attendance at the 1993 twelve-year Lha Phewa festival were able to name their subclans and to identify the principal members.
30. Fürer-Haimendorf reported that none of his informants remembered any instance of the division of a lineage that resulted in the construction of a new *khimi* (1981a:9). My informants, however, cited several examples. The Gauchan Tancang subclan originally included five other groups which now have

distinct names: Lara *phobe*, Saicyang *phobe*, Bhuicyang *phobe*, Sanke Dhorche *phobe*, and Ghera *phobe*. Ghera is now a separate subclan. The other four constitute Lara or Tancang *phobe*. Dhom *phobe* has three named subdivisions but all three share one *khimi* and have a single *jho khane*. In table 2.1, subclans with new names but using the old *khimis* listed under the original subclan; those who have new *khimis* are listed as separate subclans.

31.   Though the Sherchan Dhom *phobe* is one of the few subclans whose members are eligible to become *dhoms* or Thakali *jhākris*, there are no active *dhoms* from this subclan at present.

32.   Also called the Khumba Mela and the Bāra Barsa Kumbha Melā (N: the twelve-year festival). For a description of this festival as performed in 1981, see Vinding (1992). See also Jest (1974); Somlai (1982); and Vinding (1983).

33.   In 1993 only male clan members took advantage of these gathering centers. While there is no formal rule concerning this, there are several reasons for the gender imbalance. Families that send a single representative to the festival always send a male member of the family. Consequently, there are more males in attendance than females. Women who attend from outside Thaksatsae always accompany family members, and these families find lodging elsewhere, most commonly with relatives who live in the area or, alternatively, in the head-quarters of the various subclan *celi*, the out-married women of the subclans, who reunite during this festival.

34.   The Thakali use *guthi* (N) to refer to either land or money held in common by a clan or a named subclan.

35.   See Vinding (1981:209). Gauchan and Vinding contended that there are in-stances where individuals have been removed from the post because their work was unsatisfactory (1977:103). Fürer-Haimendorf reported that the role is largely ceremonial, involving neither power nor authority (1981a:5).

6. Codifying Culture

1.   See Manzardo and Sharma's 1975 article on the Thakali Samaj Sudhar Sangh.

2.   Other areas, such as Galkot and Darbang, had informal gatherings and orga-nizations.

3.   *Thakali Samaj Sudhar Sangh* (1971 [2028 V.S.]:3), cited in Manzardo and Sharma (1975:31).

4.   For the sake of convenience, the organizations have changed the dates on which festivals are celebrated and reduced the number of households it is obligatory to visit during the Hindu holiday of Dasain and that newlyweds are required to visit following marriage. Cost-cutting reforms have included the

elimination of certain feasts associated with funeral rites and limitations on the value of gifts given by the groom to the bride at a wedding.

5. *Thakali Samaj Sudhar Sangh* (1971 [2028 V.S.]:1), cited in Manzardo and Sharma (1975:35).

6. See, for instance, Bhattachan (1979); Gauchan (1981); Sherchan (n.d.); and the first issue of *Khāngalo* (N. S. 2037 [1980]).

7. Later, a second challenge by some of the participants forced the ad hoc committee to ask me to relinquish the existing tapes. This I did only after lengthy negotiations with a subcommittee designated by the chairman of the ad hoc steering committee. The subcommittee promised to return the tapes and to permit me to use them for my research; in return I agreed not to use verbatim any segment specified by their censors. The tapes were returned, but per our agreement this account is based solely on my handwritten notes.

8. I had been initially invited by members of the ad hoc committee and other representatives to the meeting. My attendance had also been approved by the chairman of the ad hoc committee.

9. On the morning of the fifth day, two well-known Nepali scholars arrived at the meeting. The chairman of the ad hoc planning committee, apparently desirous of avoiding another challenge to his authority, welcomed them publicly but immediately made it clear to the delegates that they had arrived uninvited.

10. At the time, the members had no accurate information on population distribution to guide this debate. My own survey completed later that year confirmed the arguments of the representatives from Baglung and Myagdi Districts.

11. There was a conscious attempt to ensure that the officers of the central committee included a representative from each clan. This is the only instance of which I am aware when clan membership was taken into consideration. Because of the web of descent and affinity, the use of clan membership as a criterion for selection does not ensure that officers are drawn from different political factions. Nevertheless, the selection of one officer from each clan was cited by some Thakali as evidence of a sincere attempt to provide diversity of representation.

12. Most of the guidelines were concerned with who should be invited to particular rituals and the maximum amount to be spent on presents and other expenses.

13. My own movements at this time were incorporated into the efficient and widespread communication network of the Thakali. I was often asked to be a courier for the central committee and for the new local chapters in areas of Khani Khuwa. This heightened my visibility and increased my access to individual Thakali.

14. Writing in 1987, I argued that the "increasing group-consciousness of the Thakali in relatively more remote areas, the growing strength of the pro-shaman, anti-Hindu factions, suggests that the reform process will move further from

the control of the urban faction and the subba group and be more influenced by traditionalists" (287).

15. See Fisher (1993). The number of member associations has grown since its formation in 1990.

7. Constructing Thakali

1. Sharma, for example, has written: "These Thakalis, who were once patrons of these Gompas, have *completely* turned away from their Tibetan religion and learning, and have been modeling their thoughts, beliefs, and practices on those of high caste Hindus" (1977:296; my emphasis). Messerschmidt has written: "By the late 19th century, the Thakalis had begun adopting Hindu social and religious forms and were beginning to abandon some forms of Buddhism and Bon, in an overt attempt to emulate their Hindu neighbors to the south" (1984:11).

2. Fürer-Haimendorf expressed doubt about the sincerity of the Thakali profession of Hinduism and suggested that aspects of Hinduism were merely camouflage for a secularization of their society (1967b:201). This suggestion is discussed below.

3. Accounts of this journey can be found in Tucci [1953] 1982, 1956.

4. *Lamaism* is often used to indicate the form of Buddhism that developed in Tibet. Tucci defends his use of the term, observing "that the term 'Lamaist,' which is inaccurate in itself, is actually appropriate in this region" ([1953] 1982:49).

5. Kawakita persisted in using the term *Takali*, though he admitted that "since 'Takali' is often aspirated as 'Thakali,' it may be right to spell the name as 'Thakali.' For instance, Hodgson spells it 'Thakoras.' Also Tucci spells the name 'Thākali.' And they are called *Thak* as well" (1957:86).

6. Kawakita is actually referring to practices associated with the Thakali *ḍhom*. *Jangri* is not a Thakali word but Nepali, usually transliterated as *jhākri*. Kawakita notes that it is pronounced *jhankri* by most of the people in Kathmandu (1957:91).

    Turner translates *jhākri* as "diviner, conjurer, wizard" (1931:231). It is more commonly glossed as "shaman." For an introduction to the *jāhkri*, see Hitchcock and Jones (1976); Hitchcock (1967); and Maskarinec (1995).

7. Iijima describes his term *Hinduization* as similar to the term *Sanskritization* used by Srinivas (1963:50 n. 2). Iijima describes Sanskritization as the adoption of vegetarianism, abstention from alcoholic beverages, and conformance of a low caste's or tribe's ritual and pantheon to that of high-caste Brah-

mans. Note that by these standards the Thakali can*not* be said to have undergone Sanskritization.

8.   "They constitute a very dynamic ethnic group found in the contact zone be-
     tween Hindu and Buddhist cultures."

9.   "Entering the Kali Gandaki valley one is struck by the plurality of religious
     forms. One moves progressively from a Hindu region to a region dominated
     by the Buddhist religion. In Thak, one finds, at the same time, Lamaist Bud-
     dhism and the magic-religious beliefs of the Thakali."

10. Snellgrove has suggested that there is no "final and clear-cut distinction" be-
     tween so-called white and black *bon* and he therefore uses the term in two
     general ways: to refer to aboriginal religion of whatever kind and the developed
     "pseudo-Buddhist" form (1961:43 n. a). He notes that it is difficult to be precise
     about the term *Bon-po*: "It is applied both to aboriginal religious practice . . .
     and to the developed form of the religion, which has organized itself by shame-
     less borrowing from Buddhism. The former is chiefly characterized by belief
     in local and personal spirits of different kinds" (1958:289–90 n. 27). Stein
     would prefer to see the term used in a more restricted sense (1952:98–100),
     but Snellgrove is closer to the Tibetan usage of the term.

     The application of this term to the varied indigenous religious practices
     common throughout the Himalayas has the unfortunate side effect of endowing
     a number of different collections of practices and beliefs with an undeserved
     and misleading analytic unity.

11. Thakuri (N), "a clan, or *thar*, of Chetris" (Turner 1931:248). Chetri (N), the
     second, or warrior, caste. Snellgrove has noted that "Thakuri derived from the
     Sanskrit thakkura meaning 'deity,' 'lord.' It was originally a title claimed by
     warriors of lordly rank, specifically by the Rajputs" (1961:19 n. a).

12. For variations of this story, see Jest 1964/65:32–33; Fürer-Haimendorf 1975;
     Manzardo 1978; and Gauchan and Vinding 1977:136 n. 13, 137 n. 14.

13. "The Thakuri, when asked, have very strongly rejected the possibility that a
     connection could exist between Thakuri and Thakali."

14. "A very cohesive group, very strongly attached to their traditions."

15. See also Fürer-Haimendorf (1966:142–43): "Until two generations ago the
     Thakalis were finally rooted in Buddhist tradition and practice. Apart from the
     performance of certain rites stemming from an older tribal religion, and in-
     volving such un-Buddhist traits as animal sacrifices, they conform to the general
     pattern of Tibetan Buddhist society."

16. While conducting research among the Thakali, I found that informants were
     sometimes unsure which label to use to describe a specific religious practice.
     In my judgment, their uncertainty did not stem from confusion but rather
     demonstrated that externally conceived traditions and categories are not always
     appropriate to describe local practices.

17. None of my informants has ever confused *ḍhom* practices with Hinduism, nor has the similarity of animal sacrifice in both traditions ever been cited as justification for the practice of *ḍhom* rituals: on the contrary, these practices were usually identified as "other than" Hindu. Some confusion was revealed by Thakalis resident in Khani Khuwa who identified *ḍhom* rituals involving animal sacrifice with Buddhism.

18. Vinding resided in Syang in 1972, 1975–78, and 1980–81.

19. Prior to Vinding's residence in Syang, one scholar lived in Marpha (Valeix 1974). Bista includes a brief section on the northern groups entitled "Panchgaonle" in his book *People of Nepal* (1967).

20. Indeed, Manzardo has argued that an orthodox Buddhist past was unlikely, and he has asserted that "it is likely that there were never very many Thakalis in the clergy" (1978:178).

21. He has since recanted this view. See his 1992 letter to the editor in *Himal* (Manzardo 1992).

22. Goffman (1959) first introduced the concept of impression management as a way of describing how individuals present themselves and their activities to others and how they control impressions formed about them. Berreman (1962) has applied the idea in a social setting not only to the activities of the subjects of his study but also to the activities of the anthropologist and his "team," examining the way in which all the individuals interacted with each other. Manzardo (1978; 1982) has employed the concept in a different way to describe what he saw as the unusually duplicitous social maneuvering of the Thakali. That individuals and collections of individuals manipulate impressions is not a startling revelation. Manzardo has claimed that what is unique about the Thakali in this regard is the degree to which they manipulate impressions, that they do it within two different cultural spheres, and that they do it as a unified group. Whereas Goffman is concerned with technique, Manzardo's interest is motive.

23. Manzardo's arguments inspired an article by Messerschmidt, who offered the tautological suggestion that the Thakali adaptation, or "strong fins," which has allowed them to adjust to the political, economic, and socioreligious "vagaries" of their situation in Thak Khola, is their ability to adapt (1984).

24. Iijima observed that the actual religious practices of the Thakali could be correlated to economic status and age: like Tucci and Snellgrove, he noted that older Thakalis, especially women, were pious Buddhists, while the rich adopted aspects of Hinduism. He also noted that though some Thakalis styled themselves Hindus, "there is not a single Hindu temple in Thak Khola, nor is there a Brahman" (1963:50).

25. For instance, while it has been argued that Buddhism plays a less important role among the Thakalis in general and Thakali migrants in particular, Vinding

argues that in the last decades it has played an increasing role in the religion of the Syang Thakali (1982:295 n. 20).

26. Tucci (1953:49) cites this as evidence of a Buddhist revival, a position not supported by most scholars who argue that Buddhism is in decline. How new the temples are is never specified.

27. A *tama patra* (N) is a copperplate on which a deed or gift is inscribed (Turner 1931:279). Fürer-Haimendorf has cited the evidence available from these (1966; 1975:141).

28. Hamilton, for example, observed that there has always been a mixture of religions in the middle hills ([1819] 1971:32–33), and Holmberg has also noted that complex religious systems are common in the middle hills of the Himalaya (1980:5).

29. Manzardo and Sharma (1975) discuss this tendency among the Thakali migrant community in Pokhara.

30. It is puzzling that rituals that have a place in the Thakali religious systems may be dismissed by an analyst because they do not fit his or her concept of traditional religious systems.

31. For exceptions, see Manzardo 1978 and Fisher 1987.

32. The goddess Narijhowa resides in a temple overlooking Khanti. She is often identified as Mahalaxmi to outsiders, particularly Nepali speakers who inquire about her, but she is also worshiped by Tibetan Buddhists. Among the Thakali, she is usually called Narijhowa. The assertion that this goddess was adopted to fill a need, as Ijima claims, is entirely speculative and, I suggest, specious. Most informants did not perceive of Narijhowa as presiding over the four clan gods of the Thakali.

33. According to Fürer-Haimendorf (1960), Iijima (1963), Manzardo (1984), Manzardo and Sharma (1975), and Sharma (1977), these reforms have been widely followed by the Thakali in Thaksatsae. Schuler (1979) and Vinding (1979/80b) claim that the reforms have been followed by less of the population than previously alleged. My own information strongly supports this latter view. Vinding (1982) suggests that some Thakali stopped eating yak after the reforms were passed but that currently most Thakali in Thaksatsae eat yak. For migrants in areas where yak is not available, of course, it is rarely an issue.

8. Beyond Sanskritization

1. The theft was planned by a Thakali who had the image taken to Kathmandu. Photographs of the statue, used to solicit a buyer, came into the hands of

another Thakali, who recognized it and alerted authorities. Cooperating with the Thakali community, the police set up a sting, caught the thief, and recovered the goddess.

2. Manzardo reported that Narijhowa was sometimes identified with Kumari, the Newar virgin goddess, a living reincarnation of Talleju, a protectress of the royal family (1985:99). This identification is apparently not widespread, and I have not been able to elicit this connection from my informants.

3. A myth recounts how Thakali hunters sighted a beautiful deer in a small forest above Narakhot. After a long pursuit they were able to corner the deer in a small cave. As they were about to shoot it, the deer transformed into a beautiful women who identified herself as the goddess Narijhowa. The men pleaded with the goddess to remain in the area and to be their protective deity. Narijhowa agreed to stay and to take on herself any misfortunes that befell the Thakali, provided that a temple be built on a cliff side overlooking the river, that the Shyopen festival be performed in her honor, and that widows or menstruating women never come into her presence. The men agreed and constructed the temple. While carrying the goddess to the temple they cam on a widow, and the goddess turned her head away in aversion. The image of Narijhowa bears the signs of her promise to take on misfortune (a blemish identified as a smallpox scar rests on her cheek) and her encounter with the widow (the images head is turned to one side).

4. See, for example, Bista (1967, 1971), Fürer-Haimendorf (1966, 1967b), Iijima (1963); Manzardo (1978), and Messerschmidt (1984).

5. Sharma, for example, has written: "These Thakalis, who were once patrons of these Gompas, have *completely* turned away from their Tibetan religion and learning, and have been modelling their thoughts, beliefs, and practices on those of high caste Hindus" (1977:296; my emphasis).

    Messerschmidt has written: "By the late 19th century, the Thakalis had begun adopting Hindu social and religious forms and were beginning to abandon some forms of Buddhism and Bon, in an overt attempt to emulate their Hindu neighbors to the south" (1984:11).

    See also Bista (1967, 1971), Fürer-Haimendorf (1966, 1967b), Iijima (1963), and Manzardo (1978).

6. Typical is Fürer-Haimendorf's persistence in describing the Thakali as "fundamentally a trading community" (1981b:175; see also 1985:141). Manzardo acknowledges that "many, if not most of the Thakali, are not traders" (1977a:63); nevertheless, his analysis focuses on "Thakalis who are involved chiefly in commercial enterprises" (1978:iv).

7. Barth notes that "practically all anthropological reasoning rests on the premise that cultural variation is discontinuous" and that there are differences that distinguish discrete cultures from one another (1969:9).

8. Earlier scholars were not unaware that the boundaries they drew were arbitrary—those peoples enclosed within the anthropologists' conceptual boundaries were often culturally, socially, politically, and economically integrated with others who fell outside of those boundaries, and there were often multiple patterns within those boundaries—but they chose to exclude such data from their analysis and conclusions.

9. Embree (1977) has fruitfully contrasted the notions of frontier and boundary with respect to regions in South Asia. I am suggesting that the same contrast can be usefully applied to group identities.

10. See the *Oxford English Dictionary*.

11. Issues of ethnic identity and distinction have commanded a great deal of attention in the anthropological literature (see, for example, Barth (1969), Berreman (1975), and Moerman (1974), where the terms *ethnic group* and *ethnicity*, like those of *caste* and *tribe*, have been defined, either implicitly or explicitly, with considerable variation in meaning. Ethnicity has sometimes been defined so broadly that it is practically synonymous with culture, and ethnic group so narrowly that it refers to well-defined interest groups. Some studies focus on the attributes possessed by tribal, caste, and ethnic units; others describe ethnicity as a status people may activate in complex political systems (Leach 1954; Lehman 1967); and still others portray ethnicity as the social organization of cultural differences that maintains social boundaries (Barth 1969). See Blake (1981), Vincent (1968), and Moerman (1978) for further discussion of this perspective on ethnicity.

12. See also Moerman (1974), Fried (1975), Dumont (1970), Leach (1954), and Lehman (1963).

13. Mayer has noted the same conditions for caste units, observing that "only in relation with other castes is the caste a significant unit" (1960:5).

14. The primordialist-instrumentalist dichotomy between the view that subjective claims to ethnic identity derive from the affective potency of primordial attachments (Geertz 1963) and the view that people with common interests coalesce into ethnic groups in pursuit of those interests (Cohen 1969a; Despres 1967) continues to orient studies of ethnicity despite a growing sense that it obscures important aspects of the phenomena under study.

15. The term *tribe*, for example, has been used in anthropological literature in at least four distinct but related ways: to indicate an evolutionary phase in the development of society; to distinguish one type of society from another (such as to distinguish noncaste society from caste society); to identify a kind of political unit; and to label any population whose members are believed to share a common culture. Not surprisingly, considerable confusion has resulted from this multiple usage.

A triple usage has been described by Moerman, who has wisely warned us to avoid confusing data with analysis and words with people: "In South-East Asia," he notes, "a society is a member of the tribal set by virtue of not being a member of the civilized set" (1974:54). Fried has noted that " 'tribe' figures prominently on the list of putative technical terms ranked in order of degree of ambiguity" (1967:154). In his essay *The Notion of Tribe*, Fried, though he admitted there was not much likelihood that he "would be able to affect common or even professional usage of the word 'tribe,' " suggested that the one usage of the term in accord with our knowledge and experience is "as a secondary sociopolitical phenomenon, brought about by the intercession of more complexly ordered societies, states in particular" (1975:114). This description is in accord with what I argue about the rise of Thakali ethnic consciousness, but it is not the only, or even the primary, sense in which other scholars have applied the term to the Thakali.

16. A number of scholars have examined the interaction between caste society and so-called tribal groups (Bailey 1960, 1961; Höfer 1979a; Dumont 1961, 1970; Fürer-Haimendorf 1957, 1960, 1967a; Iijima 1963; Mandelbaum 1972; Sharma 1977; Sinha 1965), and there have been numerous attempts to devise a topology of tribe, caste, and ethnic group in India (see, for example, Bailey 1960, 1961; Sinha 1965).

17. One alternative conceptualization envisions caste and tribe as different from one another not in kind but in degree; that is, a continuum runs from tribe to caste (Bailey 1960; Sinha 1965).

18. Barth (1969), for example, has argued that caste is but a manifestation of ethnic groups peculiar to India.

19. As Eric Wolf (1982) has argued, these attempts result in presentations of culture as bounded and unchanging billiard balls ricocheting off one another. Gerald Sider has argued that "we must reexamine the assumption, almost completely pervasive in anthropology, that a society, however bounded, has a social structure and a culture" (1986:45). See also Roseberry (1989) and Moore (1989).

20. Iijima, for example, identifies these three as the southern "Indic" region, where Hinduism is predominant; the northernmost "Tibetan" area, where "Lamaism and Bonnism are influential"; and the "Himalayan" area, which is "sandwiched between the Indic and Tibetan areas" and where the cultural characteristics are "a blending of Hinduism and Lamaism to which is added an indigenous shamanistic animism" (1963:43).

21. Numerous influences and changes over the past several decades—the Chinese occupation and the subsequent closing of the Tibetan border, Nepali-medium education, widespread migration within the middle hills regions and from the northern regions southward, and the ubiquity of Radio Nepal and to a lesser extent Nepali language print media—have affected both the distribution of

populations and cultural practices. These effects have further reduced any utility models of this type may have had.

22. One of the first descriptions of distinct groups in Nepal was Bista's classic work
People of Nepal (1967). These early descriptions presented groups as relatively
isolated and independent from relations with more encompassing elements and
forces in Nepalese society.

23. See Moerman's observation that ethnic groups are always in opposition to a
cultural system "with which they may conflict, for which they may serve, or
which they may imitate or even become, but which they can never ignore"
(1974:58). See also Leach (1954).

24. Fürer-Haimendorf's assertion recalls Dumont's claim that a tribe becomes a
caste when it recognizes the values of the caste system (1967a).

25. The question of whether there is a modification of values when tribes become
castes has been variously answered in the literature. Dumont (1961), Fürer-
Haimendorf (1966, 1967a, 1967b), Barth (1969), and Jones (1976) state clearly
that there is, while Bailey (1961), Karve (1961), and Srinivas (1961, cited in
Dumont 1970) indicate that there is not.

26. Hodgson, for example, observed that "the Himalayan population is intensely
Tribe-ish" ([1874] 1971:137).

27. See, for example, Barnett (1977), Lynch (1969), Srinivas (1967), and Sharma
(1977).

28. Lyall (1882:102, 112). Höfer calls this a "proto-theory" of Sanskritization
(1979b:187 n. 14).

29. Lévi (1905–8) and Weber ([1916] 1958) comment on the same phenomenon.

30. Lévi published the three-volume *Le Nepal* between 1905 and 1908, and Max
Weber's studies on India first appeared in 1916. Kulke (1986:99) suggests that
Weber was unaware of Lévi's work on Nepal.

31. This implication that Sanskritization may, under some circumstances, result in
de-Sanskritization is another example of the confusion created by the broad
application of the term. Srinivas seems to conflate the act of elite, or dominant
caste, emulation with the cultural character of the change that ensues. Thus
Sanskritization (understood as elite emulation) will not always result in Sanskritization (understood as the imitation or adoption of Brahmanical values).

32. For another criticism of Sanskritization, see Carroll (1977).

33. Holmberg (1980) correctly identifies these as all-Nepali holidays and rites.

9. Old Artificers in a New Smithy

1. See, for instance, the discussion in Basanta Bhattachan (1992). This is a widely
articulated view with growing support in the 1990s.

2. See Holmberg (1980:55), who cites additional examples where the employ-
    ment of a Brahman priest does not necessarily result in Sanskritization.
3. Barnett describes substantialization as the transition from castes to ethniclike
    regional caste blocs (1977:281).

Glossary

The Thakali language does not have its own script, and there is no consensus among Thakalis about how Thakali words should be written in Devanagari. In this study I have taken the most common form of Thakali words written by my informants in Devanagari script. Nepali and Thakali words have been transliterated from the Devanagari according to Turner (1931). There is no capitalization in written Nepali. I capitalize transliterated proper names as would be appropriate in English. In the following list, "N" stands for Nepali, and "T" for Thakali.

amānat (N)   system of taxation entailing collection of taxes directly by salaried employees of the government

arānsi karānsi (T)   term used by the Thakali to refer to propertyless migrants into Thak Khola

astu (N)   bone from the upper part of the head collected after cremation for deposit in the *khimi*

bahun (N)   brahman, priestly *jāt* or caste

bahunbad (N)   Brahamanism

bāis khāni (N)   lit. the twenty-two mines, sometimes used to refer generically to Khani Khuwa

Bāra Barsa Kumbha Melā (N)   lit. the twelve year festival, Lha Phewa

bāragāū (N)   lit. twelve villages, the area to the north of Panchgaon (*pāchgāu*), Baragaon

bāragāūle (N)   an individual from *bāragāū*, Baragaonle

bazār (N)   any place goods are exchanged, colloquially used to refer to towns with markets

bemchāg (T)   local record

bhāi (N)   kinship term for younger brother

Bhaṭṭachan (*commonly "Bhattachan"*) clan name, also Bhurgi

bhoṭe (N) (commonly "Bhote")   also *bhotiya*, somewhat derogatory term used to refer to people with Tibetan cultural characteristics

Bhurgi   older name for the Bhattachan clan

bon (T)   pre-Buddhist religion of the Tibetan region

bon-nāg (T)   black *bon*, the unreformed Bon practices

buḍhā (N)   village headman, see *mukiyā*

celang melang (T)   used to refer to the offspring of mixed marriages, also *khaccar* (N)

celi (N, T)   women born into a patrilineage

-chan (T)   an ending on Thakali names that indicates clan.

chang (N)   fermented alcohol, beer

Chetri (N)   a Nepalese caste, Kshatriya

chokko pāni (N)   ritually pure water

chorten (Tib.)   religious construction

cyāng (T)   refers to the temporary residences of a patrilineage set up during Lha Phewa

Cyogi (T)   older name of the Gauchan clan

dājyu-bhāi (N)   brothers

dhān rākne (N)   a premarriage ceremony by which two families indicate their intention to marry the daughter of one family to the son of another

dhārni (N)   unit of weight, about five pounds

dhikur (T)   rotating credit association

Ḍhimchen *(T)* older name for the Sherchan clan

ḍhom (T)   Thakali religious specialist

gamba (T)   leader of a patrilineal group

gāū (N)   village

Gauchan   name of a Thakali patrilineal clan, also Cyogi

ghyu (T)   extended patrilineage, also *phobe*

Gorkha   a village in central Nepal from which Pritivi Narayan Shah began his conquest of the Himalaya

gundal (T)   assistant to a *gamba* and a patrilineal group

guthi (N)   money or land held in common by a group, usually endowed by the state or individuals to fund religious or charitable functions

Hānsa Rājā *(commonly "Hansa Raja")*   name of a former ruler in Thaksatsae

ijara (N)   a tax collection system using contractors, a revenue collection contract

ijaradar (N)   contractor who collects taxes or holds an *ijara* for the management of mines

Janajāti (N) (commonly "Janajati")   a newly popular term for ethnic groups that were originally non-Hindu

jāt (N)   sort, kind, used to designate distinct groups

jhākri (N)   shaman

jho cawa (T)   yearly meeting of Thakali patrilineal groups

jho khane (N)   see *jho cawa*

joshi (N)   astrologer

juāi (N)   kinship term for son-in-law or younger brother-in-law; often used to refer to any man who has married a woman from one's family, lineage, or subclan *khaccar* (N)   mule, mongrel, bastard: offspring of parents of different *jāts*

Khāni Khuwā (commonly "Khani Khuwa") term used by the Thakali for the mining area of Baglung, Myagdi, and Gulmi Districts

khāngalo (T)   silver neck piece used for marriage ceremonies

khe (T)   kinship term for father's father, husband's father, or ancestors generally

khimi (T)   ossuary of an extended patrilineage (*ghyu*)

khimi chuwa (T)   ceremony offering change to the ancestors of a patrilineage (*ghyu*)

khimi tapne (N)   see *khimi chuwa*, part of a marriage ceremony

khola (N)   river, valley

khuwāle (N) (commonly "Khuwale")   somewhat derogatory term for the Thakali from Khani Khuwa

kiriya (N)   funeral ceremony

kul puja (N)   ancestor worship

kul devtā puja (N)   worship of the gods of a lineage

lha chuwa (T)   offering to the gods, also known as *lha chuji*

lha ḍhom (T)   a kind of *ḍhom*

Lha Yhāwā Rāngjyung (T) name of the Bhattachan clan god, the self-made yak

Lha Lāngbā Nhurbu (T) name of the Gauchan clan god, the jeweled elephant

Lha Chyurin Gyālmo (T) name of the Tulachan clan goddess, the queen crocodile

Lha Phewa (T) lit. the appearance of the gods, the Thakali festival celebrated every twelve years, the Bāra Barsa Kumbha Melā

Lha Ghāngla Singi Karmo (T)   name of the Sherchan clan goddess, the white lioness of the glacier

Malla   name of a Thukuri clan and an ancient kingdom in western Nepal

māng ḍhom (T)   a kind of *ḍhom*

mhā (T)   son-in-law

mhenḍo (T)   a representation of the deceased, made of a pot with cypress branches

mit (N)   ritual brother, male fictive kin

mitini (N)   female fictive kin

mom (T)   grandmother, female ancestor

mukiyā (N) village headman, chief, leader

mul juāi (N)   the in-law in charge of ritual performance at a *khimi tapne* or *kiriya*

mul bandej (N)   lit. main rules, constitution

Muluki Ain (N)   the legal code of 1854

Narijhowa   name of the protective deity in Nari Gomba

Newar (N) name of the group indigenous to the Kathmandu valley

panchayat (N)   a council with five members; the partyless political system of Nepal in place from 1962 to 1990

pāchgāū (N)   lit. five villages, designates a set of villages in upper Thak Khola; Panchgaon *pāchgāūle* (N)   an individual or individuals from *pāchgāū*: Panchgaonle

pāre (T)   ritual specialist of a Thakali clan, also refers to the patrilineage from which the specialists are chosen

pho khāne (N)   those who can not speak Thakali, often used interchangeably with Khuwale

phobe (T)   extended patrilineage, *ghyu*

pompar (Tib.)   king, leader

Pompar *(T)*   name of a patrilineal group

prelo (T)   year of the monkey

pumi (T)   witch

raja (N)   chief of a vassal principality

rākshi (N)   distilled alcohol

rhab (T)   account of a clan's ancestors

rhab (Tib.)   lineage, history

sādo bhāi (N)   men connected by virtue of their marriages to women of the same *ghyu* or *phobe*

Sālgi   older name for the Tulachan clan

samāj (N) (commonly *"samaj"*)   community, association

Serib   name used in Tibetan texts to refer to a historical area that may be in the upper Kali Gandaki valley, particularly Panchgaon and Baragaon

shāligram (N)   ammonite fossils found along the Kali Gandaki and considered sacred by Hindu pilgrims

Sherchan   name of a Thakali clan, also Ḍhimchen

shyopen lawa (T)   coming-of-age ritual in Thak Khola, also Kumar Jatra (N)

subbā (N) (commonly *"subba"*)   title given to a government officer

tama patra (N)   lit. copper plate, refers to the material on which government edicts were written

Thāk Kholā (N) (commonly "Thak Khola")   lit. the valley of Thak; used generally to refer to the upper Kali Gandaki valley from Ghāsā to Jomsom; used by some to refer to Thaksatsae

Thāk Khole *(commonly "Thak Khole")*   a term used to distinguish Thakali with homes in Thaksatsae from Khuwale Thakali

Thāksātsae *(N)* *(commonly "Thaksatsae")*   lit. the seven hundred Thāk, also Thak, Thag; the area of the upper Kali Gandaki from Ghāsā to Tukche

Ṭhakuri *(commonly "Thakuri")*   a high Hindu *jāt* that includes the royal family

thar (N)   clan, lineage

Terai *(N)*   the low-lying plains at the foot of the Himalayan range

thekbandi (N)   system for the collection of homestead tax through local *mukiyās* in the central hill region

thekthiti (N)   system for the collection of homestead tax through agreement with local communities *thekdar* (N)   contractor, individual authorized to collect agrarian taxes

thimten (T)   the space in a Thakali house used for rituals

Torongla   a month in the Thakali calender and a festival celebrated in this month

Tulāchan   *(commonly "Tulachan")*   name of a Thakali clan, also Sālgi

Works Cited

Allen, Nicholas J. 1978. "Fourfold Classification of Society in the Himalayas." In *Himalayan Anthropology*, ed. James F. Fisher, 7–25. The Hague: Mouton.

Anderson, Benedict, R. 1983. *Imagined Communities: Reflections on the Origin and Spread of Nationalism*. London: Verso.

Anderson, Robert T. 1966. "Rotating Credit Associations in India." *Economic Development and Cultural Change* 14: 334–39.

Appadurai, A. 1990. "Disjuncture and Difference in the Global Economy." *Public Culture* 2, no. 2.: 1–24.

Ardener, Shirley. 1964. "Comparative Study of Rotating Credit Associations." *Journal of Royal Anthropological Institute of Great Britain and Ireland* 94, no. 2: 201–29.

Bailey, F. G. 1960. *Tribe, Caste, and Nation: A Study of Political Activity and Political Changes in Highland Orissa*. Manchester: Manchester University Press.

——. 1961. "Tribe and Caste in India." *Contributions to Indian Sociology* 5: 7–19.

——. 1963. *Politics and Social Change: Orissa in 1959*. Berkeley: University of California Press.

——. 1971. *Caste and the Economic Frontier*. Manchester: Manchester University Press.

Bakhtin, Mikhail. 1981. *The Dialogic Imagination*. Trans. C. Emerson and M. Holquist. Austin: University of Texas Press.

Barnett, Steve. 1977. "Identity Choice and Caste Ideology in Contemporary South India." In *Symbolic Anthropology*, ed. J. Dolgin, D. Kemnitzer, and D. Schneider, 270–91. New York: Columbia University Press.

Barth, Frederik. 1963. *The Role of the Entrepreneur in Social Change in Northern Norway*. Bergen: Norway Universitus Press.

——. 1966. *Models of Social Organization*. London: Royal Anthropological Institute of Great Britain and Ireland.

——. 1967. "On the Study of Social Change." *American Anthropologist* 69: 661–69.

——. 1969. Introduction to *Ethnic Groups and Boundaries*, ed. Frederik Barth. Boston: Little Brown.

Beck, Stanley. 1989. "Ethnic Identity as Contested Terrain." *Dialectical Anthropology* 14: 1–6.

Belshaw, Cyril S. 1956. "The Cultural Milieu of the Entrepreneur: A Critical Essay." *Explorations in Entrepreneurial History* 7: 144–46.

Benedict, B. 1968. "Family Firms and Economic Development." *Southwestern Journal of Anthropology* 24: 1–19.

Bennett, Lynn. 1978. "Maiti-Ghar: The Dual Role of High Caste Women in Nepal." In *Himalayan Anthropology*, ed. James F. Fisher, 121–40. The Hague: Mouton.

——. 1983. *Dangerous Wives and Sacred Sisters*. New York: Columbia University Press.

Bentley, G. Carter. 1987. "Ethnicity and Practice." *Journal for Comparative Study of Society and History* 29, no. 1: 24–55.

Berglie, Per-Arne. 1976. "Preliminary Remarks on Some Tibetan 'Spirit-Mediums' in Nepal." *Kailash* 4, no. 1: 85–108.

Berreman, Gerald D. 1960. "Cultural Variability and Drift in the Himalayan Hills." *American Anthropologist* 62: 5.

——. 1962. *Behind Many Masks*. Ithaca, N.Y.: Society for Applied Anthropology.

——. 1964. "Brahmanism and Shamanism in Pahari Religion." In *Religion in South Asia*, ed. E. Harper, 53–70. Seattle: University of Washington Press.

——. 1967a. "Caste as Social Process." *Southwestern Journal of Anthropology* 23: 351–70.

——. 1967b. "Stratification, Pluralism and Interaction: A Comparative Analysis of Caste." In *Caste and Race, Comparative Approaches*, ed. A. De Reuck and J. Knight. London: Churchill.

——. 1972a. *Hindus of the Himalayas: Ethnography and Change*. Berkeley: University of California Press.

——. 1972b. "Race, Caste and Other Invidious Distinctions in Social Stratification." *Race* 13:385–414.

——. 1972c. "Social Categories and Social Interaction in Urban India." *American Anthropologist* 74, no. 3: 567–86.

——. 1975. "Bazar Behavior: Social Identity and Social Interaction in Urban India." In *Ethnic Identity: Cultural Continuities and Change*, ed. George De Vos and Lola Romanucci-Ross, 71–105. Palo Alto, Calif.: Mayfield.

Berreman, Gerald D. and Louis Dumont. 1962. "[Discussion of] Caste, Racism and Stratification." *Contributions to Indian Sociology* 6: 122–24.

Beteille, André. 1965. *Caste, Class, and Power*. Berkeley: University of California Press.

———. 1969. *Caste: Old and New*. Bombay: Asia.

Bhattachan, Basanta. 1992. "Hansaraja." *Khāngalo*.

Bhattachan, Bidya. 1992. "Nepāl ra Thakāli Mahilā." *Khāngalo*.

Bhattachan, Drupa Kumar. 1975. *Thakāli jātiko māhan porba: Ek samichhyatmak parichaya*. Bhairawa: Dainik Airmaya.

———. 1979. *Thakāli Jātiko Purtan Sanskriti Syopen lawa (Kumar Yatrako) ko ek jhalak*. Kathmandu: n.p.

Bhattachan, Krishna. 1985. "Thakaliharule aba bhannuparcha: Hami Thakali hau ra hamilai Thakali hunuma garba cha." Interview with Michael Vinding. *Phalo*, no. 2: 79–88.

Bista, Dor Bahadur. 1967. *People of Nepal*. Kathmandu: Ratna Pustak Bhandar.

———. 1971. "Political Innovators of the Upper Kali Gandaki." *Man* 6, no. 1: 52–60.

———. 1982. "The Process of Nepalization." In *Anthropological and Linguistic Studies of the Gandaki Area in Nepal*, Monumenta Serindica No. 10, 1–20. Tokyo: Institute for the Study of Languages and Culture of Asia and Africa.

Blaikie, Piers, John Cameron, David Feldman, Alan Fournier, and David Seddon, eds. 1976. *The Effects of Roads in West-Central Nepal*. A Report to ESCOR, Ministry of Overseas Development. East Anglia: Overseas Development Group, University of East Anglia.

Blake, Charles Frederic. 1981. *Ethnic Groups and Social Change in a Chinese Market Town*. Asian Studies at Hawaii, No. 27. Hawaii: University Press of Hawaii.

Blalock, H. M. Jr. 1967. *Toward a Theory of Minority Group Relations*. New York: Wiley.

Block, Anton. 1974. *The Mafia of a Sicilian Village, 1866–1960: A Study of Violent Peasant Entrepreneurs*. Oxford: Oxford University Press.

Blu, Karen I. 1980. *The Lumbee Problem: The Making of an American Indian People*. Cambridge: Cambridge University Press.

Blumer, Herbert. 1962. "Society as Symbolic Interaction." In *Human Behavior and Social Processes*, ed. A. M. Rose, 179–93. Boston: Houghton-Mifflin.

———. 1969. *Symbolic Interactionalism*. Englewood Cliffs: Prentice-Hall.

Bock, E. W. 1965. "Symbols in Conflict: Official Versus Folk Religion." *Journal for the Scientific Study of Religion* 5: 204–12.

Bonacich, E. 1973. "A Theory of Middleman Minorities." *American Sociological Review* 38: 583–94.

Bordet, P. 1961. *Recherches géologiques dans l'Himalaya du Nepal: Region du Makala*. Paris: Centre National de la Recherche Scientifique.

Borgstrom, Bengt-Erik. 1976. *The Patron and the Panca: Village Values and Panchayat Democracy in Nepal*. Stockholm Studies in Social Anthropology No. 3. Stockholm: University of Stockholm, Department of Social Anthropology.

Bougle, Celestin. 1971. *Essays on the Caste System*. Cambridge: Cambridge University Press.

Bourdieu, Pierre. 1977. *Outline of a Theory of Practice*. Cambridge: Cambridge University Press.

Brass, Paul R. 1975. *Language, Religion and Politics in North India*. New Delhi: Vikas.

Burger, Henry G. 1966. "Syncretism: An Acculturative Accelerator." *Human Organization* 25: 103–15.

Burghart, Richard. 1984. "The Formation of the Concept of Nation-State in Nepal." *Journal of Asian Studies* 44, no. 1: 101–26.

——. 1996. *The Conditions of Listening: Essays on Religion, History, and Politics in South Asia*. Ed. C. J. Fuller and Jonathan Spencer. Delhi: Oxford University Press.

Caplan, A. Patricia. 1972. *Priests and Cobblers: A Study of Social Change in a Hindu Village in Western Nepal*. San Francisco: Chandler.

——. 1978. "Hierarchy or Stratification? Two Case Studies from Nepal and East Africa." *Himalayan Anthropology*, ed. James F. Fisher, 53–66. The Hague: Mouton.

Caplan, Lionel. 1970. *Land and Social Change in East Nepal*. Berkeley: University of California Press.

——. 1974. "Inter Caste Marriages in a Nepalese Town." In *Contributions to the Anthropology of Nepal*, ed. Christoph von Fürer-Haimendorf. Warminster: Aris and Phillips.

——. 1990. " 'Tribes' in the Ethnography of Nepal: Some Comments on a Debate." *Contributions to Nepalese Studies* 17, no. 2: 129–45.

Carroll, Lucy. 1977. " 'Sanskritization,' 'Westernization,' and 'Social Mobility': A Reappraisal of the Relevance of Anthropological Concepts to the Social Historian of Modern India." *Journal of Anthropological Research* 33: 355–71.

CEDA. 1971. Seminar paper no. 2, CEDA Study Series. Seminar on Population and Development, CEDA, Kathmandu.

——. 1973. "Migration in Nepal: Implications for Spatial Development." Project proposal. Kathmandu: CEDA.

Chhetri, Ram Bahadur. 1986. "Migration, Adaptation, and Socio-Cultural Change: The Case of the Thakalis in Pokhara, Nepal." *Contributions to Nepalese Studies* 13, no.3: 239–59.

Cohen, Abner. 1969a. *Custom and Politics in Urban Africa*. Berkeley: University of California Press.

——. 1969b. "Political Anthropology: The Analysis of the Symbolism of Power Relations." *Man* 4: 217–35.

——. 1976. *Two-Dimensional Man: An Essay on the Anthropology of Power and Symbolism in Complex Society*. Berkeley: University of California Press.

——, ed. 1974. *Urban Ethnicity*. New York: Tavistock.

Cohen, Ronald. 1978. "Ethnicity: Problem and Focus in Anthropology." *Annual Review of Anthropology* 7: 379–403.

Cohn, Bernard S. 1955. "The Changing Status of a Depressed Caste." In *Village India: Studies in the Little Community*, ed. McKim Marriot, 53–77. Chicago: University of Chicago Press.

Comaroff, Jean. 1985. *Body of Power, Spirit of Resistance: The Culture and History of a South African People*. Chicago: University of Chicago Press.

Dahal. D. R., N. K. Rai, and A. E. Manzardo. 1977. *Land and Migration in Far Western Nepal*. Kathmandu: Tribhuvan University Press.

Dahal, Dilli. 1992. "Ethnic Conflict in Nepal's Terai." *Himal* 5, no. 3: 17–18.

Das, S. C. 1881. "Dispute Between a Buddhist and a Bon-po Priest for the Possession of Mt. Kailash and the Lake of Manasa." *Journal of the Asiatic Society of Bengal* 1: 206–11.

David, Kenneth, ed. 1977. *The New Wind: Changing Identities in South Asia*. The Hague: Mouton.

De Vos, George and Lola Romanucci-Ross, eds. 1975. *Ethnic Identity: Cultural Continuities and Change*. Palo Alto: Mayfield.

Despres, Leo A. 1967. *Cultural Pluralism and Nationalist Politics in British Guiana*. Chicago: Rand McNally.

Deshen, S. 1970. "On Religious Change: The Situational Analysis of Symbolic Action." *Comparative Studies of Society and History* 12: 260–74.

Dixit, Kamal. 1985. *Nunko Kojima*. Kathmandu: Salt Trading Corporation.

Dobremez, Jean-François and Corneille Jest, eds. 1974. "L'homme et le haute Montaque: L'Himalaya." *Objets et Mondes* (special edition) 14, no. 4: 205–359.

Doherty, Victor S. 1974a. "The Organizing Principles of Gurung Kinship." *Kailash* 2, no. 4: 273–301.

———. 1974b. "The Organizing Principles of Brahmin-Chetri Kinship." *Contribution to Nepalese Studies* 1, no. 2: 25–41.

Donner, Wolf. 1968. *Mustang: Observations in the Trans-Himalayan Part of Nepal*. UN-FAO Report. Kathmandu: FAO.

Dubois, Abbe J. A. 1906. *Hindu Manners, Customs and Ceremonies*. Oxford: Oxford University Press, Clarendon.

Dumont, Louis. 1961. "Caste, Racism, and 'Stratification': Reflections of a Social Anthropologist." *Contributions to Indian Sociology* 5: 20–44.

———. 1970. *Homo Hierarchicus*. Trans. M. Sainsbury. Chicago: University of Chicago Press.

Durkheim, Emile. [1915] 1964. *The Elementary Forms of Religious Life*. New York: Free.

Dutt, Nripendra Kumar. 1931. *Origins and Growth of Caste in India*. Vol. 1. London: Kegan Paul, Trench and Trubner.

Embree, Ainslie. 1977. "From Frontiers into Boundaries: From the Traditional to the Modern State." In *Symposium on Regions and Regionalism in South Asian Studies*, ed. Richard G. Fox, 255–80. Duke University Series, monograph no. 10. Durham, N.C.: Duke University Press.

Epstein, A. L. 1968. "Power, Politics, and Leadership: Some Central African and Melanesian Contrasts." In *Local Level Politics*, ed. Marc J. Swartz, 53–68. Chicago: Aldine.

——. 1978. *Ethos and Identity*. London: Tavistock.

Ferdinand, E. "Ritual Brotherhood: A Cohesive Factor in Nepalese Society." *Southwestern Journal of Anthropology* 13: 221–22.

Field, A. R. 1959. "Himalayan Salt: A Political Barometer." *Modern Review* 105, no. 6: 460–63.

Fisher, James F. 1978. "Homo Hierarchicus Nepalensis: A Cultural Subspecies." In *Himalayan Anthropology*, ed. James Fisher, 43–52. The Hague: Mouton.

——. 1985. "The Historical Development of Himalayan Anthropology." *Mountain Research and Development* 5, no. 1: 99–111.

——. 1986. *Trans-Himalayan Traders: Economy, Society, and Culture in Northwest Nepal*. Berkeley: University of California Press.

——, ed. 1978. *Himalayan Anthropology: The Indo-Tibetan Interface*. The Hague: Mouton.

Fisher, William F. 1987. *The Re-Creation of Tradition: Ethnicity, Migration, and Social Change Among the Thakali of Central Nepal*. Ph.D. diss., Columbia University.

——. 1989. "Retold Tales: Towards an Understanding of Spirit Possession in Central Nepal." *Himalayan Research Bulletin* 9, no. 2: 5–15.

——. 1992. "Notes on the Study of Thakali Culture and History." *Khāngalo*.

——. 1993. "Nationalism and the Janajati." *Himal* (March/April): 11–16.

Foster, Robert. 1991. "Making National Cultures in the Global Ecumene." *Annual Review of Anthropology* 20: 235–60.

Fox, Richard, ed. 1990. *Nationalist Ideologies and the Production of National Cultures*. American Ethnological Society Monograph Series, No. 2. Washington, D.C.: American Anthropological Association.

Francke, A. H. [1926] 1972. *Antiquities of Indian Tibet*. Part 2, *The Chronicles of Ladakh and Minor Chronicles*. New Delhi: S. Chand.

Frank, Walter. 1974. "Attempt at an Ethno-Demography of Middle Nepal." In *Contributions to the Anthropology of Nepal*, ed. Christoph von Fürer-Haimendorf, 85–97. Warminster, England: Aris and Phillips.

Fried, Morton H. 1967. *The Evolution of Political Society: An Essay in Political Anthropology*. New York: Random House.

——. 1975. *The Notion of Tribe*. Menlo Park, Calif.: Cummings.

Fürer-Haimendorf, Christoph von. 1957. "The Interrelations of Caste and Ethnic Groups in Nepal." *Bulletin of the School of Oriental and African Studies* 20: 243–60.

——. 1960. "Caste in the Multiethnic Society of Nepal." *Contributions to Indian Sociology* 4: 12–32.

——. 1966. "Caste Concepts and Status Distinctions in Buddhist Communities of Western Nepal." In *Caste and Kin in Nepal, India and Ceylon: Anthropological Studies in Hindu-Buddhist Context*, ed. Christoph von Fürer-Haimendorf, 140–60. London: Asia.

——. 1967a. "Caste in the Multi-Ethnic Society of Nepal." *Contributions to Indian Sociology* 5, no. 4: 12–32.

——. 1967b. *Morals and Merit: A Study of Values and Social Controls in South Asian Societies*. London: Weidenfeld and Nicolson.

——. 1971a. "Status and Interaction Among the High Hindu Castes of Nepal." *Eastern Anthropologist* 24: 7–24.

——. 1971b. "Tribes in Hindu Society." *Contributions to Indian Sociology* 5: 24–27.

——. 1975. *Himalayan Traders*. New York: St. Martin's.

——. 1978. "Trans-Himalayan Traders in Transition." In *Himalayan Anthropology*, ed. James Fisher, 339–57. The Hague: Mouton.

——. 1981a. "Social Change in a Himalayan Region." In *The Himalaya*, ed. J. S. Lall, 175–203. Delhi: Oxford University Press.

——. 1981b. "Social Structure and Spatial Mobility Among the Thakalis of Western Nepal." In *Asian Highland Societies in Anthropological Perspective*, ed. Christoph von Fürer-Haimendorf, 1–9. Atlantic Highlands, N.J.: Humanities.

——. 1985. *Tribal Populations and Cultures of the Indian Subcontinent*. Leiden-Cologne: Brill.

——, ed. 1966. *Caste and Kin in Nepal, India and Ceylon: Anthropological Studies in Hindu-Buddhist Contact Zones*. London: Asia.

——, ed. 1974. *Contributions to the Anthropology of Nepal*. Warminster, England: Aris and Phillips.

——, ed. 1981c. *Asian Highland Societies in Anthropological Perspective*. Atlantic Highlands, N.J.: Humanities.

Gaige, Frederik H. 1975. *Regionalism and National Unity in Nepal*. New Delhi: Vikas.

Gauchan, Prakash. 1981 (2038). *Haamro Desh Haamro Jaati (Nepaalka Thakaali-haruko): Ek Paricaya*. Kathmandu: L. S. Gauchan.

Gauchan, S. and M. Vinding. 1977. "The History of the Thakali According to the Thakali Tradition." *Kailash* 5: 97–184.

Geertz, C. 1960. "The Javanese Kijaji." *Comparative Studies in Society and History* 2: 228–49.

——. 1962. "The Rotating Credit Association: A 'Middle Rung' in Development." *Economic Development and Cultural Change* 10: 241–63.

——. 1963. *Old Societies and New States*. New York: Free.

———. 1973. *The Interpretation of Cultures.* New York: Basic.

Gellner, David. 1986. "Language, Caste, Religion, and Territory: Newar Identity Ancient and Modern." *European Journal of Sociology* 27: 102–48.

Gellner, David N., Joanna Pfaff-Czarnecka, and John Whelpton, eds. 1997. *Nationalism and Ethnicity in a Hindu Kingdom.* Amsterdam: Harwood.

Gellner, David N. and Declan Quigley. 1995. *Contested Hierarchies: A Collaborative Ethnography of Caste in the Kathmandu Valley.* Oxford: Oxford University Press, Clarendon.

Ghurye, G. S. 1950. *Caste and Class in India.* Bombay: Popular Book Depot.

Gimlette, George. 1927. *A Postscript to the Records of the Indian Mutiny.* London: H. F. & G. Witherby.

Glade, William. 1967. "Approaches to a Theory of Entrepreneurial Formation." *Explorations in Entrepreneurial History,* 2d ser, 4: 245–59.

Glover, Warren W. 1970. "Cognate Counts via the Swadesh List in Some Tibeto-Burman Languages of Nepal." In *Occasional Papers of the Wolfenden Society of Tibeto-Burman Linguistics.* vol. 3, ed. F. K. Lehman, 23–26. Urbana: University of Illinois, Department of Linguistics.

Goffman, Erving. 1959. *The Presentation of Self in Everyday Life.* Garden City, N.Y.: Doubleday.

———. 1963. *Behavior in Public Places.* Glencoe: Free.

———. 1967. *Interaction Ritual: Essays on Face-to-Face Behavior.* Garden City, N.Y.: Doubleday.

Gorer, Geoffrey. 1967. *Himalayan Village.* New York: Basic.

Graafen, Rainer and Christian Seeber. 1992–93. "Important Trade Routes in Nepal and Their Importance to the Settlement Process." *Ancient Nepal* 130–33: 34–48.

Gramsci, Antonio. 1971. *Selections from the Prison Notebooks.* New York: International.

Greenfield, Sidney M. and Arnold Strickon. 1981. "A New Paradigm for the Study of Entrepreneurship and Social Change." *Economic Development and Cultural Change* 3, no. 2: 467–99.

Greenfield, Sidney M., Arnold Strickon, and Robert T. Aubey, eds. 1979. *Entrepreneurs in Cultural Context.* Albuquerque: University of New Mexico Press.

———. 1986. *Entrepreneurship and Social Change.* Monographs in Economic Anthropology, No. 2, Society for Economic Anthropology. New York: University Press of America.

Greve, Reinhard. 1983. "A Shaman's Concepts of Illness and Healing Rituals in the Mustang District, Nepal." *Journal of Nepal Research Center* 5/6: 99–124.

Guneratne, Upali Arjun. 1994. "The Tharus of Chitwan: Ethnicity, Class, and the State in Nepal." Ph.D. diss., University of Chicago.

Gupta, Akhil and James Ferguson. 1992. "Beyond 'Culture': Space, Identity, and the Politics of Difference." *Cultural Anthropology* 7, no. 1: 6–23.

———, eds. 1997. *Culture, Power, Place*. Durham, N.C.: Duke University Press.

Gurung, Harka Bahadur. 1994. *Main Ethnic/Caste Groups by Districts Based on Population Census 1991*. N.p.

Gurung, Om. 1997. "Demographic and Environmental Efforts of the Mining Industry in the Hill Region of Western Nepal." *Studies in Nepali History and Society* 2, no. 2: 273–90.

Gutschow, N. 1994. "Kagbeni: Structural Analysis of Dendrochronological Data." *Ancient Nepal*, no. 136: 23–50.

Haarh, E. 1969. *The Yar-lung Dynasty: A Study with Particular Regard to the Contribution by Myths and Legends to the History of Ancient Tibet and the Origin and Nature of Its King*. Copenhagen: G. E. C. Gad's.

Hamilton [Buchanan], Francis. [1819] 1971. *An Account of the Kingdom of Nepal and of the Territories Annexed to the Dominion by the House of Gorkha*. New Delhi: Manjusri (Bibliotheca Himalayica).

Heide, Susanne von der. 1987. "Some Demographic Notes and a Short Description of Migratory Patterns of the Thakali." *Himalayan Culture* 5, no. 1.

———. 1988. *The Thakalis of North Western Nepal*. Kathmandu: Ratna Pustak Bhandar.

Herzfeld, Michael. 1986. "Of Definitions and Boundaries: The Status of Culture in the Culture of the State." In *Discourse and the Social Life of Meaning*, ed. P. P. Choack and J. R. Wyman, 75–94. Washington, D.C.: Smithsonian Institution Press.

His Majesty's Government of Nepal. 1992. *Constitution of the Kingdom of Nepal 2047 (1990)*. Kathmandu: Ministry of Law, Justice, and Parliamentary Affairs.

———. 1994a. *Population of Nepal by Districts and Village Development Committees/Municipalities (Population Census 1991)*. Kathmandu: Central Bureau of Statistics.

———. 1994b. *Statistical Pocket Book: Nepal 1994*. Kathmandu: Central Bureau of Statistics.

Hitchcock, John T. 1963. "Some Effects of Recent Change in Rural Nepal." *Human Organization* 22: 75–82.

———. 1965. "Sub-Tribes in the Magar Community in Nepal." *Asian Survey* 1, no. 9: 207–15.

———. 1966. *The Magars of Banyan Hill*. New York: Holt, Rinehart, and Winston.

———. 1967. "Nepalese Shamanism and the Classic Inner Asian Tradition." *History of Religions* 7, no. 2: 149–58.

———. 1974. "A Shaman's Song and Some Implications for Himalayan Research." In *Contributions to the Anthropology of Nepal*, ed. Christoph von Fürer-Haimendorf, 150–58. Warminster, England: Aris and Phillips.

———. 1978. "An Additional Perspective on the Nepali Caste System." In *Himalayan Anthropology*, ed. James Fisher 111–20. The Hague: Mouton.

Hitchcock, John and Rex Jones, eds. 1976. *Spirit Possession in the Nepal Himalayas.* New Delhi: Vikas.

Hobsbawm, Eric and Terence Range, eds. 1983. *The Invention of Tradition.* Cambridge: Cambridge University Press.

Hodgson, Brian H. [1874] 1971. *Essays on the Languages, Literature and Religion of Nepal and Tibet Together with Further Papers on the Geography, Ethnology and Commerce of Those Countries.* Varanasi, India: Bharat-Bharati.

Höfer, Andras. 1974. "A Note on Possession in South Asia." In *Contributions to the Anthropology of Nepal,* ed. Christoph von Fürer-Haimendorf 159–167. Warminster, England: Aris and Phillips.

——. 1978. "A New Rural Elite in Central Nepal." In *Himalayan Anthropology,* ed. James Fisher, 179–86. The Hague: Mouton.

——. 1979a. *The Caste Hierarchy and the State in Nepal: A Study of the Muluki Ain of 1854.* Innsbruck: Universitätsverlag Wagner.

——. 1979b. "On Re-reading *Le Nepal*: What We Social Scientists Owe to Sylvain Levi." *Kailash* 7, no. 3: 175–90.

——. 1981. *Tamang Ritual Texts, I: Preliminary Studies in the Folk-Religion of an Ethnic Minority.* Wiesbaden: Franz Steiner.

Holmberg, David M. 1980. "Lama, Shaman, and Lambu in Tamang Religious Practice." Ph.D. diss., Cornell University.

——. 1984. "Ritual Paradoxes in Nepal: Comparative Perspectives on Tamang Religion." *Journal of Asian Studies* 43, no. 4: 697–722.

——. 1989. *Order in Paradox: Myth, Ritual, and Exchange Among Nepal's Tamang.* Ithaca, N.Y.: Cornell University Press.

Horowitz, Donald. 1985. *Ethnic Groups in Conflict.* Berkeley: University of California Press.

Hopkirk, Peter. 1980. *Foreign Devils on the Silk Road.* London: Murray.

Hutt, Michael J. 1988. *Nepali: A National Language and Its Literature.* London: School of Oriental and African Studies.

——. 1991. *Himalayan Voices.* Berkeley: University of California Press.

Iijima, Shigeru. 1960. "The Thakali: A Central Himalayan Tribe." *Japanese Journal of Ethnology* 24, no. 3: 1–22. (Japanese text, English summary.)

——. 1963. "The Hinduization of a Himalayan Tribe in Nepal." *Krober Anthropological Society Papers* 29: 43–52.

——. 1977a. "Ecology, Economy and Cultural Change Among the Thakalis in the Himalayas of Central Nepal." In *Changing Aspects of Modern Nepal: Relating to the Ecology, Agriculture and Her People,* ed. Shigeru Iijima, 69–92. Tokyo: Institute for the Study of Languages and Cultures of Asia and Africa.

——. 1977b. "A Note on the Thakali's Leadership." In *Himalaya: Ecologie-Ethnologie,* ed. Corneille Jest, 427–432. Paris: Centre National de la Recherche Scientifique.

——, ed. 1977c. *Changing Aspects of Modern Nepal: Relating to the Ecology, Agriculture and Her People*. Monumenta Serindica No. 1. Tokyo: Institute for the Study of Languages and Cultures of Asia and Africa.

Jackson, David. 1976. "The Early History of Lo (Mustang) and Ngari." *Contributions to Nepalese Studies* 4: 39–56.

——. 1978. "Notes on the History of Se-Rib and Nearby Places in the Upper Kali Gandaki Valley." *Kailash* 6, no. 3: 195–227.

——. 1980. "A Genealogy of the Kings of Lo (Mustange)." In *Tibetan Studies in Honour of Hugh Richardson: Proceedings of the International Seminar on Tibetan Studies, Oxford 1979*, ed. Michael Aris and Aung San Suu Kyi, 133–37. New Delhi: Vikas.

——. 1984. *The Mollas of Mustang: Historical, Religious and Oratorial Traditions of the Nepalese-Tibetan Borderland*. Dharamsala: Library of Tibetan Works and Archives.

Jäschke, H. A. [1881] 1958. *A Tibetan-English Dictionary with Special Reference to the Prevailing Dialects*. London: Routledge and Kegan Paul.

——. 1969. *A Tibetan-English Dictionary*. 11th ed. London: Routledge and Kegan Paul.

Jest, Corneille. 1964/65. "Les Thakali: Note préliminaire concernant une ethnie du Nord-Ouest du Nepal." *Ethnographie* 58/59: 26–49.

——. 1968. "Notes sur les groupes ethniques de langue tibéto-birmane au Nepal." *Proceedings of the VIIIth International Congress of Anthropological and Ethnological Sciences*, vol. 2, 128–30. Tokyo: Science Council of Japan.

——. 1969. "Chez les Thakali, cérémonie consacrée aux ancêtres du clan." *Objets et Mondes* 9, no. 1: 59–68.

——. 1974. "La fête des clans chez les Thakalis, Spre-lo (1968)." In *Contributions to the Anthropology of Nepal*, ed. Christoph von Fürer-Haimendorf, 183–96. Warminster, England: Aris and Phillips.

——. 1975. *Dolpo: Communautés de langue tibétaine du Nepal*. Paris: Centre National de la Recherche Scientifique.

——. 1976. "Encounters with Intercessors in Nepal." In *Spirit Possession in the Nepal Himalayas*, ed. John Hitchcock and Rex Jones, 294–308. New Delhi: Vikas.

——. 1981. *Monuments of Northern Nepal*. Paris: UNESCO.

Jones, Rex. 1976. "Sanskritization in Eastern Nepal." *Ethnology* 15, no. 1: 63–75.

K. C., R. B. 1980. "Immigrant Thakalis of Pokhara: An Exercise in Urban Ethnography." M.A. thesis, Poona University.

Kantowsky, Detlef, ed. 1986. *Recent Research on Max Weber's Studies of Hinduism*. Munich: Weltforum.

Kapferer, Bruce. 1988. *Legends of People, Myths of State*. Washington, D.C.: Smithsonian Institution Press.

Karve, Irawati. 1961. *Hindu Society: An Interpretation*. Poona: Deccan College.

Kawaguchi, Ekai. [1909] 1979. *Three Years in Tibet*. Kathmandu: Ratna Pustak Bhandar.

Kawakita, Jiro. 1955. "Some Ethnographic Observations in the Nepal Himalaya." *The Japanese Journal of Ethnology* 19, no. 1: 1–57.

——. 1957. "Ethno-geographical Observations on the Nepal Himalaya." In *Peoples of the Nepal Himalaya*, ed. H. Kihara, 3:1–362. Kyoto: Flora and Fauna Society.

——. 1961. "Some Ecological Observations in Nepal Himalaya." *Japanese Journal of Ethnology* 24: 197–238. (Résumé in English.)

——. 1974. *The Hill Magars and Their Neighbors: Hill People Surrounding the Ganges Plain*. Tokyo: Tokai University Press.

Kirkpatrick, William. 1811. *An Account of the Kingdom of Nepaul, Being the Substance of Observations Made During a Mission to That Country in the Year 1793*. London: W. Miller.

Klass, Morton. 1978. *From Field to Factory: Community Structure and Industrialization in West Bengal*. Philadelphia: Institute for the Study of Human Issues.

——. 1980. *Caste*. Philadelphia: Institute for the Study of Human Issues.

Kolenda, Pauline. 1978. *Caste in Contemporary India: Beyond Organic Solidarity*. Menlo Park, Calif.: Benjamin Cummings.

Kulke, Hermann. 1986. "Max Weber's Contribution to the Study of 'Hinduization' in India and 'Indianization' in Southeast Asia." In *Recent Research on Max Weber's Studies of Hinduism*, ed. Detlef Kantowsky. Munich: Weltforum.

Landan, Perceval. [1928] 1976. *Nepal*. Kathmandu: Ratna Pustak Bhandar.

Leach, Edmund. 1954. *Political Systems of Highland Burma*. London: London School of Economics and Political Science.

Leach, Edmund R., ed. 1960. *Aspects of Caste in South India, Ceylon and North-West Pakistan*. Cambridge: Cambridge University Press.

Lears, T. and J. Jackson. 1985. "The Concept of Cultural Hegemony: Problems and Possibilities." *American Historical Review* 90: 567–93.

Lehman, F. K. 1963. *The Structure of Chin Society*. University of Illinois Studies in Anthropology, no. 3. Urbana: University of Illinois Press.

——. 1967. "Ethnic Categories in Burma and the Theory of Social Systems." In *Southeast Asian Tribes, Minorities and Nations*, ed. P. Kunstadter, 2:93–124. Princeton: Princeton University Press.

Lévi, Sylvain. 1905–8. *Le Nepal: Etude historique d'un royaume hindou*. Annales de Musée Guimet, Bibliothèque d'études, vols. 17–19. Paris: E. Leroux.

Levine, Nancy. 1987. "Caste, State, and Ethnic Boundaries in Nepal." *Journal of Asian Studies* 46: 71–88.

Lyall, A. C. 1882. *Asiatic Studies: Religious and Social*. London: Murray.

Lynch, Owen M. 1969. *The Politics of Untouchability: Social Mobility and Social Change in a City of India*. New York: Columbia University Press.

MacDonald, A. W. 1962. "Note préliminaire sur quelques jhakri du Muglan." *Journal Asiatique* 250: 107–39.

——. 1966. "Les Tamangs vus par l'un d'eux." *L'Homme* 6: 27–58.

——. 1979. "A Tibetan Guide to Some of the Holy Places of the Dhaulagiri, Muktinath Area of Nepal." In *Studies in Pali and Buddhism*, ed. A. K. Narain, 243–53. New Delhi: B. R. Publishing Corporation.

——. 1989. "Note on the Language, Literature and Cultural Identity of the Tamang." *Kailash* 15, nos. 3/4: 165–77.

MacFarlane, Alan. 1993. "A Transcription of Interview with Professor Christoph von Fürer-Haimendorf." Manuscript.

MacGregor, John. 1970. *Tibet: A Chronicle of Exploration*. London: Routledge and Kegan Paul.

Mandelbaum, D. G. 1972. *Society in India*. Berkeley: University of California Press.

Manzardo, Andrew. 1977a. "Ecological Constraints on Trans-Himalayan Trade in Nepal." *Contributions to Nepalese Studies* 4, no. 2: 63–81.

——. 1977b. "Factors in the Potential Regeneration of Thak Khola." In *Himalaya: Ecologie-Ethnologie*, ed. C. Jest, 433–441. Paris: Centre National de la Recherche Scientifique.

——. 1978. "To Be Kings of the North: Community Adaptation and Impression Management in the Thakalis of Western Nepal." Ph.D. diss., University of Wisconsin, Madison.

——. 1982. "Impression Management and Economic Growth: The Case of the Thakalis of Dhaulagiri Zone." *Kailash* 9, no. 1: 45–60.

——. 1984. "High Altitude Husbandry and the Thakalis of Thak Khola: Biology and Trade in the Himalayas." *Contributions to Nepalese Studies* 11: 21–35.

——. 1985. "Ritual Practice and Group Maintenance in the Thakali of Thak Khola: Biology and Trade in the Himalayas." *Kailash* 12, nos. 1/2: 81–114

——. 1992. Letter to the editor. *Himal* (November/December): 5.

Manzardo, Andrew and Keshav Prasad Sharma. 1975. "Cost-cutting, Caste and Community: A Look at Thakali Social Reform in Pokhara." *Contributions to Nepalese Studies* 2, no. 2: 24–44.

Marriott, McKim. 1955. "Little Communities in an Indigenous Civilization." In *Village India: Studies in the Little Community*, ed. McKim Marriott. Chicago: University of Chicago Press.

Maskarinec, Gregory. 1995. *Rulings of the Night: An Ethnography of Nepalese Shaman Oral Texts*. Madison: University of Wisconsin Press.

Mayer, A. C. 1960. *Caste and Kinship in Central India*. Berkeley: University of California Press.

Mencher, Joan. 1974. "The Caste System Upside Down or the Not-So-Mysterious East." *Current Anthropology* 15: 469–93.

Messerschmidt, Donald. 1972. "Rotating Credit in Gurung Society: The Dhikur Associations of Tin Gaun." *Himalayan Review* 5, no. 4: 23–35.

——. 1973. "Dhikur: Rotating Credit Associations in Nepal." Paper presented to the Ninth International Congress of Anthropological and Ethnological Sciences, Chicago.

——. 1976. *The Gurungs of Nepal: Conflict and Change in a Village Society.* Warminster, England: Aris and Phillips.

——. 1978. "Dhikurs: Rotating Credit Associations in Nepal." In *Himalayan Anthropology,* ed. James F. Fisher, 141–56. The Hague: Mouton.

——. 1981. "Nogar and Other Traditional Forms of Cooperation in Nepal: Significance for Development." *Human Organization* 40: 40–47.

——. 1984. "The Thakali of Nepal: Historical Continuity and Socio-Cultural Change." *Ethnohistory* 29: 265–80.

Messerschmidt, Donald and Nareshwar Jang Gurung. 1974. "Parallel Trade and Innovation in Central Nepal: The Cases of the Gurung and Thakali Subbas Compared." *Contributions to the Anthropology of Nepal,* ed. C. von Fürer-Haimendorf, 197–221. Warminster, England: Aris and Phillips

Michl, Wolf D. 1972. "Preliminary Report on the Chantel, Dhaulagiri Himalaya, Nepal." *Bulletin of the International Committee on Urgent Anthropological and Ethnological Research* (Vienna) 14:54–68.

——. 1974. "Shamanism Among the Chantel of the Dhaulagiri Zone." In *Contributions to the Anthropology of Nepal,* ed. Christoph. von Fürer-Haimendorf. Warminster, England: Aris and Phillips.

——. 1976. "Notes on the Jhankri of Ath Hajar Parbat/Dhaulagiri Himalaya." In *Spirit Possession in the Nepal Himalayas,* ed. John T. Hitchcock and Rex L. Jones, 153–64. New Delhi: Vikas.

Miller, Beatrice D. 1956. "Ganye and Kidu: Two Formalized Systems of Mutual Aid Among the Tibetans." *Southwestern Journal of Anthropology* 12: 157–70.

Mishra, T. N. 1994. "The Archaeological Research in the High Mountains of Mustang District." *Ancient Nepal,* no. 136: 147–60.

Moerman, Michael. 1967. "Reply to Naroll." *American Anthropologist.* 69: 512–13.

——. 1968. "Being Lue: Uses and Abuses of Ethnic identification." In *Essays on the Problem of Tribe,* ed. June Helm, 153–69. Seattle: University of Washington Press.

——. 1974. "Accomplishing Ethnicity." In *Ethnomethodology,* ed. R. Turner, 54–68. Middlesex: Penguin.

Molnar, Augusta. 1981. "The Kham Magar Women of Thabang." In *The Status of Women in Nepal,* vol. 2, no. 2. Kathmandu: CEDA, Tribhuvan University Press.

Montgomerie, Thomas George. 1868. "From Nepal to Lhasa and Thence Through the Upper Valley of the Brahmaputra to Its Source: Report of a Route-Survey Made by Pundit _____." *Journal of the Royal Geographical Society* 38: 129–219.

———. 1875. "Extracts from an Explorer's Narrative of His Journey from Pitgarh in Kumaon via Jumla to Tadum and Back Along the Kali Gandaki to British Territory." *Journal of the Royal Geographic Society of London* 45: 350–63.

Moore, Sally Falk. 1987. "Explaining the Present: Theoretical Dilemmas in Processual Ethnography." *American Ethnologist* 14, no. 2: 726–36.

———. 1989. "The Production of Cultural Pluralism as Process." *Public Culture* 1, no. 2: 26–48.

———. 1993. "The Ethnography of the Present and the Analysis of Process." In *Assessing Cultural Anthropology*, ed. Robert Borofsky, 326–344. New York: McGraw-Hill.

Mumford, Stan Royal. 1990. *Himalayan Dialogue: Tobetan Lamas and Gurung Shamans in Nepal*. Kathmandu: Tiwari's Pilgrims Book House.

Naroll, R. 1964. "On Ethnic Unit Classification." *Current Anthropology* 5: 283–91, 306–12.

Nepali, Gopal Singh. 1965. *The Newars*. Bombay: United Asia Publications.

Nitzberg, Frances L. 1978. "Changing Patterns of Multiethnic Interaction in the Western Himalayas." In *Himalayan Anthropology*, ed. James F. Fisher, 103–10. The Hague: Mouton, 1978.

Obidinski, Eugene. 1978. "Methodological Considerations in the Definition of Ethnicity." *Ethnicity* 5: 213–28.

Okada, F. 1957. "Ritual Brotherhood: A Cohesive Factor in Nepalese Society." *Southwestern Journal of Anthropology* 13: 212–22.

Oldfield, Henry Ambrose. 1880. *Sketches from Nepal*. London: W. M. Allen.

Olzak, Susan and Joane Nagel, eds. 1992. *Competitive Ethnic Relations*. New York: Academic Press.

Oppitz, Michael. 1968. *Geschichte und Sozialordnung der Sherpa*. Innsbruck: Universität Verlag Wagner.

Ortega y Gasset, José. 1961. *Meditations on Quixote*. New York: Norton.

Ortner, Sherry. 1984. "Theory in Anthropology Since the Sixties." *Comparative Studies in Society and History* 26, no. 1: 126–66.

———. 1989. *High Religion*. Princeton: Princeton University Press.

Parker, Barbara. 1985. "The Spirit of Wealth: Culture of Entrepreneurship Among the Thakali of Nepal." Ph.D. diss., University of Michigan.

Petech, L. 1939. *A Study of the Chronicles of Ladakh*. Calcutta: n.p.

———. 1977. *The Kingdom of Ladakh, c. 950–1842*. Rome: ISMEO.

Pignède, B. 1966. *Les Gurungs, une population himalayenne du Népal*. Paris: Mouton.

Pohl, E. and C. P. Tripathee. 1995. "Excavation at Garab-Dzong, Dist. Mustang: Preliminary Report of the Campaign 1994." *Ancient Nepal* 138: 95–106.

Phlo. 1985. Publication of Thakāli Yuwā Pariwār, vol. 1, no. 2. (Torongla 2041.)

Prindle, P. H. 1977. "The Jajmani System: A Nepalese Example." *Journal of Anthropological Research* 33, no. 3: 388–401.

Rafael, Vincente. 1993. *Contracting Colonialism.* Durham, N.C.: Duke University Press.

Rai, Ratan Kumar. 1994. *The Thakālis, Bon dKar and Lāmāists Monasteries Along the Kāli Gaṇḍaki: The Ancient Salt Route in Western Nepal.* Delhi: Book Faith India.

Ramble, Charles. 1983. "The Founding of a Tibetan Village: The Popular Transformation of History." *Kailash* 10, no. 1: 267–90.

———. 1990. "How Buddhist Are Buddhist Communities? The Construction of Tradition in Two Lamaist Villages." *Journal of the Anthropological Society of Oxford* 21, no. 2: 185–97.

———. 1992–93. "A Ritual of Political Unity in an Old Nepalese Kingdom: Some Preliminary Observations." *Ancient Nepal* 130–133: 49–58.

———. 1993. "Play by Rule in Southern Mustang." In *Anthropology of Tibet and the Himalayas*, ed. C. Ramble and M. Brauen, 287–301. Zurich: Völkerkundemuseum der Universität Zurich.

———. 1997. "Se: Preliminary Notes on the Distribution of an Ethnonym in Tibet and Nepa." In *Les habitants du toit du monde: Etudes recueillies en hommage à Alexander W. Macdonald par les soins de Samten Karmay et Philippe Sagant.* Nanterre: Société d'ethnologie.

Ramble, Charles and C. Seeber. 1995. "Dead and Living Settlements in the Shoyul of Mustang." *Ancient Nepal*, no. 138: 107–30.

Ramble, Charles and Michael Vinding. 1987. "The Bem-chag Village Record and the Early History of Mustang District." *Kailash* 13, nos. 1–2: 5–47.

Redfield, Robert. 1961. *The Little Community.* Chicago: University of Chicago Press.

Regmi, Mahesh C. 1972. *A Study in Nepali Economic History, 1768–1846.* Delhi: Manjusri.

———. 1976. *Landownership in Nepal.* Berkeley: University of California Press.

———. 1977a. "Order to Lt. Champa Singh Khadka Chhetri Regarding Arrest of Chyalpa Thakali and Others. Regmi Research Collection 33:689–96.

———. 1977b. "Petition of Subba Ram Prasad Thakali (November 1886)." Regmi Research Collection 53:195–201.

———. 1977c. "Recruitment of Troops and Auxiliaries During the Nepal-Tibet War." Regmi Research Collection 33:234–53.

———. 1977d. "The Salt Trade in Dana." Regmi Research Collection 56:353–54.

———. 1978. *Thatched Huts and Stucco Palaces.* New Delhi: Vikas.

———. 1979. *Readings in Nepali Economic History.* Varanasi: Kishor Vidya Niketan.

———. 1981a. "Monopoly Trade in Cigarettes, A.D. 1947." *Regmi Research Series* 13, no. 1: 1–2.

———. 1981b. "On Prices." *Regmi Research Series* 13, no. 1: 116.

———. 1981c. "Petition of Khamba and Thakali Traders." *Regmi Research Series* 13, no. 8: 125.

———. 1981d. "Revenue Collection in Thak." *Regmi Research Series* 13, no. 1: 10–11.

———. 1983. "Weights and Measures in Mustang." *Regmi Research Series* 15, no. 1: 80.

———. 1988. *An Economic History of Nepal, 1846–1901.* Varanasi: Nath.

Riccardi, Theodore Jr., ed. and trans. 1975. "Sylvain Lévi: The History of Nepal, Part I." *Kailash* 3, no. 1: 5–60.

Richardson, H. E. 1962. *Tibet and Its History.* London: Oxford University Press.

Risley, H. H. 1892. *Tribes and Castes of Bengal.* Calcutta: n.p.

Rosaldo, Renato. 1989. *Culture and Truth: The Remaking of Social Analysis.* Boston: Beacon.

Rose, Leo. 1971. *Nepal: Strategies for Survival.* Berkeley: University of California Press.

———. 1974. "Secularization of a Hindu Polity: The Case of Nepal." In *Religion and Political Modernization,* ed. Donald E. Smith, 31–48. New Haven: Yale University Press.

Rose, Leo and B. L. Joshi. 1966. *Democratic Innovations in Nepal: A Case Study of Political Acculturation.* Berkeley: University of California Press.

Roseberry, William. 1989. *Anthropologies and Histories: Essays in Culture, History, and Political Economy.* New Brunswick: Rutgers University Press.

Rudolph, Lloyd I. and Susan H. Rudolph. 1960. "The Political Role of India's Caste Associations." *Pacific Affairs* 33: 5–22.

Sahlins, Marshall. 1981. *Historical Metaphors and Mythical Realities: Structure in the Early History of the Sandwich Islands Kingdom.* ASAO special publications, no. 1. Ann Arbor: University of Michigan Press.

Said, Edward. 1989. *Orientalism.* New York: Vintage.

de Sales, Anne. 1993. "When the Miners Came to Light: The Chantel of Dhaulagiri." In *Nepal Past and Present: Proceedings of the France-German Conference, Arc-et-Senans, June 1990,* ed. Gerard Toffin, 94–97. New Delhi: Sterling.

Schmidt, B. 1992–93. "Dendrochronological Research in South Mustang." *Ancient Nepal* 130–133: 20–33.

Schneider, Jane and Peter Schneider. 1976. *Culture and Political Economy in Western Sicily.* New York: Academic.

Schuh, Dieter. 1990. "The Political Organisation of Southern Mustang During the Seventeenth and Eighteenth Centuries." *Ancient Nepal* 119: 1–7.

———. 1994. "Investigations in the History of the Muktinath Valley and Adjacent Areas, Part I." *Ancient Nepal* 137: 9–91.

———. 1995. "Investigations in the History of the Muktinath Valley and Adjacent Areas, Part II." *Ancient Nepal* 138: 5–54.

Schuler, Sidney. 1977a. "Migratory Traders of Baragaon." *Contributions to Nepalese Studies* 5, no. 1: 71–84.

———. 1977b. "Notes on Marriage and the Status of Women in Baragaon." *Kailash* 6: 141–52.

——. 1979. "Yaks, Cows and Status in the Himalayas." *Contributions to Nepalese Studies* 6, no. 2: 65–72.

——. 1981. "The Women of Baragaon." In *The Status of Women in Nepal*, vol. 2, no. 5. Kathmandu: CEDA, Tribhuvan University Press.

Sebring, James M. 1969. "Caste Indicators and Caste Identification of Strangers." *Human Organization* 28: 199–207.

Seeber, C. G. 1994. "Reflections on the Existence of Castles and Observation Towers in the Area Under Investigation, the South Mustang." *Ancient Nepal* 136: 81–87.

——. 1996. "Castles and Fortified Settlements: Sites for Protection and Control in Northern Mustang." *Ancient Nepal*, no. 39.

Shafer, R. 1955. "Classification of the Sino-Tibetan Languages." *Word* 11: 94–111.

Sharma, Prayag Raj. 1972. *Preliminary Study of the Art and Architecture of the Karnali Basin, West Nepal*. Paris: Centre National de la Recherche Scientifique.

——. 1977. "Caste, Social Mobility and Sanskritization: A Study of Nepal's Old Legal Code." *Kailash* 5, no. 4: 277–99.

Sherchan, Jyoti. 1992. "Thakliharuko Bastusthiti ra Chunaitiharu." *Khāngalo*.

Sherchan, Nagendra. n.d. *Lha Phewa ko Paricaya*. Self-published.

Shrestha, M. N. 1979. "Internal Migration of People in Nepal." *Eastern Anthropologist* 32, no. 3: 163–76.

Sider, Gerald M. 1986. *Culture and Class in Anthropology and History*. Cambridge Studies in Social Anthropology, 60. Cambridge: Cambridge University Press.

Silverberg, James. 1968. "Colloquium and Interpretive Conclusions." In *Social Mobility in the Caste System of India*, ed. James Silverberg. The Hague: Mouton.

——, ed. 1968. *Social Mobility in the Caste System of India*. The Hague: Mouton.

Singer, Milton B., ed. 1973. *Entrepreneurship and Modernization of Occupational Culture in South Asia*. Durham, N.C.: Duke University Program in Comparative Studies on Southern Asia.

Sinha, G. S. and R. C. Sinha. 1967. "Explorations in Caste Stereotypes." *Social Forces* 46: 42–47.

Sinha, Surajit. 1962. "State Formation and Rajput Myth in Tribal Central India." *Man in India* 42: 35–80.

——. 1965. "Tribe-Caste and Tribe-Peasant Continua in Central India." *Man In India* 42, no. 1: 35–80.

Smith, Anthony D. 1993. "Ethnic Election and Cultural Identity." *Ethnic Studies* 10: 9–25.

Smith, Donald E., ed. 1974. *Religion and Political Modernization*. New Haven: Yale University Press.

Snellgrove, David. 1958. *Buddhist Himalaya*. Oxford: Bruno Cassirer.

——. 1961. *Himalayan Pilgrimage: A Study of Tibetan Religion by a Traveller Through Western Nepal*. Oxford: Bruno Cassirer.

——. 1967. *Four Lamas of Dolpo.* Cambridge: Harvard University Press.
——, ed. and trans. 1979. "Places of Pilgrimage in Thag (Thakkhola)," by Tshampa Ngawang of Drumpa. *Kailash* 7, no. 2: 75–170.
Snellgrove, David and H. E. Richardson. [1968] 1980. *A Cultural History of Tibet.* Boulder, Colo.: Prajna.
Snellgrove, David and T. Skorupski. 1977. *The Cultural Heritage of Ladakh*, vol. 1. Warminster, England: Aris and Phillips.
——. 1980. *The Cultural Heritage of Ladakh.* Vol. 1. Warminster: Aris and Phillips.
Soen, Dan and Patrice De Camarmond. 1972. "Savings Associations Among the Bamileke: Traditional and Modern Cooperation in Southwest Cameroon." *American Anthropologist* 74: 1170–79.
Somlai, Ivan Victor. 1982. "Two Twelve-Year Festivals in the Thak Khola." *Kailash* 9, nos. 2 and 3: 159–76.
Srinivas, M. N. 1952. *Religion and Society Among the Coorgs of South India.* Oxford: Oxford University Press, Clarendon.
——. 1955. "The Social System of a Mysore Village." In *Village India: Studies in the Little Community*, ed. McKim Marriot, 1–35. Chicago: University of Chicago Press.
——. 1956. "A Note on Sanskritization and Westernization." *Far Eastern Quarterly* 15: 481–96.
——. 1963. *Social Change in Modern India.* The Rabindranath Tagore Memorial Lectures, 1963. Berkeley: University of California Press.
——. 1967. *Social Change in Modern India.* Berkeley: University of California Press.
Srivastava, Ram P. 1958. "The Bhotia Nomads and Their Indo-Tibetan Trade." *Journal of the University of Saugar* 7, no. 1, sect. A: 1–22.
Srivastava, S. K. 1963. "The Process of Desanskritization in Village India." In *Anthropology on the March*, ed. L. K. Bala Ratman, 263–67. Madras: Book Centre.
Staal, J. F. 1963. "Sanskrit and Sanskritization." *Journal of Asian Studies* 22, no. 3: 261–75.
Stein, R. A. 1952. "Recentes études tibétaines." *Journal Asiatique*, 1952: 98–100.
——. 1972. *Tibetan Civilization.* London: Faber and Faber.
Stiller, L. F. 1973. *The Rise of the House of Gorkha: A Study in the Unification of Nepal, 1768–1816.* Kathmandu: Ratna Pustak Bhandar.
Tāmāng, Bhakta Bahadur. 1995. *Tāmāng Itihās.* Kathmandu: n.p.
Tāmāng, Sitārām. 1994. *Nepālmā Janajāti Samasyā.* Kathmandu: Krishna.
Tambiah, Stanley. 1989. "Ethnic Conflict in the World Today." *American Ethnologist* 16, no. 2: 335–49.
Thakāli Sanskriti Bikas Samiti. 1979 (2036). *Toranla Smaarikaa.* Narijhowa: n.p.
Thakāli Sewā Samiti and Kendriya Krylaya. 1983 (2040). *Mul Bandej.* Kathmandu: Ganesh.

———. 1984 (2041). *Mul Bandej (pratham samsodhan)*. N.p.

———. 1992a (2049). *Thakāki Jātiko Mahān Parwa, Lha Phewa* (program for Lha Phewa).

———. 1992b (2049). *Thakāli Sewā Samiti Nepālko Bidhān*. Kathmandu: n.p.

Thases Samācār (bulletin). 1982 (N.S. 2040). Issues 1 and 2.

Tsing, A. 1993. *In the Realm of the Diamond Queen*. Princeton: Princeton University Press.

Tucci, Giuseppe. *[1953]* 1982. *Journey to Mustang*, trans. Diana Fussell. Kathmandu: Ratna Pustak Bhandar.

———. 1956. *Preliminary Report on Two Scientific Expeditions in Nepal*. Rome: IS-MEO.

———. 1980. *The Religions of Tibet*. London: Routledge and Kegan Paul. *Khāngalo*.

Tulāchan, Karun Singh. 1992. "Thakāli Jātiko Kuldevtāko Puja." *Khāngalo*.

Turin, Mark. 1995. " 'We are Thakali in 2051': A Study of Language and Ethnicity Among a Tibeto-Burman Population of Nepal." B.A. honors thesis, University of Cambridge.

———. 1997. "Too Many Stars and Not Enough Sky: Language and Ethnicity Among the Thakali of Nepal." *Contributions to Nepalese Studies* 24, no. 2: 187–99.

Turner, Jonathan and Edna Bonacich. 1980. "Toward a Composite Theory of Middlemen Minorities." *Ethnicity* 7: 144–58.

Turner, R. 1931. *A Comparative and Etymological Dictionary of the Nepali Language*. London: Routledge and Kegan Paul.

Valeix, P. 1974. "Marpha, village du Pac gau." *Objects et Monde* 14: 269–78.

Vincent, Joan. 1968. *African Elite: The Big Men of a Small Town*. New York: Columbia University Press.

Vinding, Michael. 1978. "The Local Oral Tradition About the Kingdom of Thin Garab Dzong." *Kailash* 6, no. 3: 181–94.

———. 1979. "A Preliminary Report on Kinship Terminologies of the Bodish Section of Sino-Tibetan Speaking Peoples." *Kailash* 8, nos. 3 and 4: 191–225.

———. 1979/1980a. "Marriage Systems of the Thakalis and Related Groups of the Bodish Section of Sino-Tibetan Speaking People." *Folk* 21–22: 325–45.

———. 1979/80b. "Thakali Household and Inheritance System." *Contributions to Nepalese Studies* 8, nos. 1/2: 21–45.

———. 1981. "A Note on Patrilineal Descent Groups Among the Thakalis of the Nepal Himalayas." *Folk* 23: 205–19.

———. 1982. "The Thakali as Buddhist: A Closer Look at Their Death Ceremonies." *Kailash* 9, no. 4: 291–318.

———. 1983. "A Comment on 'Two Twelve-Year Festivals in the Thaak Khola.' " *Kailash* 10, nos. 1 and 2: 5–10.

———. 1984. "Making a Living in the Nepal Himalayas: The Case of the Thakalis of Mustang District." *Contributions to Nepalese Studies* 12, no. 1: 51–106.

———. 1988. "A History of the Thak Khola Valley, Nepal." *Kailash* 14, nos. 3–4: 167–211."A History of the Thak Khola Valley, Nepal." *Kailash* 14, nos. 3–4: 167–211.

———. 1992. *Lha Phewa: The Thakali Twelve-Year Festival.* Kathmandu: Ratna Pustak Bhandar.

———. 1998. *The Thakali: A Himalayan Ethnography.* London: Serindia Publications.

Vinding, Michael and K. B. Bhattachan. 1985. "An Annotated Bibliography of the Thakalis." *Contributions to Nepalese Studies* 12: 51–105.

Wagner, Roy. 1981. *The Invention of Culture.* Rev. ed. Chicago: University of Chicago Press.

Warren, Kay, ed. 1993. *The Violence Within: Cultural and Political Opposition in Divided Nations.* Boulder, Colo.: Westview.

Weber, Max. [1916] 1958. *The Religion of India: Sociology of Hinduism and Buddhism.* Trans. H. Garth and Don Martindale. Glencoe: Free.

Williams, Brackette F. 1989. "A Class Act: Anthropology and the Race to Nation Across Ethnic Terrain." *Annual Review of Anthropology* 18: 401–44.

Williams, Raymond. 1977. *Marxism and Literature.* Oxford: Oxford University Press.

Wolf, Eric. 1956. "Aspects of Group Relations in a Complex Society: Mexico." *American Anthropologist* 58: 1065–78.

———. 1982. *Europe and the People Without History.* Berkeley: University of California Press.

Index